WELCOME

Mastery of the sea makes kings and kingdoms, empires and spheres of influence, great nations, and vassal states. Since the awakenings of mankind's awareness of the wider world, when the yearning to explore, to discover, and to develop were first recognised, those who have chosen risk and adventure have looked to the sea.

And in concert, the craft that carry them over the horizon into the unknown, from ancient times to the present day, have made history for better or worse. The warship is indicative of the inevitable conflict that has emerged, waxed and waned, as men have striven across the world's oceans. The global projection of power has grown through the centuries, along with the ambitions of political and military leaders. At times, naval power and prowess have tipped the scales in favour of one warring party or another. And in due course, the outcomes of naval battles have charted the progression of history.

From the galleys, bellies filled with oarsmen, at Salamis to the battleships and aircraft carriers that settled the issue, both Atlantic and Pacific, during World War Two, the warship has reigned mighty in its majesty and its brutal execution of orders. Even as this volume of *Great Warships of the World* is written, the major navies of the world vie for pre-eminence, jousting at sea for leverage,

ABOVE: Greek and Persian galleys clash at the decisive Battle of Salamis in 480 BC. (Wilhelm von Kaulbach Public Domain via Wikimedia Commons)

ABOVE: A Japanese bomb barely misses the US Navy aircraft carrier *Bunker Hill* during the World War Two Battle of the Philippine Sea, June 19, 1944. (US Navy via Wikimedia Commons)

ABOVE: The Royal Navy and the French Fleet collide during the Battle of the Glorious First of June, 1794. (Philip James de Loutherbourg National Maritime Museum via Wikimedia Commons)

and flying their flags in disputed waters. The great naval commanders of the ages have etched their names in our collective memory. Themistocles at Salamis, John of Austria at Lepanto, Lord Nelson at Trafalgar, John Paul Jones amid the American Revolution, Oliver Hazard Perry at Lake Erie, Sir John Tovey in the Bismarck Chase, Admiral Raymond Spruance at the Battle of Midway, and many more are remembered for their command presence.

George Washington, known as the father of his country, was the first great leader of American soldiers on land, and even he conceded in a letter to his ally, the Marquis de Lafayette: "It follows then as certain as that night succeeds the day, that without a decisive naval force we can do nothing definitive, and with it, everything honorable and glorious."

When Napoleon Bonaparte finally surrendered to the Royal Navy in 1815, he grudgingly intoned: "Wherever wood can swim, there I am sure to find the flag of England."

Through the centuries, naval power has not only served as a vital instrument of war, but ironically it has become an implement for the preservation of peace. US Navy Admiral Arleigh Burke, who served three terms as Chief of Naval Operations, observed: "For in this modern world, the instruments of warfare are not solely for waging war. Far more importantly, they are the means for controlling peace. Naval officers must therefore understand not only how to fight a war, but how to use the tremendous power which they operate to sustain a world of liberty and justice, without unleashing the powerful instruments of destruction and chaos that they have at their command."

Join us in this exploration of *Great Warships of the World*. Though an exhaustive compilation would be impossible to complete, these are representative of the tremendous influence of naval power through the ages. Welcome!

Michael E Haskew

CONTENTS

ABOVE: The expanse of the flight deck and island aboard the Japanese aircraft carrier *Akagi* are visible in this early photograph from World War Two.
(Government of Japan Public Domain via Wikimedia Commons)

ABOVE: The Japanese pre-dreadnought battleship *Mikasa* survives as a museum ship at Yokohama. (Creative Commons via Wikimedia Commons)

ABOVE: The German armoured cruiser *Scharnhorst* rolls over and sinks under the guns of British battlecruisers during the 1914 Battle of the Falklands.
(William Lionel Wyllie Cassell & Company via Wikimedia Commons)

ABOVE: Galleys and sailing ships do battle at Lepanto in 1571.
(Jan Peeters the Elder St. Paul's Church via Wikimedia Commons)

ABOVE: Lord Nelson lies mortally wounded on the quarterdeck of HMS *Victory* at the Battle of Trafalgar in 1805. (Denis Dighton National Maritime Museum via Wikimedia Commons)

ABOVE: The Nimitz-class aircraft carrier USS *Ronald Reagan* transits the Strait of Magellan in 2004 en route to the port of San Diego, California. (US Navy via Wikimedia Commons)

ISBN: 978 1 83632 091 3
Editor: Mike Haskew
Senior editor, specials: Roger Mortimer
Email: roger.mortimer@keypublishing.com
Cover Design: Steve Donovan
Cover Art: Antonis Karidis
Design: SJmagic DESIGN SERVICES, India
Advertising Sales Manager: Sam Clark
Email: sam.clark@keypublishing.com
Tel: 01780 755131
Advertising Production: Becky Antoniades
Email: Rebecca.antoniades@keypublishing.com

SUBSCRIPTION/MAIL ORDER
Key Publishing Ltd, PO Box 300, Stamford, Lincs, PE9 1NA
Tel: 01780 480404
Subscriptions email: subs@keypublishing.com

Mail Order email: orders@keypublishing.com
Website: www.keypublishing.com/shop

PUBLISHING
Group CEO and Publisher: Adrian Cox

Published by
Key Publishing Ltd, PO Box 100, Stamford, Lincs. PE9 1XQ
Tel: 01780 755131 **Website:** www.keypublishing.com

PRINTING
Precision Colour Printing Ltd, Haldane, Halesfield 1, Telford, Shropshire TF7 4QQ

DISTRIBUTION
Seymour Distribution Ltd, 2 Poultry Avenue, London EC1A 9PU
Enquiries Line: 02074 294000.

ANTIQUITY

ABOVE: This model of an early Egyptian galley from the fleet of Ramesses III resides in the National Maritime Museum of Israel. (Creative Commons Deror avi via Wikimedia Commons)

Dependent on the strong backs of men straining and sweating in dark, cramped spaces, the warships of antiquity primarily relied upon the power of their oarsmen. From the Egyptians to the Phoenicians and the Greek and Roman civilisations, maritime exploration, trade, and inevitably conflict, occurred on the high seas.

The first naval battle in history is thought to be the Battle of Alashiya, a series of three engagements between the Hittites and Cypriots that occurred approximately 1210 to 1205 BC. Scant evidence of the Hittite victory was discovered in a Hittite burial chamber, and it is only briefly mentioned among a list of military triumphs. No other details of Alashiya are known.

The Battle of the Delta, which took place around 1175 BC, is the first naval battle recorded with any mention of the action itself. In the Nile Delta, Egyptian ships led by Pharaoh Ramesses III confronted the nomadic raiders known as the Sea Peoples. A description of the battle is found on the second pylon and outer wall of the Temple of Ramesses III at Medinet Habu in ancient Thebes. The hieroglyphs and images relate elements of the clash, including the war galleys of both sides, shields and weapons at the ready, and ornately carved prows as the opponents approach one another.

Both sides deployed a version of the galley, an early vessel used as a merchantman and a combat warship, and Ramesses III was lauded for his victory. He boldly stepped forward to stop the marauding Sea Peoples, moving troops on land and winning a stirring victory against the invaders, while at sea he thwarted their plan to dominate the region.

According to an inscription, Ramesses III proclaimed: "I was prepared and armed to trap them like wildfowl. The chiefs, the captains of infantry, the nobles, I caused to equip the harbour mouths like a strong wall, with warships, galleys, and barges. They were manned completely from bow to stern with valiant warriors… being like lions roaring upon the mountaintops… As for those who had assembled before them on the sea, the full flame was in their front, before the harbour mouths, and a wall of metal upon the shore surrounded them."

The design of the ancient warships and the development of seaborne military tactics, begun in antiquity, shaped the future of war at sea and in turn the balance of power and the extent of empire building that took place centuries ago. The future of civilisation was charted at Salamis, where the Greek fleet turned back the Persian host, and Lepanto, where the fleet of the Holy League defeated the Ottoman Empire. And the great warships put to the test in ancient times have earned their places in history.

ABOVE: This tapestry depicts opposing galleys joining in seaborne combat at the Battle of Lepanto, 1571.

(Creative Commons LooiNL via Wikimedia Commons)

ABOVE: This depiction of the Battle of the Delta appears on a wall of the tomb of Ramesses III at Thebes. (Unknown Artist Public Domain via Wikimedia Commons)

GALLEY

For nearly two millennia, from the 6th century BC to the 17th century AD, the galley was the dominant seagoing vessel in the world, both in commerce and in warfare. Originating in the Mediterranean basin, the galley was used by ancient peoples including the Egyptian, Greek, and Roman civilisations. The galley not only enabled the flourishing of trade, but also projected cultural, political, and military influence across the region.

Galleys were constructed as long, slender-hulled, shallow draft and flat ships primarily powered by oarsmen. Variations on the size of the galley were directly related to the number of rows that accommodated the oarsmen, who regularly toiled in terrible conditions. The bireme, for example, included two rows of oars and stretched roughly 80ft long with a beam of 10ft. The trireme, perhaps the most familiar galley type, included three rows of oars with a length of about 130ft and beam of approximately 19ft. The triremes of the Athenian fleet, made famous in the historical writings of Herodotus, are probably the most familiar of ancient galleys.

Larger galleys included the Tessarakonteres, literally translated from the Hellenistic Greek as "40 rowed" galley, with a length of 420ft and beam of 57ft, while its superstructure reached nearly 80ft above the waterline. The Galley of Flanders

ABOVE: The Persian Admiral Ariabignes dies in battle as his galleys clash in close quarters with the Athenian fleet at Salamis. (William Rainey via Wikimedia Commons)

measured 121ft long with a 20ft beam and height of 9ft above the waterline. It was a common galley type of the Middle Ages. The actuaria was a merchant galley used by the Roman Empire for trade and transport

ABOVE: Roman soldiers are shown aboard this bireme in a temple carving dated circa 120 BC.
(Élisée Reclus via Wikimedia Commons)

of goods, while the dromon was a late Byzantine galley intended for use in naval warfare. Specifications and intended uses of galleys varied widely, and the introduction of masts and sails eventually facilitated its ocean-going capabilities across the Mediterranean Sea.

Some researchers date the earliest use of the galley to Ancient Egypt during the Old Kingdom of 2700-2200 BC, while the first Greek galleys are believed to have been developed around 2000 BC. The innovation of the bireme with its two rows of oarsmen is attributed to the seafaring Phoenicians of the eastern Mediterranean.

The use of the galley as a warship was characterised by close combat. Greek and Roman war galleys were regularly built with heavy bronze rams affixed to the prow to strike opposing warships at or below the waterline. Opposing troops boarded enemy galleys, archers fired torrents of arrows from their decks, and the warships were considered highly manoeuvrable since they did not rely on wind power in action.

Among the great battles in history that involved the galley were the Battle of Salamis, during which the Greek fleet, primarily Athenian under Themistocles, defeated the Persian host in 480 BC; the Battle of Actium in 31 BC, during which the fleet of Octavian (later Caesar Augustus) defeated the warships of Marc Antony during the final civil war of the Roman Republic, and the Battle of Lepanto when the fleet of the Holy League defeated the warships of the Ottoman Empire in 1571, effectively curbing the empire's westward expansion.

After centuries of use, the galley was replaced by the galleon, a high-hulled, multi-decked ship of war and trade that furthered exploration and trade across the globe.

ABOVE: This French galley, shown with both sails and oarsmen, was constructed in the late 17th century.
(Henri Sbonski de Passebon via Wikimedia Commons)

VIKING LONGSHIP

ABOVE: This replica Viking longship was featured at the World's Columbian Exposition in Chicago in 1893.
(Public Domain via Wikimedia Commons)

The influence of the Viking longship on Western civilization cannot be overstated. Perhaps no other aspect of the Norse culture better exemplifies the seafaring raiders and explorers of Scandinavia. Although construction varied depending on the craftsmen and location, several types of longships were produced and plied shallow waters, rivers, and indeed great oceans and expanses of the open sea. For 1,500 years the longship transported the Vikings from their coastal villages in Norway, Sweden, and Denmark across northern Europe to the British Isles, Iceland, Russia, and Greenland. In 1000, Leif Eriksson reached North America aboard such a sturdy craft.

Typically identified with its single mast and square sail, the double-ended longship was descended from the dugouts and early craft of northern Stone Age peoples. It was characterised also by its ornate prow, often carved in the image of a snake or dragon, which sometimes led Viking adversaries to call the vessels "dragon ships". Their shallow draft allowed for manoeuvring in coastal and inland waterways and landing on beaches, while either side was lined with positions for oarsmen. Several types of longships have been identified, ranging in length from roughly 50ft to more than 120ft, and their maximum speed has been estimated at more than 15kts in ideal conditions.

Longships were constructed in the clinker style, with overlapping planks nailed together and gaps stuffed with tar, wool, animal hair, and cloth for watertightness. Available timber, primarily oak or pine, depended on the location of the builder. Early steering was accomplished with a single stern-mounted oar, which was replaced in later versions around the year 1200 with a stern rudder. The smaller Karvi carried about 30 crew and warriors, while the capacity of the large Drakkar was up to 100. The snekka, commonly associated with the documented raiding of the 8th to 11th century, accommodated about 40 people.

The seaworthiness of the longship was recognised by other civilisations, including the Anglo-Saxons, while the famed Bayeux Tapestry depicts them in action during William the Conqueror's Norman invasion of Britain in 1066. Merchants from continental Europe are known to have employed the longship as well. Modern discoveries of longships have validated their strength and versatility. Historical fiction novelist Frans G Bengtsson wrote in his 1941 classic *The Long Ships*: "In a tempest neither seafarer nor warrior could stay the wind or the wave, the billow or the breaker. But a longship is for blithe sailing and merry fighting."

At least six examples of ancient Viking longships have been discovered and have provided archaeological researchers with opportunities to more fully understand their nature. Among these is the Nydam Ship, found in 1863 in a burial site in Denmark. The Nydam Ship measures 80ft in length, was powered only by oars, and dates to approximately 300 AD, evidencing early construction. It believed to be the oldest vessel recovered in northern Europe to date. The Hedeby 1, located in 1953 at the village of Hedeby in Danish Jutland, measures more than 100ft in length and was built around 985 AD. The Gjellestad Ship, found in Norway in 2018, was probably completed in the early 8th century, and preservation efforts are currently underway.

The longship finds its place among the great warships as the conveyor of Viking culture – and terror – across the northern reaches of Europe and elsewhere, while also providing Europeans with the first glimpse of the New World.

ABOVE: This section of the famed Bayeux Tapestry shows an Anglo-Saxon longship constructed in the Viking design.
(Creative Commons via Wikimedia Commons)

ABOVE: This rediscovered Viking longship has been preserved and placed on display in Oslo, Norway.
(Creative Commons Rüdiger Stehn via Wikimedia Commons)

KUBLAI KHAN'S JUNK FLEETS

Historical references to the Chinese junk stretch back to around 2800 BC, when the Emperor Fu Hsi reigned. These ships are symbolic of Chinese ingenuity and design, and their versatility has been proven through the centuries as they have been used for trade and commerce, exploration, fishing, and in warfare.

The junk has varied in size and design through the ages, ranging from 65ft to more than 98ft long. Famed European explorer Marco Polo reported seeing massive junks that stretched 400ft long with beams of 160ft constructed with 50 to 60 cabins aboard and towering high above the waterline. Evidence of the widespread use of the junk dates to the Soong Dynasty from 960 to 1129 AD, and these versatile vessels were characterised by a high stern, large flat sails with bamboo battens to enhance stability, a projecting bow, and at least two masts. The junk was designed with a flat bottom and shallow draft, capable of operating in coastal waters and on the high seas. Its sail design and steering system made the junk highly manoeuvrable.

In the late 13th century, Mongol ruler Kublai Khan, grandson of the fabled Genghis Khan and founder of the Yuan Dynasty, was at the height of his power. By brute force and cunning, he had amassed one of the world's great empires, conquering vast areas of the Asian continent into Russia, and reaching the doorstep of Europe. Remembered by many historians as barbaric and ruthless, Kublai Khan was also ambitious. On land he unleashed his famed soldiers mounted on sturdy Mongolian horses. Their combat skills, ferocity, mobility and firepower – in accurate use of the bow and arrow while at full gallop – stunned the Mongol adversaries.

A series of Mongol assaults between 1231 and 1270 subjugated the Korean peninsula. Afterwards, Kublai Khan looked eastward towards Japan. Assembling a fleet of up to 900 junks and a formidable army estimated at 16,000 to 40,000 Mongol, Korean, and Chinese men, he unleashed the host in an invasion of the Japanese home islands. The invasion fleet reached Hakata Bay in the northwest of the island of Kyushu in November 1274, and the Mongols fought a determined force of Japanese samurai warriors. Although they utilised superior tactics and weaponry, including rockets, the Mongols were unable to thoroughly defeat the Japanese. Casualties were heavy, and the Mongols elected not to pursue the Japanese as they withdrew inland.

After returning to their junks, the Mongols were subjected to a severe typhoon that is believed to have sunk approximately

one-third of their ships. They withdrew to Korea and incurred the rage of Kublai Khan for their failure.

Undeterred, Kublai Khan raised the largest invasion force yet seen by the spring of 1281. His fleet of 4,400 junks was ordered to transport 140,000 soldiers in an all-out invasion of Japan. Meanwhile, the Japanese had erected some defences, but the prospects of survival against the Mongol onslaught were slim.

In the event, however, as the Mongol host again approached Hakata Bay, the junks were caught in a massive typhoon and decimated. Estimates of the losses vary but range as high as 4,000 junks and 100,000 men drowned in the two-day maelstrom. Japan was saved from an overwhelming invasion, and the people referred to the great typhoon as Kamikaze (meaning "Divine Wind"), a phrase revived in reference to suicide pilots who defended the home islands during World War Two. Kublai Khan's designs on dominating Japan were thwarted.

Remnants of Kublai Khan's great fleet were discovered in the 1980s, and recovered artifacts are on display at the Takashima Kōzaki Historic Site in Nagasaki Prefecture.

ABOVE: This Japanese ink on paper drawing shows the defeat of the Mongol invasion fleet, shattered by the Kamikaze. (Tokyo National Museum via Wikimedia Commons)

ABOVE: Mongols fight Japanese samurai in this colourful 13th century image. (Suenaga Takezaki via Wikimedia Commons)

AGE OF SAIL

While in exile on the island of St Helena in 1816, Napoleon Bonaparte reflected on more than 20 years of war for an empire that had come to naught for France. "My arm was strong enough, it is true, to stop with a single shock all the horses of the continent," he mused. "But I could not bridle the English fleet and there lay all the mischief. Had not people the sense enough to see this?"

Indeed, the Royal Navy had held the line in the end and contributed mightily to thwarting Napoleon's dream of personal glory and the expansion of the French Empire. True, there were setbacks, but the tremendous victories achieved by Lord Horatio Nelson and the Royal Navy at the Battles of the Nile and Trafalgar, six years apart in 1798 and 1805 respectively, proved the proverbial shipwreck of Napoleon's hopes.

During the Age of Sail, the significance of naval power, projected across the globe in numerous notable instances, trebled with the rumours of war and the actual outbreak of hostilities. Extending 300 years from the 16th to the 19th century, the Age of Sail saw the influence of naval power reach an importance that has not waned since. The embryonic evolution of naval power as an extension of diplomacy as well as tool of warfare was undertaken. The mere prospect of an enemy fleet appearing on the horizon and then unleashing tons of shot and shell against a city or merchant flotilla was compelling and drove negotiators to the bargaining table more than once during the era.

Naval power enabled nations to build, develop, and defend empires and projected overarching military might across the world's oceans through the Revolutionary and Napoleonic periods and into the era of iron and steam. While the fates of nations sometimes rested on the outcomes of great naval battles, heroes emerged to set standards of conduct and dedication to duty that have become timeless. Nelson in his dying moments aboard HMS *Victory*, US Navy Captain John Paul Jones, his ageing *Bonhomme Richard* locked in a death duel with HMS *Serapis* at Flamborough Head off the coast of England, responding to a call for surrender with: "I have not yet begun to fight!" and US Navy Captain James Lawrence, who uttered the rallying cry "Don't give up the ship" while lying mortally wounded aboard his frigate USS *Chesapeake* under the guns of the frigate HMS *Shannon*.

American naval officer, strategist and historian Alfred Thayer Mahan once pronounced: "Whoever rules the waves rules

ABOVE: Lord Nelson's coat from Trafalgar, the entry point of the fatal shot visible, is on display at the National Maritime Museum in London. (Creative Commons Morio via Wikimedia Commons)

ABOVE: A pirate ship's crew boards a merchantman that has been under attack on the high seas. (Ambroise Louis Garneray via Wikimedia Commons)

the world." And so it was during the Age of Sail. Control of the sea facilitated the movement of armies on land, dictated the flow of trade among nations, and brought the mere prospect of heavy bombardment to the doorstep of hostile shores. Naval warfare became an offensive weapon, as well as a deterrent to aggression and a defence against invasion.

Warship construction, seamanship, gunnery, and firepower increased substantially over the 300 years of the Age of Sail. The navies of the great powers and their rebellious former colonies, the robber ships of barbarous pirates, the flourishing of maritime commerce, and the exploration of previously inaccessible "new worlds" came forward during this momentous time in naval history.

ABOVE: The frigates *Bonhomme Richard* and *Serapis* are shown blazing away at one another on September 23, 1789. (Irwin John David Bevan Mariner's Museum via Wikimedia Commons)

BELOW: The host of the Ming Dynasty treasure fleet is shown in this colourful 2018 painting by artist Vladimir Kosov.

(Creative Commons Vladimir Kosov via Wikimedia Commons)

TREASURE SHIPS OF THE MING EMPEROR

In 1403, the Yongle Emperor ordered the construction of his empire's treasure fleet. It was a time of Chinese military expansion, and the great ships were to demonstrate the empire's naval might and prestige across the known world. Intended as an effective diplomatic tool, the treasure fleet would sail to distant lands, firmly establishing Chinese control over trade routes, compelling foreign regimes to bend their knee to the Ming Dynasty, and returning laden with valuable tribute goods.

Between 1405 and 1433, Admiral Zheng He led the treasure fleet on seven memorable voyages. The Chinese fleet ventured into the South China Sea, Indian Ocean, coastal India, the Persian Gulf, Arabian Peninsula, and the continent of Africa. Projecting Chinese power across the globe, the treasure ships were well armed and carried contingents of troops. During their voyages, the Chinese encountered and destroyed the pirate fleet of Chen Zuyi off the coast of Sumatra in 1407 and subjugated the Kingdom of Kotte on the island of Ceylon.

The order to construct the treasure fleet was issued in 1403 and ushered in a tremendous building programme that was to augment the existing Ming fleet with nearly 3,000 additional junks by 1419. Construction was undertaken at the Longjiang shipyard in Qinhuai Province near the modern city of Nanjing.

ABOVE: The majestic treasure junk of Admiral Zheng He is shown in this 20th century drawing.

(Artist Unknown People's Republic of China via Wikimedia Commons)

The ships were large and were constructed of bamboo, pine, and fir timber. Some were between 440ft and 538ft long, with beams of up to 210ft and had nine masts and a dozen sails, although typical length was about 166ft with a beam of just over 24ft, displacement of 800 tons, and four masts. The standard treasure junk was crewed by up to 300 sailors and troops, while capable of making 5-8kts, depending on prevailing winds. They were heavily armed with an estimated 24 cannon.

The largest of the junks were called "bǎochuán" meaning treasure ships, and it is believed that more than 60 of the 317 ships that undertook the first voyage in the spring of 1405 were massive, with numerous staterooms and balconies. These earliest treasure ships sailed to Java, Sri Lanka, the

Bay of Bengal, and Palembang, among other locales, returning on October 2, 1407, and with each of the seven voyages precious silver, spices, ebony, ivory, sandalwood, cotton cloth, and other riches filled their holds. The final voyage took place from January 19, 1431, to July 1433. Admiral He is believed to have died during the return of the seventh voyage.

Subsequently, the Ming Emperor heeded the advice of Confucian courtiers and ended the treasure voyages. Apparently, the Confucians favoured miliary operations on land, and concerns had been raised regarding the cost of each lengthy expedition. As a result, many of the ships were dismantled or broken up. With their demise, the knowledge of great shipbuilding also slipped into the Chinese past.

ABOVE: This full-size recreation of a Ming Dynasty treasure junk is on display in Nanjing, China.

(Creative Commons Vmenkov via Wikimedia Commons)

MARY ROSE

ABOVE: The carrack *Mary Rose* is the most famous ship of the English Tudor Navy during the reign of King Henry VIII.
(Own scan photo by Gerry Bye original by Anthony Anthony via Wikimedia Commons)

On July 19, 1545, King Henry VIII and his privy council watched the naval Battle of the Solent unfold. The English fleet of 80 varied warships lay ready to defend against an intended French invasion of the Isle of Wight spearheaded by approximately 200 warships and support vessels. Early in the contest, one of King Henry's favourite ships, the carrack *Mary Rose*, heeled sharply to starboard and then – disaster!

Mary Rose rapidly took on water and sank in roughly six minutes, taking all but 35 of those aboard to their graves in the shallows of the Solent. The French force withdrew after the inconclusive battle, and the *Mary Rose* was mourned. Constructed between 1509 and 1511 during the period that preceded the founding of the Royal Navy, *Mary Rose* required 40 acres of timber – more than 600 oak trees. Launched at Portsmouth, she was built as a carrack, the relatively large three- or four-masted sailing ships that were commonly employed in trade, exploration, and in warfare from the 14th to the 17th century. They were characterised by their sizable forecastle and sterncastle (aftercastle) structures, and low weather decks.

Mary Rose served with the English Tudor fleet for 34 years and during the period of Henry VIII's reign, the fleet's strength grew from five warships to nearly 60. Her dimensions are uncertain, but it is believed that she displaced about 600 tons and stretched from 110ft to 148ft long. She carried an assortment of heavy cast bronze and wrought iron guns, along with smaller weapons intended to inflict casualties on enemy personnel, shred rigging, and inflict structural damage. After a major refit in 1536, *Mary Rose* is thought to have been armed with 80 to 90 guns and crewed by approximately 230 sailors with a complement of 185 soldiers. During her long career, she participated in three wars with France. On August 10, 1512, during the Battle of St Mathieu, she engaged the French warship *Grand Louise* in an exchange that is thought by some historians to have been the first-time opposing vessels with gunports fought on one another. She disabled *Grand Louise*, felling her mainmast and killing 300 men. In June 1520, *Mary Rose* sailed in escort of King Henry VIII to the French coast, where he met French King Francis I at the Field of the Cloth of Gold.

Much conjecture surrounds the story of the *Mary Rose*, including her name. While the rose represents the royal House of Tudor, some historians aver that the ship also honoured Mary Tudor, favourite sister of Henry VIII. Others believe that in keeping with the contemporary practice of giving warships Christian names, the reference to Mary is an homage to the Blessed Virgin.

The cause of *Mary Rose*'s demise remains a topic of discussion 500 years on. Some scholars attribute it to the loss of seaworthy characteristics after the 1536 refit, which added weight and made the vessel more unwieldy and likely to heel sharply in a sudden gust of wind. Further, the gunports are thought to have been left open, allowing the waters of the English Channel to sweep in and sink the majestic ship. One Frenchman offered a far-fetched claim that a cannon shot below the waterline had doomed the vessel.

After centuries lying in the mud and silt of the Solent, the wreck of the *Mary Rose* was rediscovered in 1965. Positively identified in 1971 and raised from the seabed in October 1982, about 40% of the original warship had survived the ravages of time. Archaeological studies continue, and today the fabled ship is on display along with thousands of recovered artefacts at the Mary Rose Museum in Portsmouth, Hampshire, offering a glimpse into the life and times of Tudor England.

ABOVE: The recovered structure of the *Mary Rose* is seen on display at the Mary Rose Museum in Portsmouth, Hampshire.
(Creative Commons Mary Rose Trust via Wikimedia Commons)

ABOVE: *Mary Rose* is shown during the embarkation of King Henry from Dover to Calais to meet King Francis I at the Field of the Cloth of Gold in 1520. (Jakob Kate Royal Collection via Wikimedia Commons)

VASA

T he Swedish royal battle galleon *Vasa* was an impressive sight at more than 226ft long with a beam of 38ft and towering height of 172ft from keel to the truck of her mainmast. That is until she set sail on her maiden voyage in the harbour of Stockholm on August 10, 1628.

The great ship was resplendent with fine ornate carvings and decorations that glistened in the sunlight, renderings of mythical creatures, biblical figures, and a host of symbols that represented majesty, authority and martial ardour. She was intended to carry 64 guns, 46 of which were to be newly cast bronze 24-pounders, and expectations were high that *Vasa* would be an intimidating presence, enhancing Swedish prestige and control of the Baltic Sea during a period of armed conflict with the Polish Lithuanian Commonwealth while the storm of the Thirty Years' War raged on the European continent. *Vasa*, it was said, could hurl more than 500lbs of shot at an opposing warship in a single broadside during a period in which warfare at sea was transitioning from the primary act of boarding the enemy vessel to seize control to one of subduing the adversary with accurate cannon fire.

On that pleasant summer afternoon, *Vasa* slipped into the harbour waters. A breeze, probably no more than 8kts, caused the ship to heel violently with billowing sail. In a moment, *Vasa* righted herself. Then, a second rush of wind caused the ship to topple. She sank in minutes as water gushed through her open gunports and surfaces. Vasa settled to the harbour bottom in less than 400ft of water. Thousands gasped, horrified by the spectacle that took the lives of as many as 53 of the 150 men aboard. She had sailed only about 1,300 yards.

When *Vasa* sank on her maiden voyage, it was a serious blow to the naval ambitions of Swedish King Gustavus Adolphus, who ordered the warship as

ABOVE: This model of *Vasa* reveals her grandeur prior to the tragic sinking in 1628. (Creative Commons Karolina Kristensson/SMM via Wikimedia Commons)

ABOVE: This photo reveals the top deck and scale of *Vasa* on display at one of the most visited museums in the world. (Creative Commons OneHungLow via Wikimedia Commons)

ABOVE: The recovered *Vasa* is on display at the Vasa Museum, Stockholm, Sweden. (Creative Commons Javier Kohen via Wikimedia Commons)

one of five that would replace earlier losses to violent storms and hostile action. Construction had begun in the Stockholm shipyard in 1626, under the supervision of experienced shipwrights. However, the king continually interfered, requiring structural alterations that complicated the process while continually clamouring for the ship's speedy completion. One of the king's changes added a second gun deck to the ship, which resulted in a quite unstable platform. Existing technology did not offer a solution to counter the shift in the *Vasa*'s centre of gravity to a higher position due to too much weight in her upper hull. Additional weight in the lower hull would probably have contributed to better stability, but the lowest gunports might well have become awash as *Vasa* rode lower in the water. Modern testing has indicated that only a slight breeze of 4kts would have been sufficient to precipitate the disaster.

Within seconds, all the grandeur that was *Vasa* had been lost due to Gustavus Adolphus and his persistent interference, the lack of a coherent building plan, and the flawed construction that resulted. Sofring Hanson, captain of the ship, was arrested shortly after the debacle; however, an inquest determined that there was no particular individual who could be blamed and punished. Gustavus Adolphus himself had been heavily involved in the misadventure, and Henrik Hybertsson, the most prominent master shipbuilder involved, had died in 1627.

At least 50 of the bronze cannon were recovered between 1663 and 1683, but the wreck of *Vasa* lay in the mud of Stockholm harbour for more than 300 years. Contemporary attempts to refloat the ship were abandoned. Salvage operations gained momentum in the 1950s, and Vasa was raised largely intact on April 24, 1961, the cold saltwater of the Baltic having provided protection for the vessel's oak structure from the ravages of shipworm infestation.

Although many small iron components had rusted away, an incredible number of artefacts were recovered, including sails, clothing, and leather items. These have provided a trove of information on life in Sweden and aboard naval warships during the 17th century. Conservation efforts are ongoing, and since 1988 the ship has been housed in the Vasa Museum in Stockholm, one of the most visited attractions in Scandinavia.

GOLDEN HIND

ABOVE: Sir Francis Drake gained lasting fame as an explorer and privateer aboard *Golden Hind*. (National Maritime Museum Collection via Wikimedia Commons)

Sir Francis Drake was given a privateering commission by Queen Elizabeth I in 1572, and the logical target at the time was England's empire building rival, Spain. The commission gave Drake the right to plunder Spanish shipping and property, inflicting injury and insult that would sting the court of Spanish King Philip II. Drake wasted no time.

By late July of that year, he embarked on his first voyage, reaching the Isthmus of Panama, capturing the port of Nombre de Dios, and attacking Spanish mule trains on land and treasure galleons at sea. It was the shape of things to come. For 24 years, Drake plied his craft while also achieving notoriety as an explorer and slave trader. In 1577, he commissioned his most famous warship, *Golden Hind*, best described as a mid-16th century design that bridged the transition from the carrack to the galleon.

Drake was aboard *Golden Hind* during his famed circumnavigation of the globe between 1577 and 1580. Originally named *Pelican*, the ship was renamed by Drake in mid-voyage in 1578 to honour of one of his patrons, Sir Christopher Hatton, a politician and advisor to the queen. The Hatton family crest featured a hind, or female red deer. *Golden Hind* was built beginning in 1575 and launched at Plymouth. Her length was 122ft with a beam of 20ft and draught of 9ft. She displaced 300 tons and carried 12 cannon on the lower deck and six lighter guns on her upper deck.

Drake began his famous global voyage with five ships on December 13, 1577, his crews totalling 164 sailors, about 80 of these aboard *Golden Hind*. At first, the men believed they were heading to Egypt, but Drake turned westward, rounding Cape Horn and reaching the Pacific Ocean, while four of his accompanying vessels were either

ABOVE: This artist's rendering of *Golden Hind* appeared in a 20th century history book. (Internet Archive Book Images No Restrictions via Wikimedia Commons)

lost at sea or returned to port due to storms. *Marigold*, for example, foundered and sank in a storm along with 29 crew, while *Elizabeth* became separated from the rest of the squadron and returned via the Strait of Magellan to England in 1579.

Golden Hind conducted raids on Spanish settlements along the Pacific coast of South America and some sources relate that on March 1, 1579, while sailing off the shores of Ecuador, she encountered the Spanish galleon Nuestra Senora de la Concepcion, and spent the next six days transferring treasure valued at nearly $592 million today, including a half ton of gold, 26 tons of silver, jewels, and porcelain.

Golden Hind returned to Plymouth in September 1580, and Drake was hailed a hero, knighted by the Queen in April 1581, for his achievements as an explorer and privateer.

From April 29 to May 1, 1587, Drake raised his flag aboard *Golden Hind* in a daring raid on the Spanish harbour of Cadiz, where Philip II had assembled 60 warships and dozens of support craft, some capable of carrying troops for a potential invasion of England. Drake destroyed about 10,000 tons of supplies and is believed to have damaged, sunk, or captured as many as 100 Spanish ships. The raid, sometimes called the "singeing of the beard of the king of Spain", postponed the sailing of the famed but ill-fated Spanish Armada, which was defeated by the English navy the following year.

Golden Hind continued in service with the English navy and returned to Deptford dockyard in London, where she was on display for decades before falling into disrepair and being broken up around 1662. The only known surviving piece of *Golden Hind* is a chair carved from her timbers that is housed at the Bodleian Library of Oxford University.

Several modern replicas of *Golden Hind* have been constructed and are open to the public.

ABOVE: This replica of the famed *Golden Hind* can be found in Southwark, London. (Creative Commons Jose L. Marin via Wikimedia Commons)

GALLEON

The prominent conveyor of trade, wealth, exploration, and naval power from the 16th to the 18th century was the galleon. Captains Pedro Menéndez de Avilés and Álvaro de Bazán of the Spanish navy are credited with this significant development during the Age of Sail, which emerged in the mid-1500s as a progression of the carrack and caravel designs.

The typical galleon was a full-rigged vessel with three masts, the foremast and mainmast square rigged and the mizzenmast lateen rigged. Larger galleons sometimes had a fourth mast called a Bonaventure mizzen. Galleons were also distinguishable by their long beakhead (or beak) at the bow intended as a weapon for ramming enemy ships. The hull was tapered on either side to enhance stability at sea, while the flat stern made the ship faster in favourable winds. The high, square-built stern was another characteristic of galleon design, and while the galleon was faster than other designs of its time, it was also more battleworthy as it carried more cannon than older types on two decks, capable of firing heavier broadsides. The ships were carvel built, meaning that their hull planking was laid edge to edge and did not overlap, creating a smooth surface. Their construction was generally of hardwood oak, while the masts were fashioned of softer pine.

The Spanish galleon was usually constructed with a length of 150ft and a beam of up to 50ft with a displacement of 500 to 1,000 tons. The design was developed for the purposes of long-distance trade, particularly between Europe and Asia and the New World. Its fame as the carrier of gold and treasure from Spanish territory in the Western Hemisphere across the Atlantic Ocean endures. While the galleon was employed as a transport for infantry and supplies, and as an escort for ships laden with treasure and trade goods that were otherwise susceptible to enemy privateers or pirates, the proficiency of the galleon in warfare was another catalyst for development. Documented incidents of galleons bombarding shore targets, fortresses and towns in wartime are extant as well.

ABOVE: A Danish galleon is shown in full sail in this painting of the mid-17th century.
(Privately owned at Gavno Castle Public Domain via Wikimedia Commons)

ABOVE: A Spanish galleon fires its heavy cannon in this painting by artist Cornelis Verbeeck.
(National Gallery of Art via Wikimedia Commons)

In addition to its sail power, the galleon carried a crew of up to 250, their majority utilised as rowers, while others were officers, sailors, and sometimes military troops. The earliest recorded use of the galleon in battle occurred in the late 16th century. At the Battle of Lepanto, galleons were active alongside war galleys like those that had been in use for centuries. The galleon was also the primary warship of the Spanish Armada sent by King Philip II to subdue the English navy and pave the way for invasion but which came to grief in 1588.

The only surviving original galleon is the ill-fated Swedish *Vasa*, sunk on its maiden voyage in the harbour of Stockholm and recovered in the mid-20th century.

ABOVE: This painting of the Spanish galleon Nuestra Señora de la Concepción y de las Ánimas was completed by artist Martin Amigo in 1690. (Government of Spain via Wikimedia Commons)

TURTLE SHIP

Conceived and designed by Admiral Yi Sun-sin, the great naval hero of the Korean people, the turtle ship was a decisive weapon of warfare at sea during the efforts to turn back a Japanese invasion of the peninsula in the late 16th century.

Concerns for the protection of the crew and the integrity of his warships in close fighting caused Admiral Yi to consider the construction of an ark-like vessel, its exterior completely enclosed and its roof covered with spikes to ward off would-be enemy boarding parties. Measuring up to 120ft long with a width or beam of 30 to 40ft, the turtle ship carried a crew of 80 oarsmen and a complement of 50-60 soldiers. The turtle ship was also powered by two large sails, which were lowered with the threat of impending combat. There is some speculation that the vessels were further protected by iron cladding, although no firm evidence exists. If true, then the turtle ship is possibly the first such "ironclad" warship in naval history.

Admiral Yi designed the turtle ship in 1591, and when he led a fleet of 26 Korean warships into battle at Sacheon on May 29, 1592, the single turtle ship in company was easily identifiable. Its enclosed structure was complemented by a fearsome carved dragon's head at its prow and correspondingly colourful tail at its stern. Intending to compel the opposing Japanese naval force to retire after withdrawing a substantial landing party from Korean shores, Admiral Yi used deception to lure the Japanese away from the shallow waters and into the open sea, where he defeated them, allowing a few enemy warships to survive to accomplish the desired evacuation of the shore party.

The turtle ship was distinguished in its service as the crew maintained speed while free from enemy boarders and protected from Japanese archers. Sailors moved through internal passageways, servicing

ABOVE: A scaled down replica of the Korean navy turtle ship is on display at the War Memorial Museum in Seoul, South Korea. (General Public License Feth via Wikimedia Commons)

weapons from gunports on the starboard and port sides along with cannon mounted in the bow and stern. Admiral Yi was slightly wounded during the Battle of Sacheon but remained in command throughout.

After proving its worth at Sacheon, the turtle ship was a key participant in the ensuing Korean naval effort to repel the Japanese. Three months later, Admiral Yi was warned

that another powerful Japanese naval squadron of 73 warships was approaching from the west and gathered his own force of 56 warships, including three turtle ships, north of the Kyonnaeryang Strait to defend vital shipping lanes in the Yellow Sea. When the shallow-draft Japanese ships paused along the shoals of Hansan Island, Yi realised that bringing on an engagement close to shore would negate an advantage in manoeuvrability. Again, he employed the tactic of deception, dispatching six ships as an enticement to draw the Japanese into deeper waters.

The Japanese commander, Admiral Yasaharu Wakizaka, took the bait. Pursuing the six ships, he was soon confronted with the whole of the Korean fleet which temporarily also feigned withdrawal. With the enemy charging headlong, Admiral Yi ordered an abrupt turn and deployment into the Crane Wing formation with heavier warships in the centre and lighter craft on either flank to rapidly envelope the enemy force. In minutes, a torrent of Korean cannon fire and arrows had decimated the Japanese. An estimated 47 Japanese ships were destroyed and a dozen captured.

Along with Admiral Yi, the turtle ship gained fame in the defeats of the invading Japanese. Varied designs of the turtle ship remained in service with the Korean navy into the 18th century. Modern replicas are now on display in museums, and a private company has built several for use in film.

ABOVE: This reconstructed turtle ship exhibits the fearsome dragon's head carved on its prow. (Creative Commons Moody75 via Wikimedia Commons)

ABOVE: The stern, sails, and spiked roof of the turtle ship are clearly visible in this image from the War Memorial Museum in Seoul, South Korea. (Creative Commons Steve46814 via Wikimedia Commons)

QUEEN ANNE'S REVENGE

ABOVE: This drawing of Blackbeard's flagship *Queen Anne's Revenge* was produced in 1736.
(Joseph Nicholls via Wikimedia Commons)

Before Edward Teach turned to a life of crime as a pirate on the high seas, he was likely a privateer in the service of the British crown. During Queen Anne's War of 1702-1713, he harassed and plundered Spanish shipping in the West Indies. When the conflict ended, he is believed to have learned the piracy trade under the tutelage of Captain Benjamin Hornigold.

Teach joined Hornigold's crew in 1716 and commanded a sloop in the elder pirate's small squadron of criminal vessels. Apparently, as Hornigold retired in 1717, Teach ventured on, capturing the former naval frigate, privateer and slave ship *La Concorde* near Martinique on November 28, 1717, renaming her *Queen Anne's Revenge*. Although little is known of the ship's activities prior to 1710, and her origins are somewhat unclear, it is believed that *Queen Anne's Revenge* was of French construction. Her length was 103ft with a beam of nearly 25ft. Displacing about 200 tons, she mounted 40 cannon, 30 of which are believed to have been recovered from her wreckage.

When Teach and crew captured the French ship, she was apparently loaded with a human cargo. Teach sold the slaves at market in Martinique and quickly decided to make *Queen Anne's Revenge* his flagship. Although Teach used *Queen Anne's Revenge* for nefarious purposes for less than a year, the ship gained fame – or infamy – just as Teach earned the nickname Blackbeard for his long flowing beard that some said approached his waistline. He was also said to have lit matches in his hair when approaching a victim ship to strike fear into his quarry.

Blackbeard and his crew of seafaring outlaws terrorised merchantmen in the Caribbean Sea, sailing from the waters of the Western Hemisphere to the coast of Africa while attacking merchant ships of British, Portuguese, and Dutch origin. Adjusting for inflation, the treasure stolen by Blackbeard and company is estimated to have been valued somewhere between $12.5 and $14.8 million today.

Blackbeard scoffed at acceptance of the pardon issued by King George I to pirates under certain terms, officially declining clemency in response to the governor of South Carolina, even blockading the port of Charleston in May 1718 and demanding a ransom. He subsequently settled for a chest filled with medicines in exchange for the release of hostages he had taken from the city. Weeks later, on June 10, Blackbeard ran *Queen Anne's Revenge* aground at Beaufort Inlet, North Carolina (then known as Topsail Inlet). Captain David Herriot, commander of the

ABOVE: This model of *Queen Anne's Revenge* resides in the North Carolina Museum of History.
(Creative Commons Qualiesin via Wikimedia Commons)

ABOVE: Edward Teach, better known as the pirate Blackbeard, sailed aboard *Queen Anne's Revenge*.
(Joseph Nicholls via Wikimedia Commons)

accompanying sloop *Adventure*, confirmed the incident, relating that supplies and some crewmen were transferred to his ship, which also ran aground temporarily. Some crewmen were left ashore and later rescued by pirate Stede Bonnet.

Debate as to whether Blackbeard ran *Queen Anne's Revenge* aground intentionally to disperse the crew continues today. The fabled pirate captain himself surrendered soon afterwards and accepted the King's pardon from the governor of North Carolina.

Alas, Blackbeard could not steer completely clear of his life of crime as he returned to piracy in August 1718. He was shot and killed by Royal Navy Lieutenant Robert Maynard during a fight off the Carolina coast on November 22 of that year.

The remains of *Queen Anne's Revenge* were discovered by a private research firm on November 21, 1996. More than 300 artefacts from the famed pirate ship are on display at the North Carolina Maritime Museum in Beaufort.

L'ORIENT

L'*Orient*, a magnificent example of the French Ocean-class with three decks and 120 guns, was the flagship of the fleet that opposed the Royal Navy squadron under Lord Horatio Nelson in the Battle of the Nile, also known as the Battle of Aboukir Bay, in the estuary of the great river, on August 1, 1798.

As the two fleets blazed away at one another, *L'Orient* engaged the 74-gun third-rate ships of the line, HMS *Bellerophon* and HMS *Swiftsure,* along with the diminutive 10-gun schooner HMS *Alexander.* *L'Orient* inflicted serious punishment on *Bellerophon*, which was dismasted and drifted out of the battle. However, at approximately 10pm, a tremendous explosion tore through the French flagship's powder magazine. The volcanic explosion that ensued caused both sides to pause in awe at the spectacle. More than 1,000 French sailors perished in the conflagration, but the French commander, Admiral François-Paul Brueys d'Aigalliers, was already dead from a grievous wound that severed both his legs.

Nelson had finally found and fixed the French fleet after a three-month hunt across the Mediterranean Sea, and the thorough victory at the Battle of the Nile significantly altered the plans of conquest of French General Napoleon Bonaparte during his land campaign in Egypt. In England, the resounding Royal Navy triumph was hailed and memorialised in numerous works of art. Nelson was presented with a hand-carved coffin fashioned from the remnants of the mainmast of *L'Orient* and he was subsequently laid to rest in it after his death at the pivotal Battle of Trafalgar in 1805.

Shipwright Jacques-Noël Sané designed *L'Orient*, which was the third of ten ships of her class to be constructed during the French Revolutionary and Napoleonic periods. Laid

ABOVE: L'Orient erupts in flames with the detonation of her powder magazine at the Battle of the Nile in this painting by artist George Arnald. (National Maritime Museum via Wikimedia Commons)

down at Toulon in May 1790, the ship was first named *Dauphin Royal*; however, with the ascent of the First Republic, her name was changed to *Sans-Culotte* and later to *L'Orient*. The mighty ship of the line was nearly 214ft long with a beam of more than 53ft, draught of nearly 27ft, and displacement of 5,616 tons. Cannon were situated in four locations with 32 36-pound guns on the lower deck, 34 24-pounders on the middle deck, 34 12-pounders on the upper deck, and 18 8-pounders with six 36-pound carronades on the quarterdeck and forecastle.

L'Orient was launched on July 20, 1791, and commissioned in August 1793. Early in her career, she covered the rear of the French Fleet at the 1795 Battle of Genoa,

ABOVE: While at sea, General Napoleon Bonaparte addresses French officers on the deck of L'Orient.
(Bingham, peintre anglaise, French Government via Wikimedia Commons)

exchanging fire with the British 74-gun third rates Egmont and Bedford. She became the French flagship later that year and later sailed to her terrible fate.

Aboard the 74-gun HMS *Goliath,* British sailor John Nichol witnessed the horrific demise of *L'Orient* and remembered: "When the French flagship blew up, *Goliath* was so shaken that we thought that the stern of our ship had exploded…When the firing stopped, I went on deck to see what state the fleets were in and it was a horrible sight. The whole bay was entirely covered with mutilated corpses, the wounded, the burned, wearing no clothes other than trousers. There were a few Frenchmen from the flagship *L'Orient* pressed up against the poop of *Goliath.* Poor men!"

The wreck of *L'Orient* was discovered in Aboukir Bay in 1983. French archaeologists have extensively mapped the location and recovered numerous artefacts from the site.

ABOVE: The French flagship L'Orient blazes at the centre of this painting of the Battle of the Nile by artist Thomas Luny.
(Art Renewal Center via Wikimedia Commons)

SANTISIMA TRINIDAD

ABOVE: *Santisima Trinidad* engages Royal Navy warships during the 1797 Battle of Cape St Vincent.
(Naval Museum of Madrid via Wikimedia Commons)

At the time she was launched, the Spanish first-rate ship of the line, *Santisima Trinidad*, was the largest warship in the world. Designed by Matthew Mullan, an Irish-born naval engineer who lived in Havana, Cuba, the great ship was ordered in October 1767, launched on March 20, 1769, and commissioned eight months later.

At the time of completion, *Santisima Trinidad* was 201ft long with a beam of 53ft, displacement of 4,950 tons, draught of more than 26ft, and a complement of 1,100 officers and sailors. Her initial armament consisted of 112 cannon, 30 36-pounders on the lower deck, 32 24-pounders on the middle deck, and 32 12-pounders on the upper deck, with 18 8-pounders mounted on the quarterdeck and forecastle. In 1795, the ship was redesigned with the closing of the forecastle and quarterdeck to effectively create a fourth deck. Armament was increased to a capacity of 136 guns. After sea trials, attempts were made to improve the sluggish handling of the immense vessel at the Spanish shipyards of Ferrol and Cadiz.

In the summer of 1779, more than a year after France had declared war on Great Britain and begun sending aid to the American colonies that were in revolt against the British crown, Spain followed suit. Serving as the flagship of the Spanish fleet, *Santisima Trinidad* participated in operations against British merchant shipping. In a notable encounter on August 9, 1780, she intercepted a convoy of 63 merchant ships

ABOVE: In this 20th century drawing, the massive *Santisima Trinidad* is shown with full sail.
(Jacob Hagg via Wikimedia Commons)

in the English Channel under the escort of the 74-gun HMS *Ramillies* and a pair of frigates. *Santisima Trinidad* captured 55 of the merchantmen as prizes; the outgunned *Ramillies* and other escorts made good their escape.

In 1797, *Santisima Trinidad* took part in the Battle of Cape St Vincent off the southern coast of Portugal. A Royal Navy squadron of 15 ships of the line under the command of Admiral Sir John Jervis took on a Spanish fleet nearly twice its size, and the 27 Spanish warships, under the command of Admiral Don José de Córdoba

y Ramos, were thoroughly defeated. *Santisima Trinidad* exchanged fire with at least six British warships, including the 74-gun third-rates HMS *Captain*, *Culloden*, *Orion*, *Irresistible*, and *Excellent*, and the 90-gun second-rate HMS *Blenheim*. Admiral Horatio Nelson was in command of HMS *Captain* during the battle.

Santisima Trinidad was severely damaged, losing her masts and suffering hundreds of crewmen killed or wounded. Her colours were struck, but before the British could approach to board her, the 112-gun *Principe de Asturias* and 74-gun *Infante don Pelayo* intervened and took the badly wounded *Santisima Trinidad* in tow. A few days later, as *Santisima Trinidad* limped homeward toward Cadiz, she was attacked by the 32-gun frigate HMS *Terpsichore* but managed to avoid further serious damage.

During the decisive Battle of Trafalgar in October 1805, Admiral Baltasar Hidalgo de Cisneros flew his flag aboard *Santisima Trinidad*. Light prevailing winds on the day of battle impeded her manoeuvrability and she was regularly vulnerable to opposing fire. *Santisima Trinidad* fought as many as seven different British warships and inflicted substantial damage, but she was heavily damaged as well. With at least 200 of her crew dead and 100 more wounded, she was surrendered to the 98-gun second-rate HMS *Neptune*. Taken in tow by the 98-gun second-rate HMS *Prince*, the unwieldy ship heaved in rough seas for three days. British sailors manned pumps to keep her afloat, but in the end, she was scuttled in the open sea northwest of Cadiz.

In 2009 during testing of new sonar apparatus, the Spanish navy may have located the wreck of *Santisima Trinidad* after more than two centuries at the bottom of the Atlantic Ocean. Evidence supports the conclusion, but final confirmation is pending.

ABOVE: In this 1850 painting by Richard B Spencer, *Santisima Trinidad* is shown severely damaged and without masts after the Battle of Trafalgar.
(R.B. Spencer Bonham's Auction via Wikimedia Commons)

HMS *VICTORY*

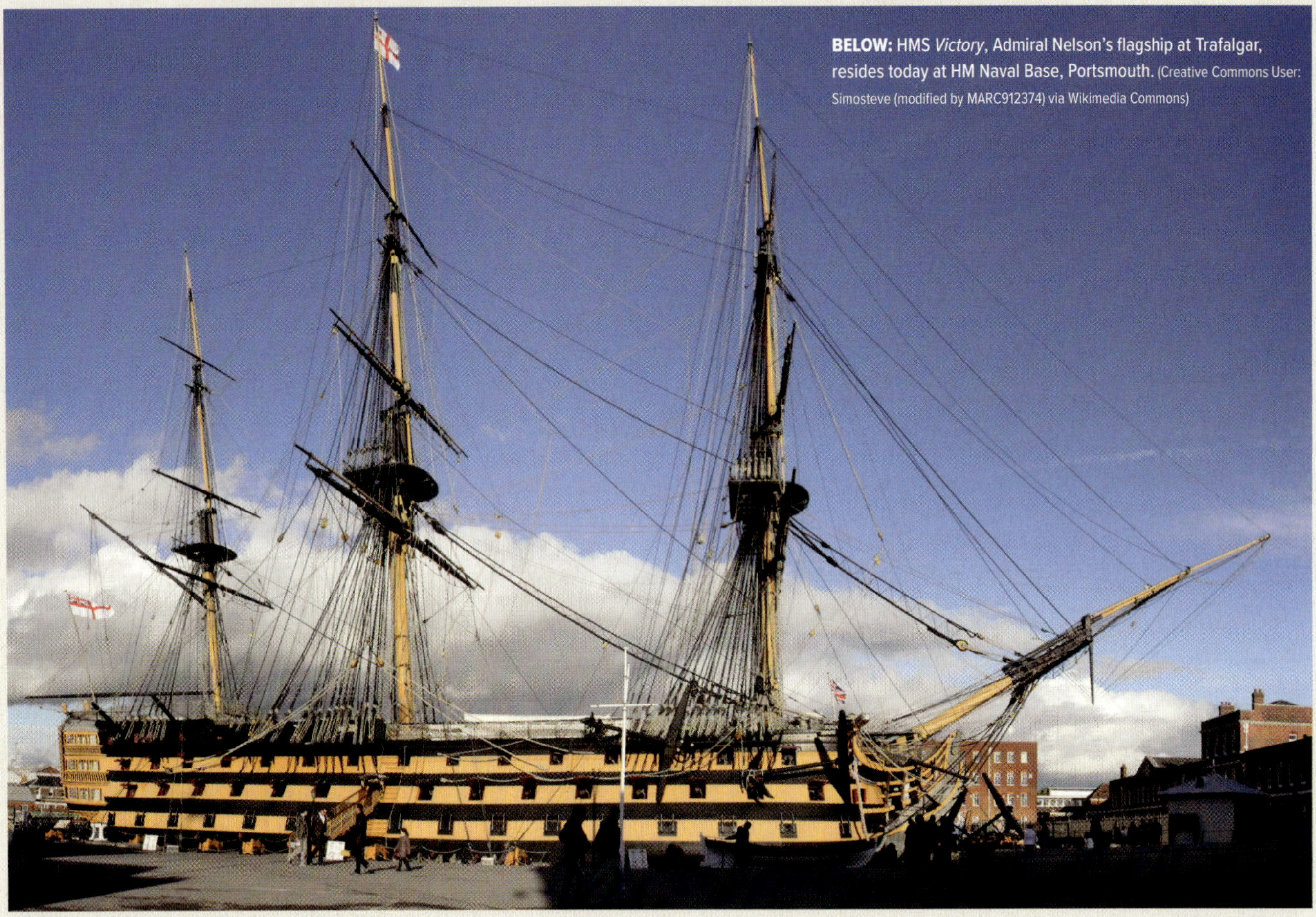

BELOW: HMS *Victory*, Admiral Nelson's flagship at Trafalgar, resides today at HM Naval Base, Portsmouth. (Creative Commons User: Simosteve (modified by MARC912374) via Wikimedia Commons)

Perhaps the most famous warship in the illustrious history of the Royal Navy, HMS *Victory* began life as a first-rate ship of the line, and after nearly 250 years in continuous service she is the world's oldest active warship still in commission. Since the early 1920s, the grand vessel has resided at Portsmouth, England, serving as the flagship of the First Sea Lord and as a museum.

Through her lengthy career during the great Age of Sail, HMS *Victory* participated in several major battles, earning the distinction as the flagship of Admiral Horatio Nelson at the decisive Battle of Trafalgar in 1805. It was on the deck of *Victory* at Trafalgar that Nelson, already a national hero after his triumph over Napoleon's fleet at the Battle of the Nile in 1798, fell mortally wounded during the fight and where he died just hours after the defeat of a combined French and Spanish fleet during the War of the Third Coalition.

HMS *Victory* was ordered by British Prime Minister William Pitt the Elder in December 1758 during the Seven Years' War, one of a dozen new ships for the Royal Navy, which had begun to exert pre-eminence among the great naval forces of the world. She was laid down the following year, launched six years later as construction was completed in 1765, and commissioned in 1778. Requiring roughly 100 acres of woodland harvest (approximately 6,000 trees), she was constructed mostly of oak but incorporated some elm, pine, fir, and lignum vitae.

With a length of just over 227ft and beam of more than 52ft, she displaced roughly

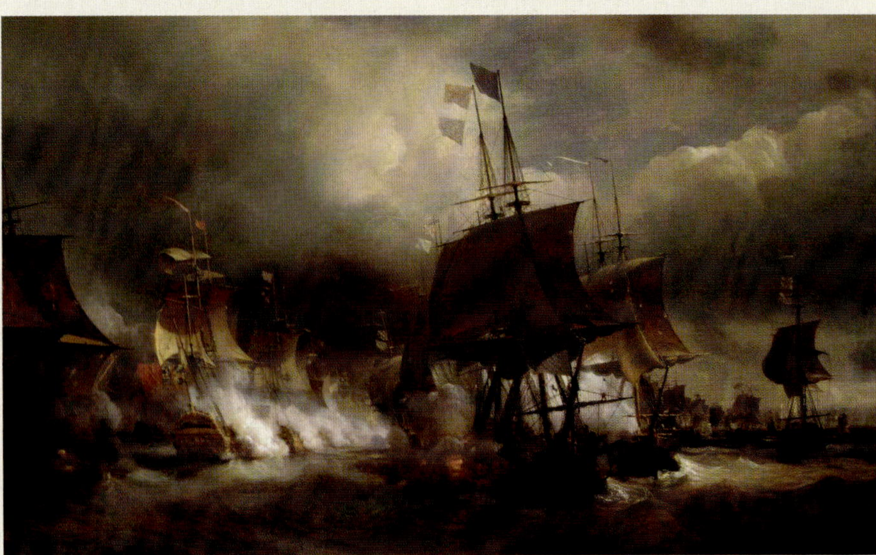

ABOVE: Warships of the Royal Navy and the French fleet collide during the First Battle of Ushant in 1778. (Theodore Gudin Museum of the History of France via Wikimedia Commons)

ABOVE: HMS *Victory*, a 104-gun first-rate ship of the line, flies the Royal Navy's blue ensign.
(Creative Neddyseagoon via Wikimedia Commons)

3,920 tons. Mounting 104 bronze cannon, her primary weapons were 30 32-pounders, and secondary armament included 28 24-pounders, 42 short 12-pounders, a pair of medium 12-pounders, and two 68-pounder carronades. *Victory* was built with three decks, and three ornate open galleries are prominent at the stern. The great cabin occupies a quarter of the space on the upper gun deck and usually served as quarters and living space for the admiral commanding, while the nearby day cabin was used as his office. *Victory* often served as the overall commander's flagship during deployments. Her crew numbered approximately 850 officers and sailors.

The hull of HMS *Victory* was sheathed in copper plating, which was a common shipbuilding practice of the time to ward off the corrosive effects of saltwater and the fouling of barnacles, and any debris encountered. Her grand magazine was perhaps the most vulnerable location aboard *Victory*, and other great sailing warships of the time, as large quantities of gunpowder were stored there. The grand magazine could hold up to 780 barrels of the volatile mixture, and even in peaceful times, the threat of fire and catastrophic explosion was ever present.

HMS *Victory* compiled an impressive service record during the Napoleonic period. She was active during the First and Second Battles of Ushant in 1778 and 1780, the siege of Gibraltar in 1782, and the 1797 Battle of Cape St Vincent. It was at Trafalgar, on October 21, 1805, however, that HMS *Victory* achieved naval immortality. Lord Nelson flew his flag aboard *Victory*, which led the 27 ships of his Royal Navy squadron into battle that day against 33 French and Spanish ships of the line off the coast of Cadiz in southwest Spain.

Prior to the commencement of the action, Nelson sent his famous signal to his command: "England expects that every man will do his duty." He ordered HMS *Victory* into the veritable gaping maw of the French and Spanish warships, at times engaging four

enemy vessels at the same time. *Victory* and the 74-gun French Temeraire-class ship of the line *Redoutable* blazed away at one another, and their masts became intertwined in the furore. A French shell struck Nelson's secretary, Warrant Officer John Scott, killing him instantly and nearly cutting his body in half.

At approximately 1.15pm, a musket ball fired by a marine sharpshooter from the rigging of the French vessel struck Nelson. The fatal round entered Nelson's left shoulder damaging ribs and lungs and severing his spinal cord before lodging in his back. Captain Thomas Hardy, captain of HMS *Victory*, saw Nelson momentarily kneeling on the quarterdeck, and the admiral whispered: "Kiss me Hardy. They have done for me at last… my backbone is shot through."

Nelson was carried below, where the ship's surgeon, Dr William Bailey, removed the ball that was still attached to a fragment of lace from an epaulette of Nelson's uniform jacket. Informed that his squadron had won a great triumph, the admiral died about three hours later. His last words were said to be: "Thank God, I have done my duty."

ABOVE: The ornate figurehead of HMS *Victory* has been restored to its early grandeur. (Creative Commons Colin Smith via Wikimedia Commons)

ABOVE: Lord Nelson, Vice Admiral of the Royal Navy, flew his flag aboard *Victory* at Trafalgar and was killed by a French marine sharpshooter.
(Lemuel Francis Abbott via Wikimedia Commons)

Severely damaged at Trafalgar, HMS *Victory* was taken in tow by the 98-gun second rate ship of the line HMS *Neptune*. The shattered flagship made port at Gibraltar, underwent temporary repairs and then sailed for England carrying the body of the fallen hero of the great naval battle. Given her age and condition, HMS *Victory* encountered another fight for survival. The Admiralty was reluctant to invest in repairs as a first-rate ship of the line, and *Victory* was relegated to second-rate with lighter guns and fewer crew. Major repairs were undertaken in 1814, and *Victory* served in the rather ignominious roles of floating depot and prison ship.

In 1831, a public outcry saved HMS *Victory* from being broken up as salvage. But still the historic warship lay derelict and continued to deteriorate for years. However, in 1921 naval historian Sir Geoffrey Callender led a fundraising campaign to save the ship, which entered drydock at Portsmouth as £120,000 was raised for early preservation.

Such a destiny seems only fitting for such a grand representative of Royal Navy history.

ABOVE: Artist John Wilson Carmichael painted this image of the opening moments of the Battle of Trafalgar in 1856.
(James Wilson Carmichael via Wikimedia Commons)

BUCENTAURE

ABOVE: The battered *Bucentaure* is shown dismasted at Trafalgar as she surrenders to the British in this painting by artist Auguste Étienne François Mayer. (Auguste Etienne Francois Mayer via Wikimedia Commons)

ABOVE: French Admiral Pierre-Charles Villeneuve surrendered *Bucentaure* to Marines from HMS *Conqueror* at Trafalgar. (Musee de la Marine via Wikimedia Commons)

Designed by famed French naval architect Jacques-Noël Sané, *Bucentaure* was the lead ship of an anticipated class of 29 80-gun third-rate ships of the line. Twenty-one of these were actually built, and the design was based on Sané's earlier Tonnant-class.

Ordered on September 16, 1802, *Bucentaure*'s keel was laid down in November, and the ship was launched on July 13, 1803. She stretched nearly 195ft with a beam of just over 50ft and displacement of just under 1,800 tons. She was built at the Toulon shipyard and carried 30 36-pounder guns on the lower deck, 32 24-pounders on the upper deck with 18 8-pounders and six 36-pounder carronades on the forecastle and quarterdeck.

Bucentaure was named after the grand state barge of the State of Venice, Bucintoro, which was destroyed by Napoleon Bonaparte's forces after his conquest of Venice in 1797. Her figurehead, in the form of a mythical bucentaur with the body of a bull and the head of a man, paid homage to the Venetian barge.

Commissioned in January 1804, *Bucentaure* became the flagship of Admiral Pierre-Charles Villeneuve, who led the Allied French-Spanish fleet at the Battle of Trafalgar on October 21, 1805. Although prevailing sentiment during a war council at the Spanish port of Cadiz had been to remain there, Villeneuve later chose to obey an order from Napoleon to sail from Cadiz to Naples, forcing the allied fleet into the decisive confrontation, its 33 ships against 27 of the Royal Navy.

When Villeneuve arrayed his warships in line of battle at Trafalgar, he counted on superior numbers and firepower to subdue the British under Admiral Horatio Nelson. However, Nelson chose to divide his command into two lines perpendicular to the French, intent on splitting his enemy in two places and separating the rear of the allied squadron from its flagship.

When Nelson took the weather line forward, his vanguard was subjected to a heavy French bombardment with little opportunity to return fire. However, once through the maelstrom, the guns of Nelson's HMS *Victory* and other Royal Navy

BELOW: Flagship of the French-Spanish fleet at Trafalgar, the third-rate *Bucentaure* flies the French Tricolour in this early 19th century rendering. (Anonymous Public Domain via Wikimedia Commons)

warships in company delivered devastating punishment to Villeneuve's fleet. Although HMS *Victory* took significant damage, nearly forcing Nelson out of the fight, once the allied enemy was split into three sections, the initiative switched to the British.

Passing through the French line between Bucentaure and the 74-gun third-rate *Redoutable*, HMS *Victory* unleashed a heavy broadside into the stern of the French flagship. The 98-gun HMS *Neptune* and 74-gun third rates HMS *Leviathan* and HMS *Conqueror* followed closely, raking *Bucentaure* with tremendous fire. the French flagship was overwhelmed amid the shattering defeat and surrendered after three hours, with 197 killed and 85 wounded. Villeneuve capitulated to Captain James Atcherley of the Marine contingent from *Conqueror*.

The defeated French admiral later wrote: "So much courage and devotion merited a better fate, but the moment has not come for France to celebrate successes on sea as she has been able to do with regard to her victories on the continent."

A crew of 71 sailors boarded *Bucentaure* and the battered ship was taken in tow. Heavy seas complicated the effort, and on October 22 when *Conqueror* gave up its prize, French officers persuaded the crew to surrender and make for the safe harbour at Cadiz amid the gale. In the foul weather, however, the port entrance was missed and *Bucentaure* crashed into the rocky shore, broke up, and sank.

USS *LAWRENCE*

On June 1, 1813, the US Navy 50-gun frigate *Chesapeake* was subdued in a brief, 11-minute engagement with the 52-gun Royal Navy frigate HMS *Shannon*. Captain James Lawrence, commander of *Chesapeake*, was mortally wounded and with his dying breath was said to have uttered the stirring cry "Don't give up the ship!"

Lawrence's death was a serious blow to his friend Captain Oliver Hazard Perry, who named his own flagship in honour of his late colleague. The brig USS *Lawrence* carried Perry into the pivotal Battle of Lake Erie during the War of 1812 as he led a flotilla of nine warships against a British squadron of six warships under Commander Robert H Barclay, on September 10, 1813. In the heat of battle, *Lawrence* was severely damaged and essentially taken out of the fight; however, Perry had already transferred his flag to *Lawrence*'s sister ship the brig *Niagara*. Perry continued the battle and finally won the day as all of the British ships were eventually captured.

When the Battle of Lake Erie was concluded, Perry sent his famous message to General William Henry Harrison: "We have met the enemy and they are ours. Two ships, two brigs, one schooner and one sloop." The outcome of the fight gave the Americans control of Lake Erie while forcing the British to abandon the city of Detroit and retire to Canada.

USS *Lawrence* was one of two Niagara-class brigs built at Cascade shipyard in Erie, Pennsylvania, by brothers Adam and Noah Brown. The construction of *Lawrence* and *Niagara* was concurrent. Both ships displaced 493 tons with length of nearly 110ft, beam of 32ft, and complement of 134 officers and sailors. Armament consisted of a pair of 12-pounder cannon and 18 32-pounder carronades. During the Battle of Lake Erie, *Lawrence* was heavily engaged with the 20-gun sloops HMS *Detroit* and

Queen Charlotte, the 10-gun brig HMS *Hunter*, and the mercantile schooner HMS *Chippawa*. After two hours of fighting and with 80% of her crew killed or wounded, Lawrence was effectively out of the battle.

With Lawrence disabled, Perry was rowed to *Niagara* to continue the fight that lasted for more than three hours. He accepted the British surrender on the deck of the battered *Lawrence*. In order to preserve her hull, *Lawrence* was sunk in Misery Bay, near Erie, Pennsylvania, in mid-1815. Sixty years later, the hull was raised from the lake bed, cut into sections, and moved to Philadelphia, where it was placed on display at the US Centennial International Exhibition in 1876. In December of that year, the pavilion housing the remnants of *Lawrence* caught fire and burned to the ground, consuming the old hulk in the process.

After the death of James Lawrence, Perry had a flag stitched bearing the last words of his friend. The flag flew at the Battle of Lake Erie, and the original survives today on display at the US Naval Academy Museum in Annapolis, Maryland.

ABOVE: Captain Oliver Hazard Perry transfers his flag from the stricken *Lawrence* to *Niagara* during the Battle of Lake Erie, 1813. (Artist William Henry Powell US Senate via Wikimedia Commons)

USS CONSTITUTION

BELOW: On July 4, 2011, USS *Constitution* fires a 21-gun salute in Boston harbour. (US Navy via Wikimedia Commons)

In the post-Revolutionary period, its fledgling navy was the first line of defence for the young United States of America. National security and standing among the nations of the world depended on the ability of the country to protect its merchant shipping from pirates and to assert itself in direct diplomacy and time of international conflict. To that end, the US Congress authorised the construction of six large frigates with the Naval Act of 1794, also known as the Act to Provide a Naval Armament, signed by President George Washington on March 27 of that year.

These great ships, *United States, Constellation, Congress, Chesapeake, President,* and *Constitution,* were intended to be larger than conventional frigates of the day, and each rendered service to its country with varying degrees of success. In the annals of US naval history, the career of USS *Constitution* stands out, resonating across time as an icon of the burgeoning power of the nation on the high seas. The third of the six new frigates, *Constitution* was constructed in the Edmund Hartt shipyard in the North End of the port of Boston, Massachusetts, launched in October 1797, and commissioned on July 22, 1798. *Constitution* remains in service

ABOVE: In this painting by artist Thomas Chambers, USS *Constitution* subdues the British frigate *Guerriere.* (Metropolitan Museum of Art via Wikimedia Commons)

today nearly 230 years later, the world's oldest commissioned warship still afloat. Preserved as a naval museum in the harbour of Boston, *Constitution* welcomes thousands of visitors at the Charlestown Navy Yard.

The big American frigates were intended to carry 44 guns with further strength and stability derived from innovative construction that included additional length, diagonal riders, lock scarfing, standard knees, and the extensive use of sturdy live oak in their wooden construction. The first ships of the new navy, the frigates were characterised by three masts, deep hull, narrow beam, and square sails. *Constitution* incorporated

timber from Maine and Georgia, and copper bolts and spikes fashioned by famed Boston silversmith Paul Revere.

Constitution was indicative of the power of the swift and heavily armed American frigates. Her principal designer was Pennsylvania-born shipwright Joshua Humphreys, named master naval constructor in 1794. Her 44 guns included 24 32-pound carronades, 30 24-pound cannon, and a single 18-pound bow chaser. With a length of 305ft, beam of more than 43ft, and displacement of 2,200 tons, *Constitution* was capable of a top speed of about 13kts with the heavy protection of her famed oak hull at 21in thick. Although officially

ABOVE: In this painting by artist Anton Otto Fischer, *Constitution* defeats the frigate HMS *Java.* (US Navy via Wikimedia Commons)

ABOVE: USS *Constitution* captures the Royal Navy sloops *Cyane* and *Levant* on February 20, 1815, in this painting by Thomas Birch. (US Navy via Wikimedia Commons)

ABOVE: Her grandeur restored, USS *Constitution* is shown underway on August 19, 2012.
(US Government via Wikimedia Commons)

mounting 44 cannon, she is believed to have carried 50 or more during some voyages.

Just months after commissioning, *Constitution* entered service during the Quasi-war with France from 1798-1801. The dispute with the prior ally stemmed from the American government concluding the Jay Treaty with Great Britain during the Napoleonic Wars and the French seizure of US merchant shipping. Under the command of Commodore Edward Preble, *Constitution* participated in the blockade of Tripoli, and chased pirate corsairs during the First Barbary War of 1803-1805.

The most significant period of *Constitution*'s service occurred during the War of 1812. On August 18 of that year, *Constitution* met the 38-gun British Royal Navy frigate *Guerriere* southeast of Halifax, Nova Scotia. *Guerriere* commenced firing first, but Captain Isaac Hull ordered the crew of *Constitution* to hold its fire until within 25 yards. In the subsequent battle, the two frigates became entangled. The extraction of the *Constitution*'s bowsprit caused *Guerriere* to shudder, and the British frigate lost both foremast and mainmast, compelling the seriously wounded Captain James R Dacres to strike his colours.

Guerriere was so heavily damaged that the ship could not be taken as a prize and was burned to the waterline the following day after British prisoners and their possessions were taken aboard *Constitution*, which made for Boston, and arrived on August 30 to cheers and wild celebration among the townspeople. During the fight with *Guerriere*, the British cannonballs seemed to have little effect on *Constitution*'s heavy live oak hull, and one American sailor shouted: "Huzzah! Her sides are made of iron! See where the shot fell out!" To this day, *Constitution* bears the nickname 'Old Ironsides'.

On the morning of December 29, 1812, *Constitution* was under the command of Captain William Bainbridge. Strange sails were spotted on the horizon off the Atlantic coast of Brazil, and the Royal Navy frigate HMS *Java*, officially carrying 38 guns but mounting 47 during the coming engagement, came into view. When the two ships closed, Captain Henry Lambert manoeuvred *Java* below *Constitution*'s stern and fired a broadside that shattered *Constitution*'s wheel and wounded Bainbridge.

Moments later, however, the Americans regained control of their ship, steering from the berth deck with a tiller connected to the rudder. The weight of *Constitution*'s broadsides and her thick hull helped Bainbridge gain the upper hand. *Java* suffered heavy damage to her masts, and Lambert was mortally wounded attempting to board his adversary. *Constitution* stood out of range of the enemy guns for a time, repairing damaged rigging, and then returned to rake the British frigate with heavy broadsides. At length, 1st Lieutenant Henry Chads surrendered *Java*. The ship was so heavily damaged that fires were lit to scuttle the hulk. *Constitution* returned to Boston on February 15, 1813, less than a week after word of her second victory over a Royal Navy frigate in six months had been received ashore.

Further victories for *Constitution* during the War of 1812 included the capture of the sloop HMS *Pictou* in the Windward Islands on February 14, 1814, and the defeat of the Royal Navy sloops *Cyane* and *Levant* east of Madeira, Portugal, on February 20, 1815. After the War of 1812, *Constitution* continued to serve, cruising the Mediterranean and other waters. After retirement from active duty, she was converted to a barracks ship in the late 19th century at the Portsmouth Navy Yard, Maine, a barn-like structure built on the historic hull.

Efforts to restore USS *Constitution* to her former glory began in the early 1900s, and her first full renovation was begun in 1925. She was formally recommissioned in the US Navy in 1931. Several subsequent restorations have been completed, the last in 2017.

ABOVE: In this 1905 photo, *Constitution* is shown as a barracks ship moored in Boston harbour.
(US Government via Wikimedia Commons)

DEMOLOGOS

The world's first warship propelled by a steam engine was developed from a plan by famed inventor Robert Fulton, whose steamship *Clermont* had established a viable passenger trade between Albany, the capital of New York, and New York City as early as 1807.

Named *Demologos*, or 'Voice of the People', the warship was a floating battery that was intended to protect New York City from the ravages of the Royal Navy during the War of 1812. As the US Congress sought to defend the country, the body authorised the construction of a steam-powered warship on March 9, 1814. Based on Fulton's design, the keel of *Demologos* was laid on June 20 of that year at the New York shipyard of brothers Adam and Noah Brown, one of three such concerns they owned.

Fulton supervised the construction of *Demologos* with a design that essentially paired two hull halves with a central paddle wheel in between. The steam boilers that fed the one-cylinder engine were placed in one side of the hull and the machinery was in the other. *Demologos* displaced 2,475 tons with a length of just over 153ft and beam of 58ft. Her top speed was 5½kts. The floating battery was steered with rudders at the stern of each hull half. Armament consisted of 30 32-pounder guns and a pair of 100-pounder (6.4in) columbiads intended for firing at enemy warships below the waterline. Most of the cannon aboard *Demologos* is said to have been captured aboard a British ship named *John of Lancaster*. In order to provide some secondary means of propulsion, Captain David Porter, first captain of *Demologos*, ordered the addition of two masts and lateen-rigged sails.

ABOVE: These views of *Demologos* reveal interior and exterior design features of the floating battery. (US Government via Wikimedia Commons)

Just days after the Treaty of Ghent was signed on December 24, 1814, formally ending the War of 1812 (although the famed Battle of New Orleans was fought on January 8, 1815, before word of the treaty had reached the opposing armies), Fulton fell seriously ill. He died of pneumonia on February 24, 1815. He did not live to see *Demologos* delivered to the US Navy in June 1816, and the floating battery had become operational too late to serve in the conflict for which it was intended. After Fulton's death, *Demologos* was rechristened as *Fulton*.

Demologos completed a number of sea trials in the summer of 1815, and a recommendation was made to use her as a training vessel, but sources say that she was never formally commissioned into the navy. She made her last trip on June 18, 1817, carrying President James Monroe from New York City to Staten Island during a tour of the northern United States. Four years later, her guns were removed and with a housing built over, she served as a receiving ship. She was initially placed in ordinary, or reserve status, at the Brooklyn Navy Yard, where an accidental explosion of gunpowder on June 4, 1829, destroyed the ship, killing 30 men and wounding many others aboard at the time.

ABOVE: Famed inventor Robert Fulton designed the steam-powered floating battery *Demologos*. (Library of Congress via Wikimedia Commons)

BELOW: Constructed of wood, the floating battery *Demologos* was the world's first warship powered by a steam engine. (US Government via Wikimedia Commons)

NAPOLEON

During an era of French naval innovation, the 90-gun ship of the line *Napoleon* ranks as one of the most significant. *Napoleon*, laid down at the Toulon arsenal shipyard on February 7, 1848, launched on May 16, 1850, and commissioned two years later, is recognised as the world's first purpose-built steam-driven battleship. The designation is accurate even though Napoleon exhibited the features of a crossover warship, a transitional vessel that still had masts and sails for primary or auxiliary propulsion, depending on the circumstance.

Napoleon, the lead ship of nine anticipated in the class, was designed by renowned French naval architect Henri Dupuy de Lôme. Notably, *Napoleon* was also the first battleship to utilise screw propulsion rather than the paddle wheel with steam as the source. The combination of steam and paddle wheel had represented an advancement in naval technology; however, the large paddle wheel and housing that were generally found either to port or starboard on contemporary warships made a tempting target for enemy fire.

Additionally, the early steam engines were somewhat underpowered, dangerous at times, and tremendous consumers of coal, which required the sacrifice of ammunition storage and other spaces that were necessarily designated as coal bunkers. The telltale plume of black smoke was also a hallmark of the coal burning warship, likely to warn an adversary of its approach.

Nevertheless, *Napoleon* optimised these requirements, including the necessary coal storage while eliminating the paddle wheel. Her introduction compelled other nations to further their research and development of steam-powered naval vessels. Ordered in 1847, *Napoleon* was just over 255ft long with a beam of nearly 56ft, draft of more than 27ft, and displacement of 5,644 tons. Although armour plating had been considered, construction was of wood with 8in of teak and oak layers providing protection. Her two-cylinder steam engine produced a top speed of 14kts, along

BELOW: Shown underway with steam and sail, the French battleship *Napoleon* is considered the world's first capital ship to use steam power and screw propulsion. (Louis Le Breton via Wikimedia Commons)

ABOVE: Black smoke curling from her stacks, the French battleship *Napoleon* rides at anchor in the harbour of Toulon. (Lauvergne Barthélemy via Wikimedia Commons)

ABOVE: Napoleon III arrives at Toulon aboard *Napoleon* on September 26, 1852. (Creative Commons Rama Antoine Léon Morel-Fatio Musée d'Art de Toulon via Wikimedia Commons)

with sustainable cruising speed that was not much slower. Among her weaponry, arrayed on two complete and one partial upper deck, were 60 30-pounder guns and 14 smaller 160mm guns. The ship's complement exceeded 900 officers and ratings.

Napoleon performed remarkably well during her 1852 sea trials, and the construction of at least one other battleship class was modified to incorporate a number of her features. Altogether, the ten Napoleon-class battleships were completed roughly during the decade from 1850 to 1860. France converted 28 older battleships from solely sail to steam as well.

Napoleon served with distinction during the Crimean War, participating in naval actions that included the bombardment of Russian shore batteries. In one operation, *Napoleon* rescued a French sailing warship whose rudder had been disabled by enemy fire, towing the stricken ship to safety primarily with its steam-powered engine. The history-making steam battleship was withdrawn from service in 1876 and broken up a decade later.

Although the British Royal Navy and other major navies around the world had undertaken their own development of steam-powered warships, the introduction of *Napoleon* caused them to accelerate the process. *A*, they rightly concluded, posed a threat that required a substantial response. The early consequence was the inception of a costly naval arms race.

IRON AND STEAM

The earliest iron-hulled warships, and those that incorporated steam propulsion, were developed in the 19th century with small gunboats entering service during the 1830s. The progress of the Industrial Revolution heavily influenced warship design, and such progress led directly to the fully ironclad warship with steam power and significantly reduced reliance on mast and sail as technology advanced. Interestingly, another major catalyst for the iron hull itself was the increasing hazard of modern armament as high explosive shells and rifled cannon were lethal to wooden-hulled warships.

Among the earliest iron warships was the gunboat *Nemesis* operated by the British East India Company, built in 1839 and acknowledged as the first iron-hulled warship in the world. Constructed by John Laird's shipyard at Birkenhead and William Fairbairn & Sons at Millwall, *Nemesis* was the first in a class of six such warships. Active during the First Opium War, she arrived in China in 1840 and earned the nickname "Devil Ship" from her Chinese adversaries.

As *Nemesis* demonstrated the potential of iron hull construction, the use of the steam engine gradually increased from an auxiliary source of power to primary, first

ABOVE: Built for the East India Company, the British gunboat *Nemesis* is considered the first iron-hulled warship in the world. (S. Bull engraver via Wikimedia Commons)

with the paddle wheel and then with the screw. Famed American inventor Robert Fulton is credited with the first use of the steam engine in warship construction with the floating battery *Demologos* of the War of 1812 period.

The introduction of the screw, originally conceived in the 3rd century by the ancient Greek mathematician Archimedes with his innovative Archimedes Screw, was accomplished by John Ericsson, a Swedish inventor residing in Great Britain, and Francis Pettit Smith, an English farmer. Smith provided public demonstrations of the screw at the Paddington Canal in 1836 and 1837, and his wooden creation was

used in the world's first screw-drive vessel, fittingly named SS *Archimedes*. Ericsson was granted a patent for his own screw propeller just six weeks after Smith received one. The Ericsson screw propeller was mounted aboard the steamboat *Francis B Ogden* in 1837 and demonstrated before the British Admiralty. Ericsson also designed the screw-driven steamboat *Robert F Stockton*, which sailed to the US in 1839. The vessel was named after a business associate of Ericsson, who encouraged his work and convinced the inventor to move to the United States.

The introduction of iron and steam revolutionised naval warfare. With the first iron-hulled warships protected further by armour plating, every wooden warship in the world was rendered obsolete. The transition to iron was necessary as demonstrated during the Crimean War when the effects of modern artillery were first experienced against wooden ship construction. The genius of John Ericsson emerged once again during the American Civil War with his design of the ironclad USS *Monitor*, which fought the Confederate ironclad CSS *Virginia* to a draw at the Battle of Hampton Roads in March 1862.

From there, warship construction continued to modernise with the introduction of heavier iron and then steel by the late 1800s. Warships were also capable of carrying increasingly heavier armament into the pre-dreadnought era as the mast and sail were inevitably relegated to the pages of history.

ABOVE: The steamship SS *Archimedes* is shown underway in 1839 with Francis Pettit Smith's screw propeller design.
(Charles Rosenberg; William John Huggins via Wikimedia Commons)

ABOVE: The US Navy paddle wheel steam frigate *Fulton*, depicted in 1851, was named after inventor Robert Fulton.
(Unknown Author circa 1855 via Wikimedia Commons)

GLOIRE

BELOW: The single row of cannon on the port side of *Gloire* is easily visible in this 1869 image.
(La Royale via Wikimedia Commons)

ABOVE: This scale model of *Gloire* resides in the Musee de la Marine in Paris.
(Creative Commons no machine-readable author provided via Wikimedia Commons)

Advancing arms technology and practical experience during the Crimean War led the French naval establishment to pursue the development of the world's first ocean-going ironclad warship in the mid-19th century.

During the Crimean War of 1853-1856, a reckoning occurred. The introduction of the Paixhans gun, the first naval gun designed to fire an explosive shell, and the Cavalli naval gun, the first such weapon to feature a rifled barrel, ignited a revolution in modern naval armament. The Paixhans gun, invented in 1821-1822 by French General Henri-Joseph Paixhans, along with the Cavalli naval gun, developed by Italian Major Giovanni Cavalli in 1845, had inflicted serious damage on wooden warships during the Crimean War.

The indication was significant enough that both Britain and France developed ironclad floating batteries to duel with Russian shore installations during the conflict while the next step in the evolution of the modern warship – ironclad construction – began to take shape. France led the way with naval architect Henri Dupuy de Lôme's design of a 5,630-ton ironclad with armour plating protecting the wooden hull. Intended to fight in line of battle such as earlier wooden warships had done, *Gloire* was to become the first in a class of three ironclad warships. Interestingly, despite its steam power, the class retained its masts and sails, evidence of the weaning process from wind to boiler and steam engine.

Gloire was laid down at the Mourillon Arsenal in Toulon on March 4, 1858, launched November 24, 1859, and completed in August 1860. When she became operational, every wooden warship in the world was functionally obsolete. Constructed of a wooden hull with timber 17in thick sheathed in armour plate up to 4.7in thick, *Gloire* was protected to nearly 18ft above the waterline and almost 7ft below. As a consequence, she rode low in the water, and her gunports in a single broadside were only 6½ft above water. She was nearly 257ft long with a beam of more than 55ft. Her single steam engine delivered a top speed in trials of more than 13kts, while 11kts was a more practical operating maximum.

The two additional ships of the Gloire-class, *Invincible* and *Normandie*, were completed in March and May 1862 respectively. The class originally mounted 36 Model 1858 6.5in muzzleloading cannon, 14 on each broadside with the remainder positioned as chase guns. These guns were largely ineffective against armour and in 1868 were replaced by rifled breechloading Model 1864 guns along with eight 9.4in and six 7.6in cannon in the centre of the gun deck and on the upper deck.

Although revolutionary, *Gloire* had a rather uneventful career in the French navy, a highlight being the escort of the imperial yacht *Aigle* with Emperor Napoleon III aboard during a voyage to Algiers in September 1860. The majority of the Gloire-class service was rendered in the Mediterranean. *Gloire* was retired in 1879 and scrapped in 1883.

ABOVE: Flying the French Tricolour, *Gloire* is shown at sea under both steam and sail power.
(French Government via Wikimedia Commons)

HMS WARRIOR

ABOVE: The restored HMS *Warrior*, berthed at Portsmouth Historic Dockyard, welcomes visitors.
(Creative Commons geni via Wikimedia Commons)

Even as the French laboured at Toulon to complete the world's first ocean-going ironclad warship, *Gloire*, the British Admiralty was well aware of the implications of such a breakthrough.

With the supremacy of the Royal Navy threatened due to the vulnerability of its venerable wood-constructed ships of the line to rifled guns and explosive shells fired from an enemy vessel that might well prove impervious to return fire, the British Empire – indeed Britain itself – might be open to invasion. Early experimentation with iron hulls had proven disappointing, even though ironclad floating batteries had been employed during the Crimean War. Nevertheless, the realisation that ironclad warships were the shape of things to come drove the Admiralty to pursue a response to *Gloire* that would even eclipse the perceived capability of the French ironclad.

Sir Baldwin Walker, surveyor of the navy and responsible for its construction programme, proposed an initial design for what was to become HMS *Warrior*. Further design and planning were carried out by Chief Constructor of the Navy Isaac Watts and Chief Engineer Thomas Lloyd. The hull of the wooden frigate HMS *Mersey* was used as a template for the iron construction, and a citadel – an armoured box – was placed amidships on the single gun deck to protect the ship's weaponry in the style described as the broadside ironclad.

Ordered in May 1859 from Thames Ironworks and Shipbuilding Company in Blackwall, London, HMS *Warrior*

ABOVE: The Royal Navy's first ironclad warships, *Warrior* and *Black Prince*, are shown at sea in this painting by Charles Edward Dixon. (Charles Dixon via Wikimedia Commons)

was laid down that summer, launched on December 29, 1860, and completed on October 24, 1861, about 14 months after *Gloire*. A sister, HMS *Black Prince*, was completed in September 1862. The hull of HMS *Warrior* was made of iron, while the armour protection was wrought iron 4½in thick with a backing of 18in of teakwood in two 9in layers laid at right angles to one another. *Warrior* was the world's first iron-hulled warship and was larger, faster, and more heavily armoured than any other contemporary rival. Her construction included the first use of watertight compartments, and the first predominant use of iron over wood with a design purpose-built to receive the heavy weight involved.

The British response to *Gloire*, intended to exceed the capabilities of the French warship, brought together an engineering combination that ushered in the era of the true ironclad. HMS *Warrior* displaced 9,284 tons with a length of 420ft and beam of more than 58ft. Her steam powerplant produced a top speed of 14kts, while she retained sails and rigging for additional or secondary propulsion if necessary. Her complement numbered roughly 700, including 50 officers and 650 ratings. Warrior was armed with 26 smoothbore muzzleloading 68-pounder guns, ten rifled breechloading 110-pounders, and a quartet of rifled breechloading 40-pounders.

Although HMS *Warrior* never fired a shot in wartime, she rendered more than 20 years of service during her prime Royal Navy career. Initially assigned to the Channel Squadron, she underwent refit and armament upgrades, then served as the guardship at Queenstown, Ireland. Among other assignments, she assisted *Black Prince* and the paddle frigate HMS *Terrible* in towing a massive drydock from Madeira, Spain, to Bermuda in 1869. By 1871 she was largely obsolete as the Royal Navy had introduced HMS *Devastation*, its first warship that did not carry sails. Various roles as a storage and depot ship, including supplying electricity at HMS *Vernon*, the Royal Navy torpedo school, were followed by ignominious use as an oil jetty. In World War Two she was used as a support ship for coastal minesweepers.

After years of consideration, restoration work was begun on HMS *Warrior* in the 1970s. Today she is a museum ship located at the Portsmouth Historic Dockyard complex, near other famous vessels including the Tudor English warship *Mary Rose* and HMS *Victory* of Trafalgar fame.

ABOVE: This 2003 photo depicts the majestically restored figurehead of HMS *Warrior*.
(Creative Commons The wub via Wikimedia Commons)

BELOW: This painting of the submarine CSS *H.L. Hunley* was completed by artist Conrad Wise Chapman in early 1864. (American Civil War Museum via Wikimedia Commons)

CSS *H.L. HUNLEY*

On the night of February 17, 1864, at the height of the American Civil War, the submarine CSS *Hunley*, in service of the rebellious Confederate states, became the first submersible warship to sink a surface ship of an enemy fleet in wartime. In doing so, however, the Rebel submarine met its own fate.

Hunley was a mere 40ft long with a diameter of only 4ft 3in. Her cramped interior was built to accommodate a crew of eight, while her construction featured a pair of watertight hatches, two conning towers, and screw propulsion operated by the crewmen with a hand crank. The small but prominent conning towers were located fore and aft, providing quite limited visibility when the craft was underway. The hatches were built into the conning towers, and crew ingress and egress was accomplished through their narrow openings at only 16½in wide and 21in long. A bench was provided to accommodate seven crewmen to operate the crank, while the first officer was positioned at the stern. From that vantage point, he could assist with cranking the shaft of the primitive submarine, which was capable of a top speed of about 4kts.

H.L. Hunley was conceived and designed by lawyer, planter and innovator H.L. Hunley of New Orleans, Louisiana, and bore the name of her creator. The submarine was constructed by the firm of Park and Lyons in Mobile, Alabama, shipped by rail to Charleston, South Carolina, and underwent two tragic

ABOVE: The submarine CSS *Hunley* rises from the depths of Charleston harbour during recovery operations on August 8, 2000. (US Navy via Wikimedia Commons)

experimental trials under the administration of the Confederate Army in which the lives of 13 sailors, including Hunley himself, were lost. For offensive purposes, Hunley carried a single torpedo filled with black powder and attached to the end of a 16ft spar, the idea being that the spar would be shoved into the hull of an enemy ship below the waterline and detonate after *Hunley* had slipped away undetected to a safe distance.

On that fateful night in 1864, Lieutenant George E Dixon, commander of the Rebel submarine, took the *Hunley*'s helm forward of the lead conning tower where the steering controls were located. Stealthily, Dixon approached the 16-gun Union sloop of war, USS *Housatonic*. At the most opportune moment, the *Confederate* crew plunged the torpedo into the enemy vessel's hull as she patrolled four miles off the mouth of Charleston harbour. Directly, a tremendous explosion ripped through the darkness. *Housatonic* sank within five minutes.

Hunley failed to return from its clandestine mission, apparently disabled and sunk in the same blast that sent *Housatonic* to the bottom. For the next 131 years, *Hunley* lay undetected on the bottom of Charleston harbour. In 1995, *New York Times* bestselling author Clive Cussler led an expedition that found the lost submarine, and in the summer of 2000 the hulk was raised to the surface amid much fanfare. Subsequent excavations of the silt-filled interior yielded a number of artefacts, including a $20 gold piece that Dixon had carried with him since the April 1862 Battle of Shiloh when the coin had deflected a Union bullet, bending it in the process, but probably saving the soldier's life. It was found in 2002 between folds of clothing during the examination of Dixon's remains.

Archaeological and preservation work continue, and CSS *H.L. Hunley* is on display to the public at the Warren Lasch Conservation Center in North Charleston, South Carolina.

BELOW: War artist William Waud sketched this drawing of the demise of the sloop of war USS *Housatonic* after a torpedo attack by the Confederate submarine *H.L. Hunley*. (Library of Congress via Wikimedia Commons)

USS KEARSARGE AND CSS ALABAMA

ABOVE: CSS *Alabama* sinks by the stern in this 19th century engraving by Louis Le Bretton. (Louis Le Bretton via Wikimedia Commons)

She was built beneath a shroud of secrecy, and her purpose was clear. The screw sloop-of-war CSS *Alabama* was constructed in the British shipyard of John Laird Sons and Company, Birkenhead. Designated as 'Hull Number 290', she was ordered by the Confederate States of America, its government intent on building a naval presence that might at least create trouble for the US Navy by raiding merchantmen and whaling vessels across the world's oceans during the American Civil War.

British neutrality laws were specific. It was permissible to build a potential warship for a belligerent country as long as it was not armed with weapons in a British port. Therefore, when in international waters, CSS *Alabama* received its complement of six muzzle-loading 32-pounder smoothbore cannon, a single 100-pounder, 7in rifled Blakely cannon, and an 8in smoothbore.

Constructed as a commerce raider, CSS *Alabama* was sleek and fast, 200ft long with a beam of nearly 32ft, and displacement of 1,050 tons. Her dual propulsion included a sail rig and a two-cylinder, single shaft

ABOVE: This photo of the deck of USS *Kearsarge* was taken in 1864 just after the sloop sank CSS *Alabama* off the coast of Cherbourg, France.

(United States Government via Wikimedia Commons)

steam engine built at John Laird and Sons that generated 300 horsepower and a top speed of 13kts. *Alabama* was launched July 29, 1862, and commissioned August 24 of that year under the command of Captain Raphael Semmes. During the next two years, *Alabama* conducted seven expeditionary raids on US shipping, spending 534 days at sea and never anchoring in a port of the Confederacy.

CSS *Alabama* ranged from the Azores to the Gulf of Mexico, the coast of New England, Bermuda, the coast of Brazil, South Africa, the Indian Ocean, Java, the South China Sea, India, and western Europe. She sank the Union paddlewheeler USS *Hatteras* and evaded numerous US Navy warships sent to hunt her down. In the process, the *Alabama* crew boarded 450 ships, captured or burned to the waterline 65 US-flagged vessels, and took more than 2,000 prisoners.

Needless to say, the havoc that *Alabama* caused also created consternation in the halls of the US government and its naval establishment. Intent on running down *Alabama* and sending this most troublesome raider to the bottom of the sea, US Navy assets hunted Semmes and his elusive raider relentlessly; at times as many as a half-dozen Union warships were tasked solely with sinking *Alabama*. At length, the career of the most famous Confederate raider came to an abrupt end on June 19, 1864, in a famous duel with the US Navy Mohican-class sloop-of-war USS *Kearsarge* off the harbour of Cherbourg, France.

Kearsarge was laid down at the Portsmouth Navy Yard, Kittery, Maine, in 1861 and commissioned on January 24, 1862. She displaced 1,575 tons with a length of just over 201ft, beam of nearly 34ft, and armament that included a pair of 11in smoothbore Dahlgren guns, four 32-pounders, and a single 30-pounder Parrott rife. Her steam power was complemented with sail rigging, and her top speed was about 11kts.

After participating in the blockade of the Confederate raider CSS *Sumter* at Gibraltar in in 1862, *Kearsarge* – named after Mount Kearsarge in New Hampshire – remained in European waters. Captain John Winslow arrived in the Azores to take command in April 1863. With orders to pursue and destroy Confederate raiders, Winslow chased CSS *Florida* and CSS *Rappahannock*. On June 12, 1864, a telegram informed him that CSS *Alabama* was at Cherbourg undergoing repairs after nearly two years at sea.

Alabama had been at Cherbourg for three days when *Kearsarge* arrived in the waters off the Netherlands on June 14 and took

ABOVE: Following their victory over CSS *Alabama*, crewmen aboard USS *Kearsarge* pause for a photograph on the sloop's deck. (Naval History and Heritage Command via Wikimedia Commons)

ABOVE: Captain Raphael Semmes posed for this photo while in command of the Confederate raider CSS *Alabama*. (National Museum of the U.S. Navy via Wikimedia Commons)

up station offshore. Semmes is noted for sending a courteous challenge to do battle with Winslow, writing of his intent to "fight the *Kearsarge* as soon as I can make the necessary arrangements". Semmes had made the decision to do battle rather than allow his ship and crew to be interned by the government of France. His confidence might have been well founded, but Semmes was unaware that Winslow had prepared *Kearsarge* for the upcoming duel.

Prior to the engagement, *Kearsarge* had been fitted with heavy chain mounted in three tiers across her starboard and port sides down to the waterline. The protective chain was then covered with planking to prevent it being visible. This addition was expected to reduce the vulnerability of the Union sloop's vital steam engine and other machinery. At the same time, *Alabama*'s ordnance had degraded during the raider's long voyage. Her powder and shot were at least two years old and perhaps much less reliable than her opponent's.

Word of the pending battle circulated quickly, and hundreds of civilians gathered on the French shoreline and aboard pleasure vessels to witness the action. *Alabama*

sortied on the morning of June 19 and opened fire on Kearsarge at 10.57am, but Winslow ordered the *Kearsarge* crew to hold its fire until the range closed to fewer than 1,000yds. The two warships circled one another at least seven times, each captain attempting to cross their opponent's bow and deliver a raking broadside while the enemy could fire only forward.

The battle lasted more than an hour, and *Alabama* scored several hits on *Kearsarge*. However, the additional armour absorbed much of the impact while some Confederate shells failed to explode. One that would have inflicted serious damage on *Kearsarge* instead lodged in the sloop's sternpost. Overall, the Confederate gunnery was poor.

In contrast, the gunners aboard *Kearsarge* fired to telling effect. The big Dahlgrens battered *Alabama* consistently. "Nearly every shot from our guns was telling fearfully on the *Alabama*," wrote Winslow in his report to US Secretary of the Navy Gideon Welles, "…I saw now that she was at our mercy, and a few more guns, well directed, brought down her flag…."

Semmes threw his sword into the Atlantic and was plucked from the sea by the British civilian yacht *Deerhound* that had carried a family to witness the battle that Sunday morning. Forty-one Confederate sailors were also rescued and made good their escape. Nineteen rebel sailors had been killed and 21 wounded, while three crewmen aboard *Kearsarge* were wounded, one dying the following day. Seventeen US Navy sailors later received the Medal of Honor for their actions.

Winslow was hailed a hero and received promotion to commodore. Semmes managed to return to the Confederate capital of Richmond, Virginia, and was promoted to admiral. He commanded an infantry unit during the 1865 evacuation of the city. The wreck of CSS *Alabama* was discovered by a French Navy minesweeper in 1984, and her wheel was recovered four years later.

ABOVE: Sailors aboard USS *Kearsarge* man an 11in Dahlgren gun during the sinking of CSS Alabama. (Julian Oliver Davidson via Wikimedia Commons)

ABOVE: French artist Édouard Manet painted this image of the sinking of CSS *Alabama* on June 19, 1864. (Philadelphia Museum of Art via Wikimedia Commons)

USS *MONITOR* AND CSS *VIRGINIA*

ABOVE: In this Currier and Ives print, *Monitor* and *Virginia* duel during the Battle of Hampton Roads.
(Currier and Ives via Wikimedia Commons)

The first combat between ironclad warships took place during the American Civil War at the Battle of Hampton Roads on March 9, 1862. The combatants were the Confederate ironclad CSS *Virginia* and the Union ironclad USS *Monitor*. Their rendezvous with destiny ended in a draw, but when the hours-long fight was over, there was no question that wooden warships were obsolescent.

When Union forces abandoned the Gosport Navy Yard in Virginia in 1861, they burned the steam frigate USS *Merrimack* to the waterline leaving the lower hull and the machinery intact. Confederate Secretary of the Navy, Stephen Mallory, an advocate for the development of ironclads to counter the strangling Union naval blockade of southern ports, spotted an opportunity.

Mallory authorised the conversion of *Merrimack* to an ironclad, and the labour was complete within nine months. The newly christened CSS *Virginia*, a casemated armoured gunboat, was ready for combat. A behemoth weighing about 4,000 tons with a length of 275ft, beam of just over 51ft and draft of 21ft, she was protected by two 4in layers of iron plating over oak and pine. Armament included a pair of 12-pounder howitzers, half a dozen 9in smoothbore Dahlgren cannon, and four rifled guns, two of them 7in and two 6.3in. A menacing iron ram was attached to the bow, and two steam engines allowed the monster to reach 6kts.

During a joint session of the US Congress on July 4, 1861, word was received that the Confederates were building an ironclad warship that might threaten the supremacy of the US Navy and even bombard Washington, DC.

BELOW: This 1871 woodcut by A.S. Barnes & Company captures the close-quarters nature of the Battle of Hampton Roads. (A.S. Barnes & Company via Wikimedia Commons)

At the time, the US Navy was busy constructing 47 new wooden warships, but within weeks US Secretary of the Navy Gideon Welles issued a proposal for a Union ironclad. An official Ironclad Board was convened and a hefty $1.5 million was appropriated for the urgent project.

Curiously, in August 1861 Swedish-American inventor John Ericsson, already well known, wrote to President Abraham Lincoln offering to participate in the design and construction of a "vessel for destruction of the rebel fleet at Norfolk and for scouring the Southern rivers and inlets of all craft protected by rebel batteries." However, the letter was intercepted by naval officers and never reached Lincoln.

A month later, the Ironclad Board authorised the construction of two broadside ironclads, *Galena* and *New Ironsides*. Cornelius Bushnell, one of *Galena*'s designers worried about the ship's stability and consulted Ericsson. The latter prevailed upon Bushnell to review his own design for a revolutionary warship. Bushnell was intrigued. He took the plans to Secretary Welles, and they were endorsed by the president. In October 1861, the Ironclad Board authorised the construction of a third warship based on Ericsson's design. He promised swift delivery and offered to repay the US government $275,000 if the venture foundered.

Construction on what would become USS *Monitor* was undertaken immediately at Continental Iron Works, Greenpoint, Brooklyn, New York. Progress was rapid, and some accounts state that *Monitor* was completed in just 98 days. USS *Monitor* was commissioned on February 25, 1862. She was 173ft long with a width of 41½ft, and draft of 10½ft. She weighed less than a quarter of *Virginia* at 987 tons. Her armament was indeed innovative; two 11in Dahlgren guns housed in a single round rotating turret that stood 9ft high centred atop the hull and protected by eight layers of 1in plating. A small pilothouse was located forward, and the deck was armoured with iron 4½in thick. A single-cylinder steam engine gave *Monitor* a top speed

ABOVE: CSS *Virginia* sinks USS *Cumberland* in Hampton Roads, March 8, 1862. (Currier and Ives via Wikimedia Commons)

ABOVE: This fanciful Kurz & Allison print commemorates the historic Battle of Hampton Roads.
(Library of Congress via Wikimedia Commons)

ABOVE: This vivid Currier and Ives print depicts the destruction of CSS *Virginia* at Norfolk, May 11, 1862.
(Currier and Ives via Wikimedia Commons)

of 8kts. The squat ironclad looked as if its deck should be awash as it sat so low in the water, and the *Monitor* was immediately described as a "cheese box on a raft".

CSS *Virginia* was completed on March 7, 1862, and went to war a day later, chugging down the Elizabeth River towards Hampton Roads at the mouth of Chesapeake Bay under the command of Flag Officer Franklin Buchanan and accompanied by five rebel steamers. Meanwhile, *Monitor* had departed Brooklyn for the Chesapeake on March 6 under the command of Captain John Worden. Battered by heavy seas, *Monitor* reached Hampton Roads on the night of March 8. However, *Virginia* had already come to call.

When Buchanan found the Union blockading fleet at Hampton Roads, he steered directly for the 22-gun sloop of war USS *Cumberland* anchored in the channel near the town of Newport News. The Rebel ironclad blazed away, and the gunners aboard

ABOVE: Swamped by the raging Atlantic Ocean, USS *Monitor* sinks on December 31, 1862, off Cape Hatteras, North Carolina. (United States Naval History and Heritage Command via Wikimedia Commons)

the wooden Union warship replied. The contest was one-sided. Impervious to enemy fire, *Virginia* rammed and sank *Cumberland* but lost her iron ram while backing away from the gaping hole. A total of 121 Union sailors were killed and 20 wounded.

Astonished at the sight, sailors aboard the 52-gun frigate USS *Congress* and the 44-gun steam frigate USS *Minnesota* were further startled when both their ships ran aground. *Virginia* turned towards the mouth of the James River and raked the helpless *Congress* for two hours. The ship burned until after midnight, finally demolished by its exploding powder magazine. Buchanan was wounded, and command of *Virginia* fell to executive officer Lieutenant Catesby ap Roger Jones, who retired on the ebb tide confident that he could return the next morning to blast the stranded *Minnesota*.

Sailors aboard *Monitor* heard the reports of cannon, but the Union ironclad arrived too late to take part in the action of March 8.

The morning of March 9, 1862, was shrouded in fog, but *Virginia* plodded within range of Minnesota just after 8am, and fired a broadside. Lookouts spotted an odd vessel approaching, and within a few minutes the historic battle was joined. *Monitor* opened fire from just yards away, and *Virginia* responded with a broadside that rattled every inch of the Union ironclad. The opponents hammered one another for four hours, and one hit from *Virginia*'s rifled stern guns temporarily blinded Worden as he peered through *Monitor*'s pilothouse vision slit. When the ironclads pulled apart to assess damage then opted to retire, each claimed victory.

The battle itself was inconclusive, but the world took note.

CSS *Virginia* was burned by her own crew at Norfolk on May 11, 1862, to prevent the ironclad from falling into the hands of advancing Union troops. USS *Monitor* was sunk while under tow in a violent storm off Cape Hatteras, North Carolina, on December 31 of that year. Her wreck was discovered in 1973, and two years later she was declared the first US national marine sanctuary. Artefacts, including the round turret, are on display at the USS Monitor Center, Mariners' Museum, Newport News, Virginia.

USS *OLYMPIA*

During the brief 1898 Spanish-American War and the overwhelming victory of American arms, the pre-dreadnought protected cruiser USS *Olympia* came to symbolise the burgeoning power of the United States Navy.

Olympia served as the flagship of Commodore George Dewey during the pivotal Battle of Manila Bay, when the US Asiatic Squadron thoroughly defeated the Spanish Pacific Squadron under Admiral Patricio Montojo. In company with *Olympia* were the protected cruisers *Baltimore*, *Raleigh*, and *Boston*, and gunboats *Concord* and *Petrel*. During the one-sided fight, eight Spanish ships were destroyed, set ablaze by the accurate gunnery of the Asiatic Squadron. The Spanish force was nearly annihilated with at least 167 killed and 214 wounded. American warships suffered no appreciable damage, and just seven sailors were wounded.

Commodore Dewey surveyed the disposition of the enemy in Manila Bay while his command braved the inaccurate fire of Spanish shore batteries. As the enemy came within range of the American guns, roughly 5,500yds, Dewey turned to Captain Charles Gridley, commander of *Olympia*, and famously declared: "You may fire when you are ready, Gridley."

Arcing east to west, the Americans closed the distance and fired steadily. The cruiser *Reina Christina*, flagship of the hapless Spanish squadron, opened fire as the distance closed but was forced to retire under a heavy barrage. After inflicting significant damage on the Spanish, Dewey withdrew amid reports that ammunition was running low. He ordered his command to eat breakfast, verified that stocks of shells were sufficient, and renewed his attack in the late morning. In just a few hours, the battle was over. The American warships had fired a total of 5,859 shells.

ABOVE: Commodore George Dewey stands on the bridge of USS *Olympia* during the Battle of Manila Bay.
(US Naval Historical Center via Wikimedia Commons)

ABOVE: This image of the protected cruiser USS *Olympia* from the port bow was taken in 1902.
(US Navy via Wikimedia Commons)

When word of the overwhelming victory reached the US, Dewey was proclaimed a national hero and *Olympia* secured its honoured place in the annals of the US Navy.

The pre-dreadnought protected cruisers built for the US Navy in the late 19th and early 20th century had steel construction and curved armoured decks that sloped toward the waterline. Though their armour and armament were less than those of contemporary battleships, they were faster with a top speed of up to 23kts. The contract for *Olympia*'s construction was awarded to Union Iron Works of San Francisco, California, in the spring of 1890 with a projected cost of nearly $1.8 million, more than $62 million today.

Olympia was laid down on June 17, 1891, launched on November 5, 1892, and commissioned on February 5, 1895. With a length of just over 344ft, beam of 53ft, and displacement of 5,676 tons, she was powered by a pair of steam engines with six coal-fed boilers. Her armament included four 8in guns in twin turrets fore and aft, ten 5in guns, 14 smaller 57mm weapons, a single 37mm gun, four Gatling guns, and six torpedo tubes.

Returning to the United States in 1899, *Olympia* was placed in reserve. Reactivated in 1902, she served in the Caribbean and as a training ship for midshipmen of the US Naval Academy. During World War One she patrolled the US East Coast, and in 1918 transported troops to Russia. In October 1921, she transferred the remains of the US Unknown Soldier of the Great War from Le Havre, France, to Washington, DC.

Olympia was decommissioned in 1922. She was refurbished as a museum ship 35 years later. The world's oldest steel warship still afloat, USS *Olympia* is open to the public at Penn's Landing in Philadelphia.

ABOVE: USS *Olympia*, the world's oldest steel warship remaining afloat, is located in Philadelphia.
(Creative Commons Acroterion via Wikimedia Commons)

USS *MAINE*

ABOVE: The wreckage of the battleship USS *Maine* lies awash in Havana Harbour. (US Navy via Wikimedia Commons)

"Remember the *Maine*! To hell with Spain!" The slogan reverberated across the United States, whipping war sentiment to a frenzy.

In 1895, the people of Cuba rose up against their Spanish masters in a bid for independence. The Spanish dominion over the island was deemed cruel and inhumane, and the US government watched the struggle with growing humanitarian concern – along with a commitment to protect American investment and business interests.

In January 1898, the battleship USS *Maine* was dispatched to the Cuban capital's harbour, its military might conveying a message that some viewed as conciliatory towards Spanish officials in Cuba while also intending to provide protection of American citizens threatened by continuing violence. Sailing from Key West, Florida, on order of President William McKinley, *Maine* arrived at Havana on January 25 and anchored peacefully.

Three weeks later, at 9.40pm on February 15, a tremendous explosion devastated *Maine* and at least 260 of her 350 crew were killed in the blast. Sabotage was suspected and major US newspapers of the day carried war-mongering headlines that stirred public sentiment against Spain.

In March, a US Navy court of inquiry concluded that *Maine* had been destroyed by a mine. The court did not openly rule that Spain had been responsible, but the conclusion was readily apparent. On April 25, the United States declared war on Spain. Without firing a shot in anger, USS *Maine* – half submerged in Havana harbour – had provided the proverbial spark that ignited the Spanish-American War, a brief and one-sided affair that ended in US domination after roughly four months of fighting, and favourable terms concluded with the signing of the Treaty of Paris in December 1898.

USS *Maine* was the lead ship in its pre-dreadnought class, which included USS *Texas*. Her construction was undertaken at the New York Navy Yard on October 17, 1888, and concluded nine years later, sometime after formal commissioning on September 17, 1895. Delays in receiving adequate armour plating, shortcomings in available US industrial support, and a fire that destroyed critical blueprints led to *Maine* being functionally obsolescent when she entered service.

Nevertheless, *Maine* struck an impressive profile with a length of more than 324ft, a beam of 57ft and a displacement of 6,789 tons. Twin steam engines were powered by eight boilers, raising a top speed of more than 16kts. She was armed with twin 10in main guns turreted fore and aft, and offset to port and starboard to increase their lateral range of fire. Secondary armament included six 6in guns, seven 57mm guns, four 37mm guns, and four torpedo tubes. Prior to her rendezvous with fate, USS *Maine* served with the navy's North Atlantic Squadron along the east coast of the United States and in the Caribbean.

Although the true cause of the fatal explosion that left *Maine* a demolished hulk has never been determined, Admiral Hyman Rickover led a private investigation into the tragedy during the mid-1970s that concluded the explosion was caused by a fire ignited in one of the ship's coal bunkers. In 1911, the hulk of *Maine* was raised from the mud of Havana harbour, and a year later the wreckage was towed into the Strait of Florida and sunk with military honours.

Maine's mast was transported to Arlington National Cemetery, where it was placed on a granite base to serve as a memorial to those killed aboard the ship.

ABOVE: USS *Maine* steams in the open sea in this 1895 painting. (US Government via Wikimedia Commons)

ABOVE: The battleship USS *Maine* was photographed from her starboard side in 1898. (National Museum of the US Navy via Wikimedia Commons)

ABOVE: The pre-dreadnought battleship *Mikasa* sits on display at dockside in Yokohama, Japan. (Creative Commons 江戸村のとくぞう via Wikimedia Commons)

IJN *MIKASA*

On May 27, 1905, prior to the decisive Battle of Tsushima, Admiral Heihachiro Togo, commander of the Imperial Japanese Navy Combined Fleet, declared: "The existence of the Empire depends on this battle. Japan expects this day the courage and energy of every officer and every man in the fleet, Togo."

The message was conveyed to the entire fleet from Togo's flagship, the pre-dreadnought battleship *Mikasa*, and was reminiscent of Lord Nelson's famous signal prior to the Battle of Trafalgar a century earlier. Indeed, the resounding Japanese victory at Tsushima over the Baltic Fleet of Imperial Russia has been characterised as the "Trafalgar of the East".

In the half century from the opening of feudal Japan to Western trade by the US fleet under Commodore Matthew Perry to the Russo-Japanese War, the modernisation of Japan was astonishingly rapid. In the context of industrialisation and emerging national identity, the Japanese military developed and expanded in anticipation of future territorial conquests, together with the spread of the island nation's hegemony in the Pacific and the Asian mainland.

Stark evidence of the imperialist awakening in Japan is found in the career of Togo's flagship at Tsushima, where his superb skill and superior tactics crushed the enemy fleet and contributed substantially to the Japanese victory over Russia in the 1904-1905 war, the first time in history that a traditional European power and Caucasian country had been defeated by the forces of an Asian nation.

Throughout its modernisation, the Japanese naval establishment sought to emulate the vaunted British Royal Navy, from order and drill to uniforms and fighting ships. When the Japanese embarked on their naval build-up, they sought the assistance of the British for the shipbuilding expertise and technology to accomplish the task. *Mikasa* was a pre-dreadnought

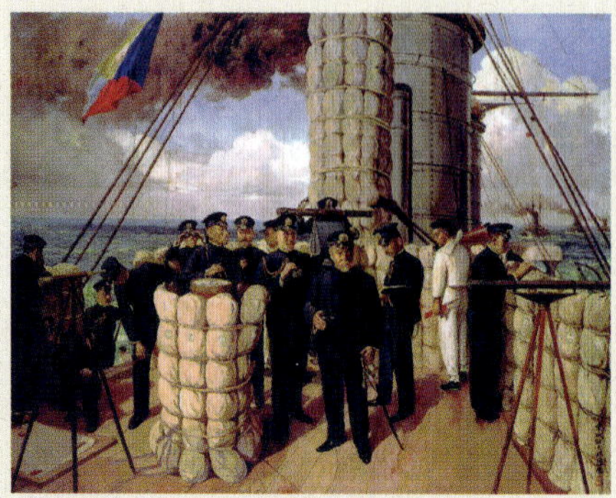

ABOVE: Admiral Togo stands on the deck of *Mikasa* just prior to the Battle of Tsushima. (Shotaro Tojo via Wikimedia Commons)

ABOVE: From the deck of *Mikasa*, Admiral Heihachiro Togo led the Imperial Japanese Navy to victory at Tsushima in 1905. (Government of Japan via Wikimedia Commons)

battleship characteristic of the major navies across the world from the 1880s to 1907, when the design was rendered obsolete by the introduction of the British battleship HMS *Dreadnought*. Pre-dreadnought battleships had a mix of a few turreted

ABOVE: *Mikasa*'s forward main battery of 12in guns was a formidable opponent in its day.
(Creative Commons Monado via Wikimedia Commons)

large-calibre guns supplemented by smaller rapid-firing armament, heavy steel armour protection, and coal-fired steam engines.

At the turn of the 20th century, Japanese naval might had proven a primary component of the country's military prowess. However, the performance of its Matsushima-class armoured cruisers during the First Sino-Japanese War of 1894-1895 had been disappointing. Therefore, a renewed ten-year construction programme was undertaken to include six new armoured cruisers and six battleships. *Mikasa*, the sole ship of her class and built in Great Britain, was the last of the six battleships. Ordered in 1898, construction began the following January at the Vickers shipyard in Barrow-in-Furness. *Mikasa* was launched November 8, 1900, commissioned on March 1, 1902, and named after Mount Mikasa, a mountain which rises in Nara Prefecture.

Mikasa was built as a modified Formidable-class battleship, displacing 15,380 tons with a length of 432ft and beam of 76ft. Her twin vertical steam engines, fed from 25 Belleville boilers produced a top speed of 18kts. Armament included four 40-calibre 12in guns mounted in two turrets, one fore and one aft, built by the Elswick Ordnance Company. These guns were operated by electricity and hydraulics, or by hand with magazine storage capacity of 240 rounds, each weighing 850lb.

The main batteries were capable of firing at a rate of three rounds every two minutes, with a range of roughly 15,000yds. Secondary armament included 14 rapid-firing Elswick 6in guns along with 20 12-pounders, a dozen 47mm 2.5- and 3-pounder weapons, and four torpedo tubes. The ship's complement totalled 836 officers and sailors.

With the outbreak of war against Russia, *Mikasa* participated in the Battle of Port Arthur on February 9, 1904. Engaging both shore batteries and Russian warships, *Mikasa* was struck by a pair of 10in shells that inflicted some damage and wounded seven crewmen. During the Battle of the Yellow Sea on August 10, *Mikasa* took the forward position at the head of the column of Japanese battleships. She engaged the Russian battleships *Tsesarevich* and *Poltava*, inflicting slight damage against her opponents' heavy armour. She absorbed 20 hits from Russian shells, which silenced her aft 12in gun turret and killed or wounded 125 of her crew.

At Tsushima, *Mikasa* was the lead Japanese ship once again as Admiral Togo executed the classic naval manoeuvre of crossing the Russian "T". The movement initially exposed the Japanese fleet to enemy fire without the ability to substantially reply, but once it was completed, the full weight of Togo's guns could be brought to bear on the enemy, while only the forward or stern guns of the Russian ships could acquire targets. Early in the battle, *Mikasa* took the brunt of the Russian fire, including hits from six 12in shells and 19 6in rounds. By the end of the battle, she had sustained 40 hits, although none inflicted serious damage.

In turn, *Mikasa* joined with the battleship *Asahi* and the armoured cruiser *Azuma* to engage the Russian battleship *Suvorov*, which was set ablaze and temporarily forced out of action with jammed steering. Mikasa also launched torpedoes and fired on the battleship *Borodino*. One of *Mikasa*'s main 12in guns was put out of action when a shell exploded prematurely in its barrel. The battle ended in a thorough rout of the Russian squadron, *Mikasa* having fired 124 12-inch shells and taken 113 casualties.

ABOVE: This photo of *Mikasa* was taken in February 1905, three months before the historic Battle of Tsushima.
(Sakai City Maritime History Science Museum Collection via Wikimedia Commons)

ABOVE: The flag of the Rising Sun flies from the prow of *Mikasa*. Note the chrysanthemum crest just below.
(Creative Commons Monado via Wikimedia Commons)

On the night of September 11, 1905, six days after the Treaty of Portsmouth ended the Russo-Japanese War, *Mikasa* was moored at Sasebo, Japan, and suffered a magazine explosion that sank her in the harbour. After being refloated, she underwent repairs and armament upgrades, returning to service in 1908. During World War I, *Mikasa* served on coastal patrol duties, and in the 1921 expedition to Siberia amid the Russian Civil war, she ran aground near Vladivostok but did not sustain serious damage.

Mikasa was deactivated on September 23, 1923, in accordance with the terms of the Washington Naval Conference of 1921-1922. The Japanese government petitioned the other signatory countries and received permission to preserve the old battleship as a memorial, immobilised with her guns and engines removed. Damaged in World War Two, she was later repaired and remains open to the public at Yokosuka as the only surviving example of a pre-dreadnought battleship in the world.

BELOW: Painted in camouflage, the Revenge-class battleship *Royal Sovereign* is pictured underway in the Indian Ocean.
(Collections of the Imperial War Museums via Wikimedia Commons)

HMS *ROYAL SOVEREIGN*

The Revenge-class battleship HMS Royal *Sovereign* was not deemed sufficiently combat ready to participate in the epic Battle of Jutland in the spring of 1916, and her service with the Royal Navy's Grand Fleet through the remainder of World War One was unremarkable. However, during World War Two, the venerable battleship became the only such vessel to serve with the navies of two Allied nations in the conflict.

HMS *Royal Sovereign* was laid down on January 15, 1914, at His Majesty's Dockyard, Portsmouth, launched on April 29, 1915, and commissioned in May 1916. She was the last of her class following *Revenge, Ramillies, Resolution,* and *Royal Oak,* which was infamously sunk at anchor in Scapa Flow by the Nazi submarine U-47 in 1939. *Royal Sovereign* displaced 30,451 tons with a length of nearly 621ft, beam of 88½ft, and draft of almost 34ft. She was powered by four Parsons steam turbines that were supplied with steam by 18 oil-fired Babcock & Wilcox boilers. The propulsion system produced 40,000 shaft horsepower and a top speed of 23kts.

The Revenge-class was heavily armed with eight 15in Mk I guns in four turrets, paired fore and aft. Secondary armament consisted of 14 single-barrel 6in guns, a pair of single 3in guns, four single 47mm guns, and a quartet of 21in torpedo tubes. *Royal Sovereign* was protected by substantial armour, including 13in thickness across her main belt at the waterline, up to 4in on the deck, and 11in along portions of the superstructure.

ABOVE: HMS *Royal Sovereign* is shown underway in September 1943 after being refitted at the Philadelphia Navy Yard. (Collections of the Imperial War Museums via Wikimedia Commons)

Royal Sovereign was present at Scapa Flow on May 30, 1916, when Admiral Sir John Jellicoe ordered the Grand Fleet to sea a day before the Battle of Jutland. However, Jellicoe reportedly chose not to order the battleship to

ABOVE: The main 15in batteries of HMS *Royal Sovereign* bark during gunnery training in World War One.
(Collections of the Imperial War Museums via Wikimedia Commons)

sortie due to its crew's inexperience. After the Great War, *Royal Sovereign* joined the Home Fleet in 1919 and was subsequently assigned to the 1st Battle Squadron of the Atlantic Fleet. She steamed into the Mediterranean Sea in the 1920s during unrest between Greece and the Ottoman Empire, while also rescuing Russian refugees fleeing the Bolsheviks during that country's civil war.

While the Queen Elizabeth-class battleships of World War One vintage underwent modernisation during the inter-war years, the battleships of the Revenge-class did not, receiving only some improvements to their antiaircraft batteries before the outbreak of World War Two in 1939. From 1940-1941, *Royal Sovereign* performed convoy duties with the Home Fleet and escaped an attack by an Italian submarine without damage. In September 1942, she was ordered to the United States for a major refit which required a full year to complete. Returning to service, she was assigned for only a month to convoy duty in the Indian Ocean before being ordered to Britain for placement in reserve.

After reaching Scapa Flow, *Royal Sovereign* was loaned to the Soviet Navy and renamed *Arkhangelsk.* Departing Britain on August 17, 1944, she joined the escort of convoy JW 59, which was attacked by a German U-boat, generating erroneous reports of torpedo hits on the battleship. Soviet sailors took over the former *Royal Sovereign* at Polyarny near Murmansk. She was returned to the Royal Navy in February 1949, and was scrapped later that year.

POTEMKIN

ABOVE: This photo of a leader of the Potemkin mutiny was taken just after his arrest in Romania.
(Stead's Review via Wikimedia Commons)

Their meat ration was unfit for human consumption. Their officers regularly dealt out abuse. Living quarters were cramped and almost uninhabitable. So said the sailors of the Imperial Russian Navy aboard the battleship *Potemkin*.

When *Potemkin*'s doctor inspected the meat and declared that it was edible, the crew exploded like a powder keg and the battleship became a flashpoint of the Revolution of 1905. The mutiny aboard *Potemkin* occurred on June 27, 1905, and involved many of the ship's complement that included over 700 disgruntled sailors.

The Revolution of 1905 had begun in January of that year in protest at the harsh rule of the House of Romanov, particularly Tsar Nicholas II, who had reigned since November 1894. Riots broke out in major cities across Russia, and martial law was declared in some areas. Before the unrest quieted in June 1907, more than 15,000 people had died and the Tsar had ostensibly given up some of his dictatorial power with the formation of a constitutional monarchy and a legislative assembly known as the Duma.

When the sailors aboard *Potemkin* lashed out at their superiors at least two senior officers were killed outright. Others were said to have been thrown overboard as the pre-dreadnought battleship sailed from the port of Sevastopol in the Crimea to the Ukrainian port of Odessa. From there, *Potemkin* sailed to Constanta, Romania, but a request to replenish food and supplies was declined. Moving on

to Feodosiya, Ukraine, another request for supplies was turned down. The crew returned to Constanta and surrendered to Romanian officials after opening the sea cocks to flood the ship. Some crewmen were captured by Russian authorities, tried, and sentenced to death or exile in Siberia.

The famous incident was recounted in the classic 1925 film *Battleship Potemkin* directed by Sergei Eisenstein. The film, though banned for years by the Soviet regime of Josef Stalin, remains a classic of international cinema.

Potemkin, named after Grigory Potemkin, a prominent soldier, statesman, and lover of Empress Catherine the Great, was laid down at the Nikolaev Admiralty Shipyard in Mykolaiv, Ukraine, on October 10, 1898, after three years of planning. She was commissioned into the Black Sea Fleet of the Imperial Russian Navy in 1903. An improvement over earlier Russian pre-dreadnought designs, *Potemkin* displaced 12,600 tons with a length of nearly 379ft, beam of 73ft, and draft of 27ft. She was powered by a pair of steam engines that raised a top speed of 16kts, and her armament consisted of twin 12in guns in turrets fore and aft, 16 6in guns, 14 75mm and six 47mm weapons, and five torpedo tubes.

In a 1909 accident, *Potemkin* sank a Russian submarine, and in 1911 the battleship ran aground. In World War One, name changed to *Panteleimon*, she

participated in the Battle of Cape Sarych against a Turkish naval squadron. In 1915, she participated in the bombardment of Turkish fortifications. She was captured by the Germans at Sevastopol in May 1918 and later disabled by the British to prevent her use by the Bolsheviks in the civil war that followed the Revolution of 1917. *Potemkin* was ultimately abandoned and scrapped by the Soviets in 1923.

ABOVE: This poster advertised Sergei Eisenstein's classic 1925 film *Battleship Potemkin*.
(Government of Russia via Wikimedia Commons)

ABOVE: The Russian pre-dreadnought battleship *Potemkin*, later renamed *Panteleimon*, was the scene of a 1905 mutiny. (Фотография из коллекции Юрия Чернова via Wikimedia Commons)

DREADNOUGHT, WORLD WAR ONE, INTERWAR ERA

ABOVE: HMS *Lion*, flagship of battlecruiser commander Admiral David Beatty at Jutland, leads the British battlecruiser line into the maelstrom. (Charles Dixon via Wikimedia Commons)

ABOVE: Delegates pause during the signing of the Washington Naval Treaty of 1922.
(US Government via Wikimedia Commons)

For three centuries, the British Royal Navy ruled the waves; certain and tangible evidence of the military might of the empire. By the turn of the 20th century, however, Imperial Germany was active in building a navy to challenge British pre-eminence on the high seas. For Germany to achieve the prestige of its own empire – its proverbial place in the sun – a strong navy was a prerequisite.

At the same time, the awakening of a military power in the Far East, Imperial Japan, spawned a new awareness of the strategy and tactics that would characterise future naval engagements. At Tsushima, the Japanese navy dealt a staggering blow to the Baltic Fleet of the Imperial Russian Navy, and demonstrated its capabilities. While the great strides of the Japanese at sea were heavily influenced by the Royal Navy and numerous capital ships of the rising power were actually produced in British shipyards, the ironic extension brought yet another challenge to the existing naval balance of power.

Nations began to explore the theory of the "big gun" battleship, with armour protection, speed, and most consequentially a suite of heavy guns all of the same calibre. When HMS *Dreadnought* emerged in 1906 as the reality of the big gun concept, the state of naval warfare was radically changed. A major arms race ensued as nations built their own modern warships to maintain parity or even attempt to achieve primacy.

At the epic Battle of Jutland and other naval battles of World War One, modern warships blasted away at one another, the strengths and weaknesses of designs and weaponry laid bare. Particularly of note was the performance of the Royal Navy battlecruisers, capital ships mounting heavy 15in main guns. The Achilles heel of the battlecruiser, however, was its

ABOVE: The tonnage of the battleship USS *North Carolina* and other capital ships was limited by treaty during the interwar years. (US Navy via Wikimedia Commons)

sacrifice of armour protection for speed. In direct combat with the battleships of the German High Seas Fleet, the battlecruiser was weighed in the proverbial balance and found wanting.

After the Great War with the surrender of Germany's fleet and its scuttling at Scapa Flow in an act of defiance, the former belligerents' acknowledged that further big gun warship development was in the offing. The submarine had become a proven weapon of the future, and the stirrings of aircraft carrier development were undertaken.

In order to curb the continuing arms race and achieve a naval balance of power across the globe, the Washington Naval Treaty of 1922 established a ratio of 5:5:3, effectively limiting the expansion of the Royal Navy, the US Navy, and the Imperial Japanese Navy. For every five capital ships the US and Great Britain constructed, Japan was allowed to build three. After all, the British had an extensive empire to defend while the Americans were obliged to patrol both the Atlantic and Pacific to protect their coastlines. Japan was perceived as only responsible for national interests in Asia and the Pacific. The Washington agreement also limited the size of capital ships to 35,000 tons.

Later, the London Naval Treaties of 1930 and 1936 introduced new restrictions on the size and number of warships that nations could produce in the vain hope of preventing another world war. However, in due course these terms were shunted aside. Bigger, more powerful warships were the wave of the future, not to mention the advent of naval air power.

SMS *KAISER BARBAROSSA*

Kaiser Wilhelm II of Imperial Germany was convinced that his nation required a powerful navy to support expansionist yearnings and the growth of an empire that would rival other European powers at the turn of the 20th century. His commitment to a modern navy was evidenced with the construction of pre-dreadnought battleships for at least 25 years prior to the outbreak of World War One.

Kaiser Barbarossa was the fourth of the five Kaiser-class battleships built for the Kaiserliche Marine, laid down at Schichau-Werk, Danzig, on August 3, 1898, launched on April 21, 1900, and commissioned into service in June 1901. The other battleships in the class included *Kaiser Friedrich III*, *Kaiser Wilhelm II*, *Kaiser Wilhelm der Grosse*, and *Kaiser Karl der Grosse*. Indicative of the class, *Kaiser Barbarossa* was among the frontline battleships of the German Navy until the construction of the Westfalen-class, in response to Britain's HMS *Dreadnought*, was undertaken in 1907.

ABOVE: Smoke pours from her funnels as SMS *Kaiser Barbarossa* steams at full speed.
(Cassier's Magazine Public Domain via Wikimedia Commons)

ABOVE: This majestic illustration of SMS *Kaiser Barbarossa* at sea was completed by artist Oscar Parkes in 1908. (The Navy League Annual Public Domain via Wikimedia Commons)

Kaiser Barbarossa displaced 11,599 tons with a length of 411ft, beam of 67ft, and draft of 27ft. Her three triple expansion steam engines propelled three screws with 14,000 shaft horsepower and delivered a top speed of 17½kts. The battleship was protected by an armour belt of 11.8in with up to 2.6in on the decks, and nearly 10in on the turrets. Her powerful armament consisted of four 9.4in guns mounted in twin turrets in barbettes fore and aft, 18 5.9in guns, a dozen 3.45in guns, 12 machine guns, and six 17.7in torpedo tubes. Between 1907 and 1910, *Kaiser Barbarossa* was one of four Kaiser-class battleships to undergo a modernisation which included reduced superstructure, removal of the stern torpedo tube, the addition of a pair of 3.45in guns, and increased height of the two funnels.

The Kaiser-class battleships were the first of their type ordered for the German Navy since the introduction of the Brandenburg-class, its first modern battleships, in 1889. During her commissioning cruise, *Kaiser Barbarossa* sailed to Spain. She visited Norway and Great Britain during manoeuvres and training cruises, and reached China during the Boxer Rebellion. Following the outbreak of World War One in 1914, the battleship was mobilised along with her sisters for coastal defence in Battle Squadron V, patrolling the Baltic and North seas. The Kaiser-class battleships were withheld from major combat roles during the Great War due to shortages of trained crews and the risks inherent with operating older types of warships against more modern Allied classes.

Kaiser Barbarossa was decommissioned in 1916 and converted to a floating prison in the port of Wilhelmshaven, where she housed Allied prisoners of war. With the signing of the Treaty of Versailles, Germany removed the old battleship from its naval list. *Kaiser Barbarossa* was sold for scrap and broken up at Rüstringen in 1919.

ABOVE: The German pre-dreadnought battleship SMS *Kaiser Barbarossa* is shown prior to the outbreak of World War One. (Library of Congress via Wikimedia Commons)

HMS *DREADNOUGHT*

By 1900, Admiral John 'Jackie' Fisher's vocal support of an all big gun battleship was full throated. Fisher had already collaborated with engineer WH Gard, chief constructor of the Royal Dockyard in Malta, on the topic, and their conceptualisation of such a naval weapon of war was ambitious.

By the autumn of 1904, Fisher was serving as First Sea Lord, and the big gun concept had made progress. After consulting with fellow Royal Navy officers on the size of the primary armament such battleships should carry, Fisher was persuaded to increase the guns from 10in to 12in, conceding a more rapid rate of fire for simply better destructive power. Fisher used the term "untakeable" to describe his idea of a battleship that was not only fast but possessed of overwhelming firepower. His early specifications had also included a top speed of 21kts, and by the end of the year a Royal Navy Committee on Designs had been formed with Fisher as its chairman.

Taking under review the concept noted as Design B, the committee evaluated both battleship and battlecruiser designs that incorporated the 12in naval gun, the required speed and armour that was adequate for protection against enemy shells. Secondary armament was shunted away in the process with the exception of anti-torpedo boat weapons. While the committee contemplated, Fisher was adamant that the new warship should have not only broadside firing capability but also offensive and defensive armament sufficient for engagement fore and aft.

Among the designs considered, the E designate included three twin-gun turrets, D with six twin-gun turrets, and G with six twin turrets located fore, aft, and on each

ABOVE: The powerful battleship HMS *Dreadnought* is shown at sea in 1906, when she ruled the waves.
(US Navy via Wikimedia Commons)

beam. The H variant included ten 12in guns in five twin turrets with three located on the centreline and one turret at each beam. The H configuration was ultimately chosen, and the keel of HMS *Dreadnought* was laid at His Majesty's Dockyard, Portsmouth, on October 2, 1905. Construction was accomplished at an astonishing rate, with launching in February 1906 and commissioning in December of that year. The build was accomplished in a calendar year and demonstrated the skill and adaptability of the workers at the Portsmouth Dockyard.

The incorporation of turrets intended for the existing Lord Nelson-class battleships also speeded the process.

When HMS *Dreadnought* entered service, her capabilities shocked the world, and the big gun battleship was destined to dominate naval construction and warfare for more than three decades. Fisher once commented: "Fear God and Dreadnought" while assessing her power. Another contemporary opined: "The *Dreadnought* was not just a ship; it was a revolution."

HMS *Dreadnought* was the first capital ship to utilise steam turbines for propulsion, her quartet delivering 26,350 shaft horsepower to a set of four propellers to generate a top speed of just over 21kts. Eighteen Babcock

ABOVE: HMS *Dreadnought* exhibits a terrible splendour in this illustration by artist William Frederick Mitchell, completed in 1907. (William Frederick Mitchell 1907 edition of Brassey's Naval Annual via Wikimedia Commons)

ABOVE: First Sea Lord Admiral 'Jackie' Fisher (left) and other Admiralty Lords attend a naval review in 1907.
(Queen Alexandra's Christmas Gift Book, published by the Daily Telegraph, 1908 via Wikimedia Commons)

rendered generally obsolete. Her performance was eclipsed by the next generation of superdreadnought battleships that were faster and carried heavier calibre guns.

Dreadnought underwent extensive sea trials in home waters and in the Mediterranean Sea in 1906. She made port calls at Gibraltar and other locales before transiting the Atlantic Ocean for Port of Spain, Trinidad, in early 1907. She returned to Portsmouth in March of that year for adjustments and corrections that were needed as revealed during the cruise. From 1907 to 1911, *Dreadnought* served as the flagship of the Royal Navy Home Fleet. She was assigned to the 1st Division of the Home Fleet in March 1911 and participated in the fleet review during the coronation of King George V.

During World War One, HMS *Dreadnought* served as flagship of the 4th Battle Squadron operating in the North Sea out of the anchorage at Scapa Flow. Her most significant action of the Great War occurred in coastal waters at Pentland Firth in the north of Scotland on March 18, 1915. *Dreadnought* rammed and sank the German submarine U-29, slicing the craft in two, and became the only battleship known to have intentionally rammed and sunk an enemy submarine. *Dreadnought* missed the Battle of Jutland in May 1916 due to an ongoing refit.

She was retired from active service in February 1919, sold for scrap two years later, and then broken up at Thos W Ward facilities at Inverkeithing, Scotland, in 1923.

& Wilcox boilers fed the two paired sets of direct drive turbines that were manufactured by Parsons under agreement with primary machinery contractor Vickers, Sons & Maxim. The turbines replaced older piston-driven reciprocating triple expansion steam engines.

Armour protection was considered adequate but not to impede the warship's speed. It ranged from 8 to 11in on the waterline belt, 4 to 6in nearing bow and stern, 11in at critical bulkheads, ¾ to 4in on the decks, 4 to 11in at the barbettes, 3 to 11in on the turrets, and 8 to 11in on the conning tower. The revolutionary *Dreadnought* stretched 527ft long with a

beam of just over 82ft and draft of nearly 27ft. Her lengthened hull provided enhanced hydrodynamic qualities, allowing the big ship to glide through the water more efficiently. She displaced over 18,000 tons and 21,845 tons fully loaded.

Along with *Dreadnought*'s main 12in guns, the anti-torpedo boat weaponry consisted of 27 single QF 12-pounder guns. Five 18in torpedo tubes and four Maxim machine guns were also installed. The ship's complement included 773 officers and ratings.

Taken in total, the attributes of HMS *Dreadnought* required a response from the world's rival naval establishments. Germany, for example, began the development of its Nassau-class and Helgoland-class battleships, which were launched beginning in 1908.

By the outbreak of World War One, however, HMS *Dreadnought* was herself

ABOVE: This view of *Dreadnought*'s armament includes a twin 12in gun turret with QF 12-pounders mounted above.
(Library of Congress via Wikimedia Commons)

ABOVE: Admiral Sir John 'Jackie' Fisher, First Sea Lord from 1904-1910 and again in 1914-1915, was an advocate for the construction of HMS *Dreadnought*.
(National Portrait Gallery via Wikimedia Commons)

ABOVE: These QF 12-pounder guns were mounted atop a main battery turret aboard HMS *Dreadnought*.
(Library of Congress via Wikimedia Commons)

U-20

In the spring of 1915, amid World War One, transatlantic ocean travel was hazardous. The German government had issued its warning that unrestricted submarine warfare would target those merchantmen and passenger ships that were believed to be carrying contraband to aid the British war effort. Those who chose to book passage on ocean liners between the United States and Great Britain literally risked their lives.

So it was that on May 7, 1915, the British-flagged Cunard liner *Lusitania* was steaming 11 nautical miles off Ireland's Old Head of Kinsale. At 2.10pm, the afternoon calm was shattered by the impact of a single torpedo fired by the German submarine *U-20*. *Lusitania* sank in 18 minutes and 1,195 people perished, 128 of them Americans. In a flash, *U-20* had become not only an instrument of war, but also a linchpin of international relations.

Although the United States was not a direct belligerent, the country was, in fact, supplying Great Britain with critical resources including munitions. Under the current conditions, *Lusitania* was considered a legitimate target as far as the Germans were concerned. Actually, early in the war British warships had stopped, searched and turned around American vessels bound for German ports. One major distinction had clarified the situation, though. The Germans were killing American citizens on the high seas. The British were not.

ABOVE: Kapitanleutnant Walther Schweiger commanded *U-20* when the submarine sank the liner *Lusitania* on May 7, 1915. (Creative Commons Bundesarchiv Bild via Wikimedia Commons)

While the Royal Navy was the largest and strongest in the world, Germany did not have the resources in warships to contest British naval supremacy or to blockade British ports. The alternative of the U-boat, however, was viable. The submarines were cheap to produce and German shipyards could turn them out in meaningful numbers. A cordon of U-boats therefore might sink enough ships to deprive Britain of the staples of war and perhaps even starve the island nation into submission.

Since the outbreak of hostilities, US President Woodrow Wilson had straddled

ABOVE: Shown second from left in this group of German submarines, *U-20* is moored at the port of Kiel in 1914. (Library of Congress via Wikimedia Commons)

ABOVE: *U-20* sustained heavy damage and was destroyed by her crew after running aground on the Danish coast in 1916. (Library of Congress via Wikimedia Commons)

the fence, hoping to remain neutral but aware that relations with Imperial Germany were steadily eroding. He had campaigned for a second term as president with the slogan: "He kept us out of war." However, with each passing day, Wilson's ability to maintain such a posture was slipping away, and his hopes for continuing neutrality became more of an exercise in wishful thinking. After Britain declared the North Sea a war zone in 1914, Germany responded in February 1915 with its policy of unrestricted submarine warfare, asserting that any enemy merchant ship encountered in the waters around the British Isles would be sunk without warning, contrary to maritime prize rules then in effect that specified such ships were to be stopped by a surfaced submarine, and their passengers and crew removed to safety before the ship was torpedoed.

U-20 was a Type 19 German submarine, ordered in November 1910, her keel laid on November 7, 1911, at Kaiserliche Werft, Danzig, and launched in December 1912. She was commissioned in August 1913, and was under the command of Kapitanleutnant Walther Schweiger on that fateful spring day nearly two years later. *U-20* was 210½ft long with a beam of 20ft, and displacement of 650 tons. She was equipped with four torpedo tubes, located in pairs fore and aft, and carried six torpedoes. A 105mm deck gun was installed for anti-ship use as well. Her crew included four officers and 31 sailors. *U-20* was powered by batteries while submerged with a top speed of 9½kts and a single-shaft

ABOVE: Sometime prior to the outbreak of World War One, *Lusitania* arrives in port, possibly at New York. (Library of Congress via Wikimedia Commons)

diesel engine while travelling on the surface with a top speed of just over 15kts.

Visibility was poor on the morning of May 7, 1915, and Schweiger had three torpedoes left. In the two days prior, *U-20* had sunk the steamers *Earl of Lathom*, *Candidate*, and *Centurion*. When an officer aboard *U-20* spotted *Lusitania*, the prospects were not favourable for attack, but when *Lusitania* altered course and turned, Schweiger took advantage of the opportunity. His log states that only one torpedo was fired, and he was said to have been so disturbed by the chaotic scene that unfolded after the initial torpedo impact and a secondary explosion, that he declined to fire a second "into this crushing crowd of humanity trying to save their lives".

When word of the sinking reached the United States, anti-German sentiment soared. In a speech three days later, Wilson did not mention the sinking of *Lusitania* directly but said: "The example of America must be a special example. The example of

America must be the example not merely of peace because it will not fight, but of peace because peace is the healing and elevating influence of the world and strife is not. There is such a thing as a man being too proud to fight. There is such a thing as a nation being so right that it does not need to convince others by force that it is right."

The sinking of *Lusitania* was not alone among the provocations that eventually compelled Wilson to ask for and receive a declaration of war against Germany in April 1917. American lives were lost aboard other ships sent to the bottom by U-boats, and political intrigue also played a significant role. However, the significance of the *Lusitania* tragedy cannot be overstated.

ABOVE: The neutrality policy of US President Woodrow Wilson was assailed after *U-20* sank *Lusitania*. (Harris & Ewing via Wikimedia Commons)

During the course of World War One, *U-20* completed seven patrols and sank 37 ships of 145,830 total tons. She was destroyed by her crew on November 4, 1916, after running aground on the Danish coast. Schweiger went on to command *U-88* and was killed in action on September 15, 1917, when the U-boat struck a floating mine. He was 32 years old.

For decades, the British government denied that *Lusitania* was carrying any munitions, however, in 1982 it was made public that an examination of internal documents revealed the passenger ship was transporting approximately 4.2 million rounds of small arms ammunition with other war-related cargo at the time she was sunk.

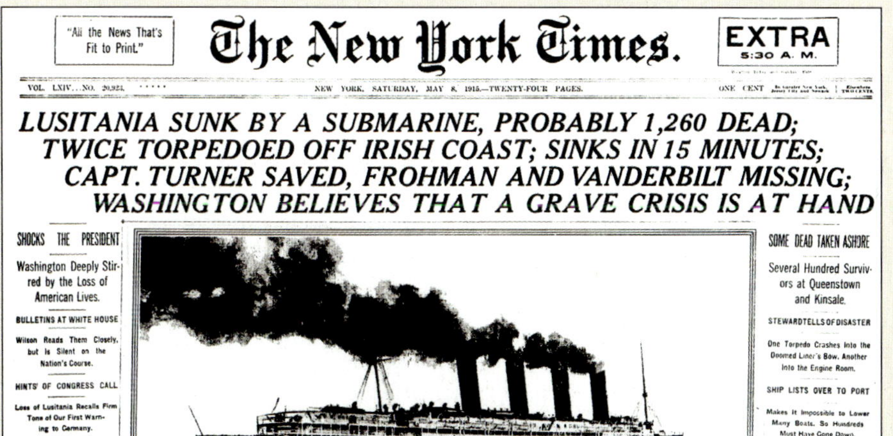

ABOVE: The front page of the May 8, 1915, edition of the New York Times relates the news of *Lusitania*'s sinking. (The New York Times via Wikimedia Commons)

DON'T MISS OUT ON OTHER KEY MILITARY MAGAZINE SPECIALS

If you'd like information about Key Publishing's military books, magazine specials, subscription offers and the latest product releases sent directly to your inbox. **Scan here »»**

SMS SCHLESWIG-HOLSTEIN

Laid down on August 18, 1905, at the Germaniawerft shipyard in the harbour of Kiel, SMS *Schleswig-Holstein*, named after the province in northwest Germany, was launched in December 1906, and commissioned in July 1908.

The last of the five pre-dreadnought Deutschland-class battleships ordered for the Kaiserliche Marine, *Schleswig-Holstein* was already obsolete by the time she slid down the ways at Kiel. Despite such circumstances, she was destined to earn lasting fame – or infamy – a generation later. After entering the harbour at the free city of Danzig on the pretext of a goodwill visit, she fired the first shots of World War Two in Europe, targeting Polish military installations at Westerplatte.

Schleswig-Holstein and her sisters displaced about 14,000 tons with length of nearly 419ft, beam of nearly 73ft, and draft of 27ft. They were protected by 9.4in of belt armour and 11in of steel on the turrets. Three triple expansion steam engines propelled three screws at a maximum speed of just over 19kts. Original armament consisted of four 11in guns in twin turrets fore and aft,

ABOVE: The German battleship *Schleswig-Holstein* fires her main guns at the Polish Westerplatte military installations in September 1939. (Government of Poland Public Domain via Wikimedia Commons)

ABOVE: German soldiers stand on the deck of the battleship *Schleswig-Holstein* in the harbour at Danzig in September 1939. (Creative Commons Bundesarchiv Bild via Wikimedia Commons)

14 6.7in guns, 22 3.5in guns, and six 17.7in torpedo tubes. This configuration was altered during refits in 1926 and 1939.

Schleswig-Holstein engaged in training exercises with the II Battle Squadron of the High Seas Fleet after commissioning and made summer cruises to Norway, her crew winning Kaiser Wilhelm II's gunnery award for accuracy in 1913. Despite her obsolescence, the battleship participated in the epic May 31, 1916, Battle of Jutland, taking a hit from a 12in shell fired by the

British dreadnought battleship HMS *New Zealand*, which inflicted slight damage but killed three sailors and wounding nine others. During the subsequent night action, *Schleswig-Holstein* scored a direct hit on the British destroyer HMS *Onslaught*, which had just torpedoed and sunk the German battleship *Pommern*. The accurate fire killed the captain of the British destroyer and caused numerous other casualties.

By 1917, *Schleswig-Holstein* served as a depot ship at Bremerhaven; a conversion to a barracks ship at Kiel followed the next year. Retained at the conclusion of the Treaty of Versailles, the battleship was modified with a second funnel during her 1920s refit and named flagship of the fleet in 1926.

ABOVE: The pre-dreadnought battleship SMS *Schleswig-Holstein* fired the first shots of World War Two in Europe. (Creative Commons Bundesarchiv Bild via Wikimedia Commons)

In 1935, the German Navy was renamed the Kriegsmarine under the Nazi regime, and *Schleswig-Holstein* was reconfigured as a training ship by mid-1936.

On August 25, 1939, *Schleswig-Holstein* made port at Danzig and moored near the ammunition depot at Westerplatte with 225 soldiers below decks. Sometime after 4am, the old battleship opened fire on the shore target, signalling the first hostile shots of the greatest armed conflict of the 20th century. For several days, *Schleswig-Holstein* supported ground operations ashore.

After returning to Germany, *Schleswig-Holstein* spent months as a training ship before recommissioning into active Kriegsmarine duty in February 1944. While undergoing refit at Gotenhafen, she was hit three times by Royal Air Force bombers and heavily damaged, finally to be scuttled before falling into Soviet hands. After the war she was raised and towed to shallow water near the Estonian coast in the Gulf of Finland, where the Soviet Navy used the hulk for target practice for decades.

The wreckage of *Schleswig-Holstein* remains visible lying on the seabed. Her bell was later put on display at the Bundeswehr Military History Museum in Dresden.

USS *TEXAS*

ABOVE: The battleship USS *Texas* lies just off New York harbour after returning from service during World War One. (Naval History and Heritage Command via Wikimedia Commons)

Even as the battleship HMS *Dreadnought* rendered early capital ships of the world's navies obsolete, the development of even heavier battleships with even bigger guns was already underway. When *Dreadnought* emerged in 1907, her dominance was immediate but the years that followed led to the development of the "super dreadnought", which lasted essentially until the end of World War One and the negotiations of the 1922 Washington Naval Treaty that at least temporarily slowed a decades-long naval arms race.

The battleship USS *Texas*, second and last of the New York-class battleships built between 1911 and 1914 for the US Navy, was laid down at Newport News Shipbuilding in Virginia on April 17, 1911, launched on May 18, 1912, and commissioned on March 12, 1914, only three weeks before the United States entered World War One. The battleship was built to bring the US capital ships to parity with the modern warships then being built by European countries.

Texas displaced 27,000 tons empty and 34,000 fully loaded. Her length was more than 572ft, beam just over 106ft, and draft 28½ft. Her two vertical triple expansion steam engines produced 28,100 shaft horsepower and a top speed of 21kts. Armour protection ranged from 6½in along the belt to 12in on the barbettes and conning tower. Her armament consisted of ten 14in guns in five twin turrets, leading some naval observers to conclude that, at the time she was launched, *Texas* joined her sister *New York* among the most powerful battleships afloat. Secondary armament included five 5in guns, ten 3in anti-aircraft guns, and 76 additional 40mm and 20mm antiaircraft weapons.

The New York-class battleships were designed to replace the preceding Wyoming-class and were originally intended to carry a dozen 12in guns in six turrets. However, the new 14in naval gun was housed in two turrets fore, two aft, and one amidships, supporting the contention that *New York* and *Texas* were truly super dreadnoughts.

During her first commissioned cruise, *Texas* sailed to Vera Cruz, Mexico, to support the temporary occupation of the city. She joined the Atlantic Fleet at mid-year and remained in that assignment until January 1918. She crossed the Atlantic and joined the British Grand Fleet with the US Navy's 6th Battle Squadron in the North Sea during the Great War, returning to American waters in December 1918.

USS *Texas* was ordered to the Pacific in mid-1919 and designated BB-35 the following year. After cruising to European ports in 1924, she underwent a major refit in 1925 and then served in both the Atlantic and Pacific for the next six years. In 1937, she was assigned exclusively to the Atlantic Fleet.

By 1941, USS *Texas* was conducting convoy escort operations in the Atlantic, protecting merchant vessels from German U-boats during the undeclared naval war

ABOVE: A German shell falls between the battleships USS *Texas* and USS *Arkansas*, from whose deck this photo was taken, during action off the coast of Cherbourg, France, in 1944. (US Navy via Wikimedia Commons)

with Nazi submarines that preceded US entry into World War Two. In November 1942, *Texas* fired her heavy guns in support of Operation Torch, the Allied invasion of North Africa. After further convoy escort duty, her main and secondary batteries bombarded targets on the coast of German-occupied French Normandy in support of the D-Day landings on June 6, 1944. She later duelled with German shore batteries during the battle for the French port city of Cherbourg, taking two hits from the enemy guns. Before transferring to the Pacific, *Texas* supported the Allied landings in southern France during Operation Dragoon.

During the Pacific War, *Texas* supported the American landings on Iwo Jima and Okinawa, and was assigned to the proposed invasion of Japan when the war ended on September 2, 1945. She was decommissioned and stricken from the navy roll in 1948. Donated to the state of Texas that year, she was on display at San Jacinto for many years. Having undergone extensive refurbishment, USS *Texas* is expected to reopen as a floating museum in 2025, docked at the port of Galveston.

BELOW: While undergoing preservation work, USS *Texas* is docked at Galveston in November 2024. (Creative Commons Jaro Nemčok via Wikimedia Commons)

BELOW: The dreadnought battleship HMS *Iron Duke* was the flagship of the British Grand Fleet at Jutland. (Collections of the Imperial War Museums via Wikimedia Commons)

HMS *IRON DUKE*

Named after Arthur Wellesley, 1st Duke of Wellington and the victory over Napoleon in the historic 1815 Battle of Waterloo, HMS *Iron Duke* earned fame in her own right as the flagship of the Royal Navy Grand Fleet with Admiral John Jellicoe aboard during the 1916 Battle of Jutland.

Fought in the North Sea off the Danish peninsula, the Battle of Jutland was a pivotal engagement in naval history, seen largely by historians as a tactical victory for the German High Seas Fleet in terms of damage inflicted but a strategic victory for the Royal Navy in that the Germans did not sortie in such strength again for the duration of World War One.

HMS *Iron Duke* was laid down at the Portsmouth Dockyard on January 12, 1912, the lead ship of four in her class, including HMS *Marlborough*, *Benbow*, and *Emperor of India*. She was launched on October 12, 1912, and commissioned in March 1914, five months before the outbreak of the Great War. All four Iron Duke-class battleships were launched within a year during the feverish naval arms race that gripped European navies in the early 20th century.

Iron Duke displaced 25,401 tons with a length of nearly 623ft, beam of 90ft, and draft of 29½ft. Her 18 Babcock & Wilcox boilers fed four Parsons steam turbines and four screw propellers to produce 29,000 shaft horsepower, and a top speed of slightly more than 21kts. The Iron Duke-class battleships were the last of the Royal Navy ships to use coal as their primary fuel source. Armour protection included 12in along the belt, 11in at the turrets, and 10in for the barbettes. After the Battle of Jutland, it was determined by the Admiralty that armour protection should be augmented in many of the existing warships, and *Iron Duke* received an upgrade in October 1916.

The dreadnought battleship mounted main armament of ten 13.5in Mk V guns in five twin turrets, a dozen 6in guns, two 76mm and four 47mm guns, and a quartet

ABOVE: The battleship HMS *Iron Duke* and escorting destroyers are shown in action at the height of the Battle of Jutland in this painting by artist Charles Edward Dixon. (Christie's via Wikimedia Commons)

ABOVE: In another vivid image of the Battle of Jutland, the main batteries of HMS *Iron Duke* roar on the evening of May 31, 1916. (Sothebys via Wikimedia Commons)

of 21in torpedo tubes. In 1914, *Iron Duke* became the first Royal Navy battleship to be armed with anti-aircraft guns, a pair of 12-pounders.

Upon completion, HMS *Iron Duke* exhibited characteristics that were both outdated and modern, as noted in her fuel and aircraft defence configurations. She underwent sea trials in the autumn of 1913 and then transferred with the Home Fleet, later designated the Grand Fleet, to the major anchorage at Scapa Flow, in the Orkney Islands of Scotland, as World War One loomed. During the early months of the war, *Iron Duke* participated in a steady training regimen, occasional sweeps of the northern and southern North Sea, and sortied but did not engage the enemy in the early 1915 Battle of the Dogger Banks.

ABOVE: HMS *Iron Duke* and her sister HMS *Marlborough* lead a line of Royal Navy Grand Fleet battleships in 1918.
(United Kingdom Government via Wikimedia Commons)

the historic Battle of Jutland. During the balance of the Great War, *Iron Duke* operated in the North Sea, conducting periodic sweeps and limited offensive and defensive operations.

During the interwar years, *Iron Duke* served as flagship of the Royal Navy Mediterranean Fleet and during Allied operations in the Russian Civil War of the early 1920s, as well as the Greco-Turkish War of 1919-1922. She transported refugees from the Greek city of Smyrna, which was devastated by a major fire in September 1922.

In 1930, the London Naval Treaty specified that the four Iron Duke-class battleships were to be either scrapped or rendered unserviceable as warships. With much of her armament and armour removed, *Iron Duke* was converted into a gunnery training vessel and continued as such until the outbreak of World War Two in September 1939. Relocated to Scapa Flow as a harbour defence ship, she was damaged by German bombers in October, and run aground to prevent her sinking.

HMS *Iron Duke* remained useful as an anti-aircraft platform until the end of the war and was refloated in April 1946. She was scrapped at Glasgow in the late 1940s, and her bell has been preserved on display at Winchester Cathedral.

Routine operations followed, but in January 1916 the battleship collided with the tanker *Prudentia* at Scapa Flow. While the latter sank, *Iron Duke* was undamaged.

After Royal Navy intelligence picked up German radio traffic that indicated a significant sortie of the High Seas Fleet in late May 1916, the Admiralty ordered the Grand Fleet to put to sea. The Germans had hoped to lure a portion of the Royal Navy's strength into a trap and destroy it. In the event, Admiral Jellicoe led 28 dreadnought battleships and nine battlecruisers in an attempt to cut off the Germans' 24 dreadnought and pre-dreadnought battleships, six light cruisers, and a complement of smaller warships during their return to the haven of the estuary of the River Jade.

The Battle of Jutland opened with a clash between opposing battlecruisers, and by 6pm the main British battle line made contact with the Germans. *Iron Duke* was the ninth dreadnought in the Royal Navy line with the 4th Battle Squadron. Within 15 minutes of engaging the enemy, a pair of large-calibre shells fell dangerously close to *Iron Duke* but did no damage. A few minutes later, after closing the range to 26,000yds, Admiral Jellicoe's flagship opened fire on the German dreadnought SMS *König*. Her accurate gunnery scored an estimated seven hits on the enemy ship, wreaking severe damage.

Shortly afterwards, *Iron Duke* joined several other British warships in raking the damaged German cruiser SMS *Wiesbaden*, which later sank. German destroyers engaged, but *Iron Duke* scored no hits in the melee. One enemy destroyer was sunk during a torpedo attack that materialised minutes later, and *Iron Duke* has historically been credited with the decisive blows, although evidence as to which British warship fired the deadly salvoes remains unclear.

After searching for damaged enemy ships on the morning of June 1, *Iron Duke* returned to Scapa Flow before noon, having sustained no damage during the battle. Her main batteries had fired 90 rounds and her secondary guns 50 rounds during

ABOVE: With awnings erected for shade, the battleship HMS *Iron Duke* is shown at anchor in Port Said, Egypt.
(Dutch National Museum of World Cultures via Wikimedia Commons)

ABOVE: Officers walk the deck of the battleship HMS *Iron Duke,* while a destroyer is moored alongside in February 1917.
(Library and Archives Canada via Wikimedia Commons)

HMS *INVINCIBLE*

ABOVE: First of the Royal Navy battlecruisers, HMS *Invincible* was launched in 1907.
(United Kingdom Government via Wikimedia Commons)

The battlecruisers of the dreadnought era were a British concept, and the favourite of Admiral John "Jackie" Fisher, Admiral of the Fleet and twice First Sea Lord. HMS *Invincible* was the first warship of her kind to enter service with the Royal Navy, commissioned on March 20, 1909.

The battlecruisers carried heavy guns comparable to those of battleships yet they were lightly armoured in comparison, essentially sacrificing armour protection for speed. The idea was relatively simple. Battlecruisers carried the firepower to destroy any inferior forces encountered, while their great speed allowed them to sail swiftly out of danger if confronted by superior numbers of enemy warships. In either of these roles, the battlecruiser seemed equal to the task. However, the design was never meant to maintain position in a battle line, slugging it out with the enemy for an extended period – which is precisely what occurred at the epic Battle of Jutland in May 1916, when three Royal Navy battlecruisers, *Indomitable*, *Queen Mary*, and *Invincible* were blown up and sunk by German fire.

HMS *Invincible* was the lead ship of her class, laid down on April 2, 1906, at the yard of WG Armstrong, Whitworth & Co, Ltd, at Tyneside. She was launched on April 13, 1907, and HMS *Inflexible* and HMS *Indomitable* followed. *Invincible* was 567ft long with a beam of 78½ft, draft of 30ft, and displacement of 17,530 tons. Her armour belt was 4 to 6in thick with 7in on turrets and barbettes and up to 2½in on the deck. Her 31 Yarrow boilers and two

direct-drive steam turbines produced 41,000 shaft horsepower and a top speed of 25½kts. Armament consisted of eight 12in guns in twin turrets, 16 single-mounted 4in guns, and five 18in torpedo tubes.

Invincible joined the Home Fleet in March 1909, but refits were necessary for her main turrets to work properly, and the problem was not corrected until a general refit got underway at Portsmouth in the spring of 1914. World War One broke out in August, precluding the installation of a modern fire-control system.

At the end of August, *Invincible* participated in the Battle of Heligoland Bight before heading south in November in search of a powerful German battle squadron that had destroyed the Royal Navy West Asia Squadron at the Battle of Coronel. Under the command of Admiral Doveton Sturdee, *Invincible* and *Inflexible,* along with supporting cruisers, engaged the Germans, under Admiral

Maximilian Graf von Spee, on December 8, 1941, in the Battle of the Falklands, sinking the armoured cruisers Scharnhorst and Gneisenau, and two other enemy warships.

At Jutland, *Invincible* was the flagship of Admiral Horace Hood and the Third Battlecruiser Squadron, ranging ahead of the main body of the Grand Fleet. *Hood* came to the rescue of the cruiser Chester, set upon by four German light cruisers, and along with *Indomitable* pounded the enemy's *Wiesbaden* around 6pm. Minutes later, *Invincible* engaged German battlecruisers of the High Seas Fleet's First Scouting Group.

Hood shouted an order to his gunnery officer: "Your firing is very good. Keep at it as quickly as you can. Every shot is telling." However, as a bank of fog lifted, silhouetting *Invincible* against the sun, the German battlecruisers *Derfflinger* and *Lützow* fired three salvoes. At least one enemy shell struck *Invincible*'s Q Turret, blowing its roof off and causing adjacent magazines to detonate. At 6.34pm, *Invincible* broke in two amid a towering explosion that was later attributed to her light armour protection compounded by poor ammunition handling among her crew.

Admiral Hood and 1,025 others died, while only six of *Invincible*'s complement survived the catastrophe. The controversy surrounding the Royal Navy battlecruiser concept continues today. *Invincible*'s wreck was discovered in 1991 in 180ft of water.

ABOVE: Under Admiral Horace Hood, the battlecruiser HMS *Invincible* steams into action at Jutland.
(Creative Commons Royal Museums Greenwich via Wikimedia Commons)

ABOVE: After blowing up during the Battle of Jutland, the severed halves of HMS *Invincible* protrude from the water.
(Collections of the Imperial War Museum via Wikimedia Commons)

SMS *EMDEN*

SMS *Emden* was the second and last of the Dresden-class light cruisers ordered for the German Kaiserliche Marine in 1905, differing from her sister in propulsion. While *Dresden* was fitted with a dozen boilers and Parsons steam turbines, *Emden* retained an older system of a dozen boilers with a pair of triple expansion steam engines.

Laid down at Kaiserliche Danzig on November 1, 1906, *Emden* was launched on May 26, 1908, and commissioned on July 10, 1909. She displaced 3,664 tons with a length of just over 388ft, beam of slightly more than 33ft, and draft of about 18ft. Her top speed was 23½kts. Built for endurance, she mounted 10 4.1in guns located in forecastle, broadside, and aft turrets, eight 2in guns, and a pair of 17.7in torpedo tubes.

Soon after commissioning, *Emden* steamed for the Pacific by way of South America. When World War One erupted, she was in port at the German trade centre of Tsingtao, China, under the command of Captain Karl von Müller. A day after Germany declared war on Imperial Russia, August 2, 1914, Emden captured the Russian steamer *Ryazan*, which was later converted into the German commerce raider *Cormoran*. Müller was then ordered to briefly join the East Asia Squadron in the Indian Ocean and was released thereafter to conduct independent raiding against targets of opportunity.

On October 28, Müller launched a surprise attack on the Allied anchorage at Georgetown, Penang. Sailing into the harbour disguised as a British cruiser, *Emden* torpedoed, shelled, and sank the Russian cruiser *Zhemchug* and then sank the French destroyer *Mousquet* before making good her escape.

During the next three months, Müller gained a reputation for skill and chivalry,

ABOVE: The German cruiser SMS *Emden* is shown underway in 1910 prior to her combat career in World War One. (Creative Commons Bundesarchiv Bild via Wikimedia Commons)

while audacity was the watchword aboard *Emden*. The diminutive German cruiser sank or captured at least 20 Allied merchant ships totalling nearly 71,000 tons and sailed more than 30,000 nautical miles. *Emden* singlehandedly disrupted the Indian Ocean shipping lanes and bombarded the Burma Oil Company storage facilities at Madras, India. Her exploits caused insurance rates in Britain to skyrocket and a near panic ensued.

The brief but spectacular career of *Emden* came to an end on November 9, 1914, as she initiated a raid on the Cocos Islands in the eastern Indian Ocean to disable the British cable and wireless station there. The Australian cruiser HMAS *Sydney*, commanded by Captain John Glossop, was dispatched to the area when the wireless operator sent a distress signal. *Sydney* was faster, more manoeuvrable, and more heavily armed than *Emden*, with

ABOVE: Captain Karl von Müller led the cruiser SMS *Emden* on a brief but spectacular raiding campaign. (New York Times via Wikimedia Commons)

eight 6in main guns. Standing out of range of *Emden*'s main weaponry, *Sydney* pounded the German warship into submission. Müller ran *Emden* aground with 134 dead to avoid sinking. Her survivors became prisoners of war.

The hulk of *Emden* was degraded by heavy wave action, and her remains were scrapped in the 1950s. Karl von Müller, a recipient of the Pour le Mérite, attempted to escape captivity and was repatriated after the Great War. He died from complications of malaria aged 49 in 1923.

BELOW: The battered remains of the German light cruiser *Emden* lie beached on North Keeling Island, Cocos. (State Library of Victoria via Wikimedia Commons)

AURORA

The last of three Pallada-class protected cruisers built for the navy of Imperial Russia, *Aurora* followed *Pallada* and *Diana*. Laid down on May 23, 1897, at the Admiralty Shipyard in St Petersburg, she was launched on May 11, 1900, and commissioned in July 1903.

Aurora holds two distinctions. The first had repercussions worldwide as one of her guns fired the initial shot of the Bolshevik October Revolution of 1917. Anchored in the Neva River near St Petersburg, the cruiser fired a blank round from its forecastle gun in the direction of the Winter Palace of Tsar Nicholas II to signal the beginning of the uprising.

The second distinction that *Aurora* holds is its survival of the debacle that befell the Russian Baltic Fleet in the historic Battle of Tsushima during the Russo-Japanese War of 1904-1905. The Japanese fleet, under the command of Admiral Heihachiro Togo, decimated the Russian armada under Admiral Zinovy Petrovich Rozhestvensky on May 27, 1905. *Aurora* was struck by numerous Japanese shells and sustained serious damage but managed to remain afloat. After the battle, she limped to safety at Manila harbour in the Philippines to be interned by the neutral US government, and was later returned to the Russian navy. Re-entering service in the Baltic Sea in 1906, *Aurora* was redesignated as a training ship.

Meanwhile, *Pallada* was torpedoed during the 1904 Japanese attack on Port Arthur, stripped of her guns that were installed as shore batteries, and then sunk in the harbour by fire from heavy Japanese 11in howitzers.

ABOVE: This 1905 photograph of *Aurora* reveals some of the damage sustained during the Battle of Tsushima.
(Government of Russia Public Domain via Wikimedia Commons)

Diana survived both the Russo-Japanese War and World War One to be scrapped at Bremen, Germany, in 1922.

Aurora and her sisters displaced 6,731 tons with length of nearly 416ft, beam of 55ft, and draft of almost 21ft. Three vertical triple expansion steam engines provided 13,000 shaft horsepower and a top speed of 19kts. They were armed with eight turreted 6in main guns, 24 11-pounder guns, eight 1-pounders, and three 15in torpedo tubes. Armour protection ranged from 2in on deck to 3in at the slopes, and 6in on the conning tower.

ABOVE: The historic cruiser *Aurora* moored in the harbour at Leningrad in the summer of 1961.
(Creative Commons Wilford Peloquin via Wikimedia Commons)

ABOVE: Photographed in 1903, the protected cruiser *Aurora* steams in the open sea.
(Government of Russia Public Domain via Wikimedia Commons)

In late 1916, *Aurora* was transferred to St Petersburg to undergo an extensive refit. Within weeks, revolutionary fervour had gripped the city, and the crew of the warship held a meeting to organise a revolutionary committee. Most of the ship's complement then joined the Bolsheviks prior to the beginning of the uprising, but her commander, Captain Mikhail Nikolsky, was killed as he attempted to quell the insurrection aboard his ship.

Aurora returned to service as a training ship in 1922, and her guns were removed for the defence of Leningrad during World War Two. She was heavily damaged by German bombs and artillery fire, and sank in September 1941. After the war, she was restored and became a museum ship at Leningrad (St Petersburg) in 1957. Since then, she has undergone several restorations and remains open to the public there.

IJN *HOSHO*

The first aircraft carrier designed and built for the purpose from the keel up was *Hosho* of the Imperial Japanese Navy. Laid down on December 16, 1920, at the Asano Shipbuilding Company, Tsurumi-ku, Yokohama, Japan, *Hosho* had originally been conceived as a naval tanker or seaplane carrier. However, the observations made by Japanese naval officers attending demonstrations of air operations aboard the British carrier HMS *Furious* prompted the Japanese military establishment to chart an alternative course.

Hosho was launched on November 13, 1921, and towed to the Yokohama Naval Arsenal for completion prior to commissioning on December 27, 1922, seven months before the British introduced the second purpose-built aircraft carrier in the world, HMS *Hermes*. *Hosho* was small in comparison to her British and American contemporaries, displacing only 7,400 tons. She was powered by eight Kampon Ro Go boilers with a pair of Kampon geared steam turbines, producing 30,000 shaft horsepower and a top speed of 25kts. Originally designed to carry up to 32 aircraft, primarily fighters and torpedo bombers, her number was scaled back

ABOVE: The Japanese aircraft carrier *Hosho* sails in Tokyo Bay shortly after completion in 1922. (Government of Japan via Wikimedia Commons)

to 23, and in practical operations *Hosho* maintained about 15 planes.

Hosho was designed with funnels at starboard and an original superstructure design was replaced entirely in the spring of 1919 with a small starboard island that allowed an unobstructed operation of the entire 552ft flight deck, which sloped down the forward edge to assist with aircraft take offs. The flight deck ran the entire length of the carrier, and *Hosho*'s beam measured 59ft with a draft of just over 20ft. The flight deck was levelled during later refits, and a system of lights and mirrors was installed along its length to provide good sight pictures for pilots attempting to land. For anti-aircraft defence, *Hosho* originally carried six 5.5in guns and a complement of 3.1in weapons. Her crew totalled 512 officers and sailors.

Two aircraft hangars were completed below the flight deck with elevators installed to move planes for launch and servicing after recovery. During World War Two the flight deck was enlarged to accommodate more modern aircraft, but this rendered

Hosho unstable and incapable of large-scale operations in the open sea.

Hosho shared an early assignment, along with other carriers, specifically serving as a platform for the refinement of air operations at sea and the development of aircraft carrier combat doctrine. In 1932, she launched raids against Chinese positions around the city of Shanghai. After a 1935 refit, she was deployed a second time with the outbreak of the Second Sino-Japanese War in 1937. At the end of that year, she was placed in reserve prior to the outbreak of World War Two. In 1941, *Hosho* sortied with the Pearl Harbor attack force, and the following year she participated in the Battle of Midway with the main body of Admiral Isoroku Yamamoto's fleet. After another refit in 1944, she was transferred to the training fleet, and surrendered to the Allies during the occupation of Japan.

Hosho was scrapped by the Kyowa Shipbuilding Company of Osaka in 1946-1947.

ABOVE: This photo was taken beneath the narrow flight deck of *Hosho* in 1945, looking towards the carrier's forecastle. (US Navy via Wikimedia Commons)

HMS *EAGLE*

By the early 1920s, the world's three major naval powers, Great Britain, the United States, and Japan, were increasingly emphasising their aviation capabilities as evidenced by the flurry of aircraft carrier production that was ongoing. Among these major powers, no fewer than six aircraft carriers were either in service or under construction by the middle of the decade.

When the armistice was signed to end the Great War, the Royal Navy's 14,500-ton *Argus* was operational, while two other aircraft carriers, *Eagle* and *Hermes*, were under construction. *Eagle* was converted from the hull of a dreadnought-era battlecruiser, while *Hermes* was the first Royal Navy aircraft carrier purpose built from the keel up.

At 22,200 tons, HMS *Eagle* was laid down on January 22, 1913, at the Elswick shipyard of Armstrong, Whitworth & Co Ltd, Newcastle upon Tyne. She was launched on June 8, 1918, and completed on April 13, 1920. Sir E H Tennyson d'Eyncourt, Royal Navy director of naval construction, supervised the transition from battlecruiser to aircraft carrier with a flight deck that extended 670ft, the full length of the hull. No island or mast construction was incorporated above the flight deck, and the carrier's beam stretched nearly 98ft, while its draft was almost 25ft.

Thirty-two Yarrow steam boilers produced steam for the four Parsons geared turbines that generated 50,000 shaft horsepower and a top speed of 24kts. A suite of nine 6in guns was mounted for defence against enemy surface ships, and four 4in anti-aircraft guns were installed. HMS *Eagle* was capable of accommodating from 20-30 naval aircraft of various types. During the period, naval flight operations were evolving, and practical experience gained from *Argus* and from flight trials conducted by *Eagle* off the coast of Sicily in 1920 led to a redesign of the latter in the autumn of that year, which took until 1923 to complete. The same

BELOW: This image of the aircraft carrier HMS *Eagle* was taken during sea trials in the 1920s. (Collections of the Imperial War Museums via Wikimedia Commons)

ABOVE: The aircraft carrier HMS *Eagle* steaming in the open sea sometime during the 1930s. (US Navy via Wikimedia Commons)

information gleaned during flight trials brought on two redesigns of *Hermes* while she was still under construction.

Following the completion of her refit, HMS *Eagle* was commissioned on February 20, 1924. Her revised configuration included an island on the starboard side of the flight deck to facilitate the launch and recovery of planes and ease navigation, along with the addition of a second funnel. Two masts were installed atop the island, with the gunnery fire control station positioned forward.

Hermes, redesigned by d'Eyncourt from a seaplane carrier concept, was launched on September 11, 1919, and was decidedly smaller than *Eagle* at 11,020 tons. Her length was 598ft with a flight deck extending 570ft. Although the two aircraft carriers were closely linked during their construction and early service, they were not sisters. During the interwar years, HMS *Eagle* sailed with the Mediterranean Fleet and served on the China Station.

With the outbreak of World War Two, *Eagle* had just completed a refit in Singapore and joined other Royal Navy warships in the hunt for German merchantmen in the Pacific and Indian oceans. She was again active in the Mediterranean and met her fate while escorting the critical Pedestal convoy bound from Majorca to the embattled island of Malta. On August 11, 1942, four torpedoes from the German submarine *U-73* ripped into HMS *Eagle*, and she sank in less than four minutes, taking 160 of her complement of 830 officers and ratings to their deaths.

BELOW: After being struck by four torpedoes from the German submarine *U-73*, HMS *Eagle* lists heavily to port before sinking, August 11, 1942. (Collections of the Imperial War Museums via Wikimedia Commons)

USS *LANGLEY*

Although the US Navy's interest in carrier aviation had begun in the waning years of World War One, it was not until March 1922 that USS *Langley*, converted from the old collier *Jupiter* first commissioned in 1913, became its first aircraft carrier in service.

The conversion of *Jupiter* to *Langley* was authorised in the summer of 1919 and begun at the Norfolk Navy Yard in Virginia by the spring of 1920 when the ship was officially renamed after Samuel Pierpont Langley, an American aviation pioneer. The conversion involved the removal of the collier's superstructure with the relocation of its two funnels to the port side aft along the flight deck, which ran the 542ft length of the hull. A single elevator was installed, and power was supplied by three boilers

with a General Electric turbo-electric system generating 7,200 shaft horsepower and a top speed of 15½kts. The propulsion system eliminated the need for coal as a fuel source.

Langley's beam was 65½ft wide, her draft just over 22ft, and her displacement 11,500 tons. She was designated CV-1 – C standing for "carrier" and V indicating the use of aircraft that were heavier than air. Her flight deck resembled the canopies common on pioneer Conestoga wagons of the American West earning the new carrier the nickname "Covered Wagon". Her flight deck was constructed on steel girders above the hull, and the space between her flight deck and the original Jupiter main deck allowed space for up to 36 aircraft, most of which were slow biplanes since her short length restricted take-off and landing operations.

ABOVE: A torpedo hit completes the scuttling of the aircraft carrier and seaplane tender USS *Langley* on February 27, 1942. (US Navy via Wikimedia Commons)

Early sea trials were conducted in the Atlantic in 1924.

Like the Japanese carrier *Hosho*, *Langley* served as a floating laboratory for the development of carrier-borne air operations. Among the innovations first utilised with aircraft operating aboard *Langley* was the tailhook that was intended to grasp arresting cables stretched across the flight deck and connected to a braking system to assist with landings.

By the mid-1930s, progressive aircraft carrier designs had rendered *Langley* obsolescent, and she was converted to a seaplane tender at Mare Island Navy Yard near San Francisco, California. By 1937, *Langley* was on station in the Pacific supporting seaplane patrol activity, and later ferrying aircraft during the early months of US involvement in World War Two. On February 27, 1942, *Langley* was attacked by 16 Japanese dive bombers while ferrying 32 Curtis P-40 Tomahawk fighter planes from Fremantle, Australia, to the Dutch East Indies.

Langley took five bomb hits, and 16 sailors were killed outright. She came to a halt and developed a serious list to port. When it became evident that she could not be saved, *Langley* was scuttled by torpedoes from an escorting destroyer. Her final losses included 288 killed in action.

ABOVE: The collier *Jupiter* undergoes conversion to the aircraft carrier USS *Langley* at Norfolk Navy Shipyard in 1921. (US Navy via Wikimedia Commons)

ABOVE: Biplanes line the flight deck of the aircraft carrier USS *Langley* in this 1927 photograph. (US Navy via Wikimedia Commons)

BELOW: The battleship HMS *Rodney* fires on the crippled *Bismarck* at the climax of the epic chase, May 27, 1941. (United Kingdom Government via Wikimedia Commons)

WORLD WAR TWO

The conflagration of World War Two marked a definitive period in the evolution of the warship. The advent of naval air power made the aircraft carrier queen of the seas, supplanting the grand floating fortresses of the Battleship Era.

At the same time, the submarine became an even greater influence on the course of the conflict as British Prime Minister Winston Churchill later asserted in his 1949 memoirs: "The only thing that ever really frightened me was the U-boat peril." Meanwhile, submarines of the US Navy ravaged the Japanese merchant fleet in the Pacific, strangling the island nation and causing strongholds across its far-flung empire to wither on the vine.

From the earliest days of World War Two, control of the seas was imperative. The Battle of the Atlantic raged throughout 1939-1945, first with the Nazi U-boats wreaking havoc, while Kriegsmarine surface raiders posed a significant threat to Allied convoy traffic. Then, the pendulum swung towards the Allies with the introduction of improved technology in submarine detection, escort warships, surveillance aircraft, and the development of the hunter-killer group, a naval task group with the sole mission of sinking Nazi U-boats.

The early Battle of the River Plate, in which the Nazi pocket battleship *Graf Spee* was scuttled after duelling with the Royal Navy cruisers *Exeter* and *Ajax* and

ABOVE: Kriegsmarine officers celebrate the return of their U-boat to the French port of St Nazaire after a war patrol in 1942. (Deutsches U-Boot-Museum Stiftung Traditionsarchiv Unterseeboote via Wikimedia Commons)

ABOVE: A US Navy Grumman F6F Hellcat fighter lands on the flight deck of the aircraft carrier USS *Lexington* during the Battle of the Philippine Sea. (US Navy via Wikimedia Commons)

the New Zealander cruiser *Achilles*, the epic hunt for the great Nazi battleship *Bismarck*, the Channel Dash of German warships in 1942, the Battle of the North Cape in which the German battlecruiser *Scharnhorst* was sunk under the guns of the battleship HMS *Duke of York*, and the X-Craft midget submarine attack on *Bismarck*'s sister *Tirpitz* marked the high stakes game of cat and mouse at sea.

The military establishment of Imperial Japan, its nation on a collision course with the United States, understood that mastery of the vast Pacific Ocean was a requirement for the extension of the so-called Greater East Asia Co-prosperity Sphere. Therefore, the pre-emptive attack by naval aircraft flying from the decks of six aircraft carriers,

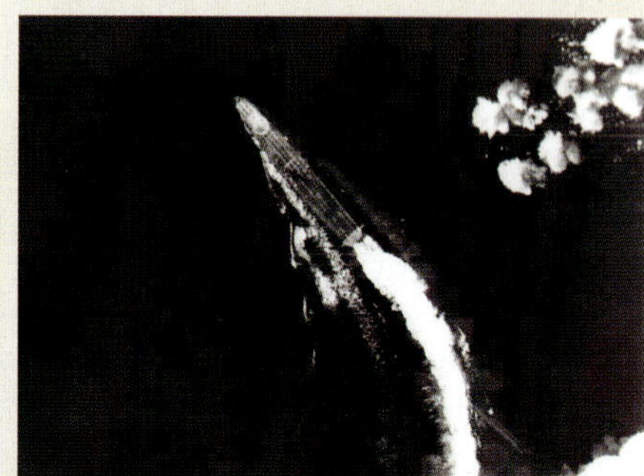

ABOVE: The Japanese aircraft carrier *Hiryu* manoeuvres violently to avoid bombs from American planes during the Battle of Midway. (US Navy Photo USAF-3725 Naval History and Heritage Command via Wikimedia Commons)

struck the first blow of the Pacific "Carrier War" against the anchorage of the US Pacific Fleet at Pearl Harbor, Hawaii, disabling and sinking several battleships, and other vessels.

World War Two across the vast Pacific brought the aircraft carrier into its own and confirmed the notion of air supremacy's critical role in the safety of capital ships. Just three days after Pearl Harbor, Japanese warplanes sank the battleship HMS *Prince of Wales* and the battlecruiser HMS *Repulse*, designated Force Z and sent without air cover to bolster the defences of Singapore. Japanese aircraft carriers ranged across the Indian Ocean, and drove elements of the Royal Navy to the sanctuary of East Africa. Naval battles swirled around the Solomon Islands during the fight for Guadalcanal, and a hard-pressed US Navy finally won control.

During the long island-hopping campaign, and the thrust west and north from Australia through New Guinea and the Philippines toward the Japanese home islands, the Allied forces that made long marches and amphibious landings were dependent on supply and defence from the sea. From transport of men and materiel to shore bombardment and air support, to the great ocean battles that saw the destruction of the Imperial Japanese Navy, Allied naval assets were critical components of the eventual victory.

At the 1942 Battle of Midway, the course of the Pacific War was dramatically altered with the sinking of four Japanese aircraft carriers, *Akagi*, *Kaga*, *Soryu*, and *Hiryu*. While the three American carriers, *Enterprise*,

ABOVE: Allied aircraft fly over the battleship USS *Missouri* and an assemblage of naval might in Tokyo Bay as Japan surrenders, September 2, 1945. (National Archives and Records Administration via Wikimedia Commons)

Hornet, and *Yorktown*, risked everything, and *Yorktown* was lost. Japan's defensive naval war then became a litany of defeat, first at the Battle of the Philippine Sea in June 1944 and then the great Battle of Leyte Gulf that October. Both Japanese super battleships, *Yamato* and *Musashi*, were sunk, absorbing severe punishment from American planes, before the war ended in 1945. The instrument of surrender was signed on the deck of the battleship USS *Missouri* in Tokyo Bay.

With the aircraft carrier ascendant, nuclear power and the jet engine in their infancy, the decades that followed World War Two were demonstrative of the requirement to "show the flag". The roles of major navies as instruments of political and military might, projecting power, increased on an unprecedented scale.

ABOVE: The battleship HMS *Duke of York* leads the battleship HMS *Nelson*, battlecruiser HMS *Renown*, aircraft carrier HMS *Formidable*, and cruiser HMS *Argonaut* off North Africa. (Collections of the Imperial War Museums via Wikimedia Commons)

BISMARCK AND TIRPITZ

Although inter-war research and development of modern warships had been restricted by the terms of the Treaty of Versailles, the German Navy (Kriegsmarine) of the Nazi era managed to conduct clandestine work on the new design of the Bismarck-class battleship. The result included two of the most infamous capital ships of World War Two: *Bismarck* and *Tirpitz*.

Although they were constructed on the modified hull design of the Baden-class superdreadnought of the Great War period, the new battleships mounted advanced fire-control and radar apparatus, demonstrated significant firepower, and were soundly constructed. In total, they were formidable opponents of the Royal Navy, and caused the Admiralty great concern for the safety

ABOVE: The Nazi battleship *Tirpitz* is festooned with decoration during her launching ceremonies. (Creative Commons Bundesarchiv Bild via Wikimedia Commons)

ABOVE: In this photo, taken on May 27, 1941, *Bismarck* is shown under fire from *King George V* and *Rodney* shortly before sinking. (Collections of the Imperial War Museums via Wikimedia Commons)

of both trans-Atlantic troop and merchant convoy traffic.

Bismarck, which was sunk at the conclusion of an epic chase in the spring of 1941, was laid down at the Blohm & Voss Shipyard in Hamburg on July 1, 1936, launched on February 14, 1939, and commissioned on August 24, 1940. Although ostensibly built to the 35,000-ton limit specified in the Washington Naval Treaty of 1922, she displaced 50,900 tons fully loaded. Her length

stretched nearly 814ft with a beam of more than 118ft, and draft of nearly 35ft. She was armoured with a belt of up to 12½in, 4¾in on the steel portions of her deck, and up to 14¼in on her turrets. Main armament included eight 15in guns in paired twin turrets fore and aft, 12 5.9in guns, and 16 105mm and 37mm guns, along with 12 20mm guns for anti-aircraft purposes. Her three geared steam turbines generated 138,000 shaft horsepower and a top speed of 29kts.

ABOVE: The Nazi battleship *Bismarck* is shown in 1940 shortly after entering service with the Kriegsmarine. (Creative Commons Bundesarchiv Bild via Wikimedia Commons)

Although designated as *Bismarck*'s sister, *Tirpitz* was some 2,200 tons heavier due to wartime modifications. Among other differences, *Tirpitz* carried two double hangars for reconnaissance aircraft near the mainmast, while *Bismarck* was constructed with a single hangar. *Tirpitz* was laid down at Kriegsmarinewerft Shipyard in Wilhelmshaven on November 2, 1936, launched on April 1, 1939, and commissioned into the Kriegmarine on February 25, 1941.

The elimination of the threat posed by both *Bismarck* and *Tirpitz* was of highest priority for the Admiralty during the Battle of the Atlantic. When *Bismarck* sortied from Götenhafen, Poland, on May 18, 1941, to commence a commerce raiding career, she was spotted, and the Royal Navy marshalled forces to interdict and sink her. The ensuing chase was one of the most storied in naval history.

ABOVE: The German battleship *Tirpitz* lies camouflaged in a Norwegian fjord. (Government of the United States via Wikimedia Commons)

In company with the heavy cruiser *Prinz Eugen*, *Bismarck* fought the venerable battlecruiser HMS *Hood* and new battleship HMS *Prince of Wales* in the Denmark Strait during her attempted breakout into the Atlantic. In the brief May 24, 1941, battle, *Hood* was sunk but *Bismarck* sustained damage from three hits, one of them fouling a significant amount of fuel oil. *Bismarck* was shadowed by British cruisers – particularly HMS *Norfolk* and HMS *Suffolk,* soon joined by *Prince of Wales* which had sustained damage in the Denmark Strait fight – and aircraft as she turned for the safety of the port of Brest in occupied France. Hoping to come within range of Luftwaffe air cover and support from U-boats, Admiral Gunther Lütjens separated *Bismarck* from *Prinz Eugen* on May 25, turning southeast towards potential sanctuary.

The German behemoth nearly succeeded in reaching her destination, but a desperate airstrike by Fairey Swordfish, anachronistic biplane torpedo aircraft, launched from the deck of the aircraft carrier *Ark Royal* on the evening of the 26th, resulted in a hit that jammed her steering so that she could turn only in a circle. As Royal Navy forces, including the battleships HMS *King George V*, flagship of Admiral John Tovey the Royal Navy commanding officer,

ABOVE: A photographer on board the German heavy cruiser *Prinz Eugen* took this photo of *Bismarck* in May 1941. (Creative Commons Bundesarchiv Bild via Wikimedia Commons)

and HMS *Rodney*, along with a host of cruisers and destroyers closed in, *Bismarck*'s fate was sealed.

At approximately 8.45am on the morning of May 27, 1941, *Bismarck* was finally cornered about 400 miles west of Brest. Both British battleships sighted their quarry at about the same time. The 14in guns of King George V and 16in guns of *Rodney* pounded the virtually immobile *Bismarck* for roughly 90 minutes. *Bismarck* fought back valiantly, firing her main batteries and straddling *Rodney* before each of her turrets in turn fell silent. By 10.15am, *Bismarck* had taken heavy casualties, and been reduced to a battered hulk belching smoke and flame.

With his battleships short of fuel and concerned with reports that U-boats lurked in the area, Tovey ordered a turn for home waters after directing the cruiser *Dorsetshire* to fire torpedoes to finish off the German battleship. This was accomplished, but conjecture persists to this day as to whether *Bismarck* was sunk by enemy fire or scuttled by her

crew. Due to the U-boat threat, British warships remained on the scene long enough to rescue only 110 survivors from a complement of 2,300 as *Bismarck* slid beneath the waves at 10.39am.

Tirpitz was the repeated target of Royal Air Force bombers as she sought shelter in Götenhafen and Kiel, as well as several fjords along the coastline of Norway. Her presence in northern waters maintained a constant threat to Allied convoys bound for the Soviet Union and elsewhere. Although the raids inflicted some damage, *Tirpitz* remained a viable threat and periodic reports that she intended to sortie heightened the sense of urgency at the Admiralty that she should be disposed of permanently.

After the frustrations of the RAF bombing raids, specially trained Royal Navy crews exhibited tremendous bravery in executing Operation Source, an attack with midget submarines dubbed X-Craft, against the mighty *Tirpitz* as she lay at anchor in Kafjord, Norway, on September 22, 1943. The British raiders managed to gain entry to the fjord, avoid anti-torpedo nets and patrol craft for a time, and plant limpet mines that inflicted enough damage to keep the great battleship out of action for six months. Two Royal Navy raiders received the Victoria Cross for heroism during the operation.

Afterwards, RAF air attacks against *Tirpitz* resumed, and she was finally sunk in Tromsö fjord on November 12, 1944, having fired her main 15in batteries only once during the bombardment of installations on the island of Spitsbergen 14 months earlier. The British bombers that finally sank *Tirpitz* dropped 12,000lb Tallboy bombs to accomplish the job.

ABOVE: Smoke from bombs and her own anti-aircraft fire, swirl around the German battleship *Tirpitz* during a raid by planes of the Royal Navy Fleet Air Arm in April 1944. (Collections of the Imperial War Museums via Wikimedia Commons)

HMS *KING GEORGE V*

Constructed following a ten-year ban under the terms of the Washington Naval Treaty of 1922, and following the updated guidelines of the First and Second London Naval Treaties of 1930 and 1936, the battleship HMS *King George V* was the lead ship of her class, all laid down by the summer of 1937, and completed by August 1942. The five also included HMS *Prince of Wales*, *Duke of York*, *Anson*, and *Howe*.

King George V was laid down at the Vickers Armstrong shipyard, Newcastle upon Tyne, on January 1, 1937, launched on February 21, 1939, and commissioned on October 1, 1940. Displacing 42,076 tons fully loaded, she stretched 745ft in length, with a beam of 103ft, and draft of nearly 33ft. Her four steam turbines produced 110,000 shaft horsepower and a top speed of 28kts, while armour protection was up to 15in in the belt, 6in on armoured decks, and 13in on main turrets and barbettes.

The battleship's 14in main guns, specified by the terms of the Second London Naval Treaty, were arranged in quadruple turrets fore and aft, with a twin turret behind and above the forward quadruple mount. Secondary armament was initially 16 133mm dual purpose guns and 32 2-pounder pom-pom anti-aircraft guns. Additional pom-poms were fitted during World War Two.

King George V gained lasting fame as the flagship of Admiral John Tovey during the pursuit and sinking of the German battleship *Bismarck* in May 1941. The five battleships of her class operated around the globe during World War Two and were

ABOVE: Admiral John Tovey stands on the deck of HMS *King George V*, flagship of the Home Fleet, in February 1943.
(Collections of the Imperial War Museums via Wikimedia Commons)

the last class of Royal Navy battleships to see action in the great conflict. Only *Prince of Wales*, which participated in the *Bismarck* chase when brand new, was lost in combat. She succumbed to Japanese bombers and torpedo planes, along with the battlecruiser *Repulse* in the South China Sea off the coast of Malaya on December 10, 1941.

King George V joined the Home Fleet at Scapa Flow in late 1940, proceeding to transport Lord Halifax, Ambassador to the United States, across the Atlantic and then escorting the eastbound Convoy BX104 to the British Isles. She provided escort during the British and Norwegian Commando raid against German industrial targets on the Norwegian Lofoten Islands in March 1941.

On May 22 of that year, *King George V* weighed anchor, with Admiral Tovey aboard, when reports of *Bismarck*'s inaugural sortie were received by the Admiralty. In company with the aircraft carrier *Victorious*, and a complement of escorting cruisers and destroyers, the search for the German battleship lasted five rigorous days. During the deadly game of cat and mouse, *Bismarck* managed to elude shadowing British cruisers and aircraft more than once. Meanwhile, Tovey co-ordinated the convergence of separate naval forces, some coming up from the Mediterranean, to finally subdue the Nazi battleship.

ABOVE: The battleship HMS *King George V* enters the harbour at Guam in the Pacific, in 1945.
(US Navy via Wikimedia Commons)

However, it had been a near-run thing. Tovey had been ready to concede and turn for home, his capital ships low on fuel. But a single torpedo hit from a Fairey Swordfish biplane rendered *Bismarck*'s helm only able to answer in a complete circle. She was battered mercilessly about 400 miles off the French coast and sank on May 27.

Following the *Bismarck* saga, *King George V* performed further escort duty, colliding with the destroyer HMS *Punjabi* while guarding Convoy PQ15 in May 1942, and sustaining heavy damage while the destroyer was cut in two and sank. The battleship underwent repairs and then supported Operation Husky, the Allied landings in Sicily, in the summer of 1943.

After an extensive overhaul, *King George V* transferred to the Pacific in the autumn of 1944, and took part in operations in the Dutch East Indies, the Okinawa campaign, and the bombardment of targets in the Japanese home islands. Along with her three surviving sisters, the battleship was placed in reserve in 1950. All were scrapped by the end of the decade.

ABOVE: The battleship HMS *King George V* trains her heavy 14in guns at sea in 1941.
(Collections of the Imperial War Museums via Wikimedia Commons)

BELOW: This photo of HMS *Hood* was taken in March 1924 around the time of the Empire Cruise. (Government of Australia via Wikimedia Commons)

HMS *HOOD*

Between the world wars the sleek battlecruiser HMS *Hood* was the pride of the Royal Navy. Participating in fleet exercises and routine operations in the Atlantic and Mediterranean, she also ventured far and wide while "showing the flag" for Great Britain across the far-flung empire. In 1923-1924, *Hood* participated in a circumnavigation of the globe known as the "Empire Cruise", weighing anchor in numerous British colonies, South Africa, Canada, Australia, and New Zealand.

Originally laid down at the John Brown & Company shipyard in Clydebank, Scotland, on May 31, 1916, the very day of the epic Battle of Jutland, her construction was temporarily halted during the Great War to assess the blueprints in the wake of the loss of three Royal Navy battlecruisers in the memorable fight. The result of Admiralty reconsideration was a heavier design with increased hull belt armour, a slightly slower speed, and increased attention to the calibre and placement of secondary weaponry to complement her 15in main batteries.

Hood thus became the lead ship in an anticipated class of four battlecruisers including *Rodney*, *Howe*, and *Anson* – all three of which were laid down but cancelled by the autumn of 1918, based on intelligence that the Germans had ceased their own construction of major warships. *Hood* was the only battlecruiser of the class completed; her keel officially re-laid on September 1, 1916. Launched on August 22, 1918, and commissioned in May 1920, *Hood* was representative of a generation of capital ships championed by First Lord of the Admiralty John 'Jackie' Fisher, who saw the battlecruiser as a means of screening naval forces and protecting British communication lines – faster and lightly armoured in comparison to a battleship but mounting the same heavy-calibre guns.

Sacrificing armour protection for speed was a hallmark of the battlecruiser, and some observers have concluded through the years that this feature contributed to the dreadful losses at Jutland and 25 years later to the demise of *Hood* in the May 24, 1941, Battle of the Denmark Strait, when in company with the battleship HMS *Prince of Wales*, she exploded and sank in approximately three minutes during a duel with the German battleship *Bismarck* and her consort the heavy cruiser *Prinz Eugen*. The theory that a 15in shell from *Bismarck* found a "chink" in *Hood*'s armour, which caused the fatal detonation of an ammunition magazine, has been challenged, and the debate continues as to the actual cause of *Hood*'s loss with only three survivors from a complement of over 1,400.

Despite the terrible blow inflicted with her sinking, *Hood* was a magnificent warship. Noted for her streamlined hull, she displaced 44,600 tons, with top speed of 32kts delivered by 24 oil-fed Yarrow boilers and four Brown Curtis geared steam turbine engines delivering 144,000 shaft horsepower. Her armament included eight 15in guns paired in four turrets fore and aft, a dozen 5.5in guns, four 4in and four 3-pounder anti-aircraft guns, and six 21in torpedo tubes. She was nearly 861ft long, with a beam of more than 104ft, and draft of 32ft fully loaded.

Hood's resting place was located in July 2001, and exploration has furthered discussions concerning the cause of her unfortunate demise. The ship's bell was retrieved in August 2015 during an exploration led by Paul Allen, co-founder of Microsoft.

ABOVE: A pair of *Hood*'s aft turret 15in guns are seen trained to their extreme arc of travel.
(US Navy via Wikimedia Commons)

ABOVE: This dramatic painting of the sinking of *Hood*, with the battleship *Prince of Wales* in the foreground, was created by artist JC Schmitz-Westerholt.
(US Naval Historical Center via Wikimedia Commons)

HMS ARK ROYAL

At 6.30pm on the evening of May 26, 1941, the aircraft carrier HMS *Ark Royal* turned into the wind to launch its second mission of the day, 15 antiquated Fairey Swordfish biplane torpedo bombers of 825 Squadron, Fleet Air Arm. The target was the fleeing German battleship *Bismarck*, nearing the cover of Luftwaffe aircraft and Kriegsmarine U-boats, and then the sanctuary of the port of Brest in German-occupied France.

It was a last-ditch long shot to slow the enemy after days of Royal Navy pursuit of the Nazi battleship, but it was the only British card left to play. The Swordfish fliers pressed on through the gloom, and then a torrent of anti-aircraft fire. Miraculously, they scored two hits, one inconsequential amidships, but the other decisive, jamming the battleship's rudder at 15° port so that she could steer only in a circle and await her doom just hours away.

And it was this incredible sequence of events that made HMS *Ark Royal* perhaps the most famous Royal Navy warship of World War Two. Nevertheless, her combat career was relatively brief and her loss, hardly befitting such a distinguished lady of the sea, generated a wave of controversy.

Designed in 1934 under the terms of the Washington Naval Treaty, *Ark Royal* was laid down at Cammell Laird shipyard, Birkenhead, on September 16, 1935, launched April 13, 1937, and commissioned December 16, 1938. With a hull length of 721½ft, flight deck of 800ft, and beam of nearly 28ft, she was powered by six Admiralty boilers and three Parsons geared steam turbines with a top speed of 31kts. Her complement included nearly 1,600 officers and ratings, and she could carry up to 60 aircraft in six squadrons, most of them

ABOVE: The aircraft carrier HMS *Ark Royal* launches and recovers Fairey Swordfish torpedo bombers at sea in 1939. (US Navy via Wikimedia Commons)

Swordfish, Blackburn Skua dive bombers, or Blackburn Roc fighters.

Ark Royal participated in the hunt for the German pocket battleship Graf Spee in 1939 and supported the ill-fated British operations in Norway in the spring of 1940. By the time of the *Bismarck* chase, she was assigned to Force H in the Mediterranean and moved north with her complement of Swordfish under Admiral James Somerville, who ordered the desperate gamble of May 26.

Following the drama of the *Bismarck*, *Ark Royal* ferried fighter planes to the embattled Mediterranean island of Malta. After completing one of these deliveries, she was en route to port at Gibraltar on November 13, 1941, when she was spotted by the German submarine *U-81*. A single torpedo struck the carrier amidships and tore a gaping hole 130ft long in her starboard side, causing tremendous

ABOVE: The aircraft carrier HMS *Ark Royal* lists heavily to starboard after being fatally struck by a German torpedo on November 13, 1941. (Collections of the Imperial War Museums via Wikimedia Commons)

flooding. *Ark Royal* soon developed a precipitous list to starboard of more than 20°.

Subsequent efforts to tow the stricken carrier were fruitless. The following day *Ark Royal* capsized, broke in two, and sank 22 nautical miles east of Europa Point, the southernmost tip of Gibraltar. Only one British sailor died in the sinking, but something had gone wrong. What could cause the carrier of more than 22,300 tons to succumb to a single German torpedo?

A board of inquiry was convened, and the court-martial of Captain Loben Maund, the carrier's commanding officer, followed in February 1942. Maund was found guilty of negligence in the sinking, although his conviction was tempered with the acknowledgment that his concern for the crew had been his priority. Maund continued in the Royal Navy and held several high command positions.

Ark Royal, it was concluded, had come to her ignominious end in part because of her dependence on electric power, knocked out when boilers and other mechanical equipment flooded. With the hard lesson learned, the design of the follow-on Illustrious-class carriers then under construction was altered to provide more protection for critical internal spaces.

ABOVE: This 1938 photo of HMS *Ark Royal* reveals the extension of the aircraft carrier's flight deck beyond her stern. (US Navy via Wikimedia Commons)

VITTORIO VENETO

Launched on July 25, 1937, the battleship *Vittorio Veneto* was the second Regia Marina capital ship of the Littorio-class. Fascist dictator Benito Mussolini nurtured ambitions that the Mediterranean Sea would, as in the days of ancient Rome, once again become an Italian lake. *Vittorio Veneto* was intended to make that dream a reality.

Indeed, *Vittorio Veneto* became the most famous warship of the Italian Navy during World War Two, participating in several engagements with the British Royal Navy. Although Italian dominance of the Mediterranean was never achieved, the battleship outlived the fascist regime and was eventually scrapped at La Spezia in the early 1950s.

One of four planned Littorio-class battleships, *Vittorio Veneto* was among the most powerful and modern warships of her era. Designed by General Umberto Pugliese and engineer Francesco Mazullo, she was the first battleship built in excess of the 35,000 ton restrictions imposed by the Washington Naval Treaty of 1922. *Vittorio Veneto* displaced 41,400 tons and was ordered on June 10, 1934. Other battleships in her class included the lead *Littorio*, *Roma*, and *Impero*, the last of which was laid down at the Ansalo shipyard in Genoa in May 1938, but never completed.

Named after the Italian military victory over Austria-Hungary at the Battle of *Vittorio Veneto* in World War One, the battleship was laid down on October 28, 1934, launched on July 25, 1937, and commissioned on April 28, 1940. She was constructed at the Cantieri Riuniti dell'Adriatico (CRDA) in Trieste. The battleship was 780ft long with a beam of nearly 108ft, and draft of 31ft. Her innovations included Gufo E.C. 4 radar, the first Italian battleship so equipped. The apparatus was capable of detecting surface targets at a range of more than 18½ miles and aircraft at a distance of nearly 50 miles. Her armour was notable, with a main belt of

ABOVE: *Vittorio Veneto* and *Littorio* fire their main 15in batteries during sea trials in 1940. (Regia Marina via Wikimedia Commons)

11in, secondary belt at roughly 2¾in, deck armour of up to 6½in, and turrets protected by 14in on the main batteries. Powered by four steam turbines developing 133,771 shaft horsepower fed by eight oil-fired Yarrow boilers, her top speed was 30kts. She incorporated an innovative anti-torpedo system invented by General Pugliese.

Vittorio Veneto carried three IMAM Ro. 43 reconnaissance float planes or Reggiane

ABOVE: Down by the stern after taking a torpedo hit during the Battle of Cape Matapan in March 1941, *Vittorio Veneto* withdraws from the action.

(Government of Italy via Wikimedia Commons)

Re 2000 fighters that were launched from a catapult at her stern.

Armed with nine 15in main guns located in two turrets forward and one astern, *Vittorio Veneto* boasted that the penetrative power of their rounds made them the most potent guns of their calibre in history. Secondary armament included a dozen 6in guns in four triple turrets, four 120mm guns, 12 90mm guns, and 40 lighter 37mm, and 20mm anti-aircraft weapons.

During World War Two, *Vittorio Veneto* patrolled the Mediterranean in the hope of intercepting British convoy traffic in the autumn of 1940. She was present in the harbour of Taranto on the night of November 11, 1940, but came through the daring British torpedo bomber raid unscathed before moving on to Naples, where she was named flagship of the Regia Marina. She was undamaged during the inconclusive Battle of Cape Spartivento against a heavier squadron of the Royal Navy at the end of the month.

Vittorio Veneto was struck by a single British aerial torpedo during the Battle of Cape Matapan in March 1941, suffering substantial flooding with a notable list. After repairs at Taranto, she put to sea again in August and was attacked in the Strait of Messina by the British submarine HMS *Urge*. A single torpedo hit again put the battleship out of action – this time until early 1942. After operating at sea through November, she relocated with the balance of the Italian fleet to La Spezia, and was seriously damaged by American bombers. After Italy surrendered in September 1943, *Vittorio Veneto* ended up in the Suez Canal for the duration of World War Two.

ABOVE: The Italian battleship *Vittorio Veneto* is shown at anchor prior to completion in 1940.
(Naval History and Heritage Command via Wikimedia Commons)

IJN *YAMATO* AND *MUSASHI*

The largest battleships ever built, sisters *Yamato* and *Musashi* were also the most powerful battleships of their era. They were armed with the largest calibre guns ever mounted on a warship and became symbols of the might of the Imperial Japanese Navy during the years of World War Two in the Pacific. Both massive battleships participated in naval campaigns during the war, and both were sunk by swarms of US Navy bombers and torpedo planes.

Plans for *Yamato* and *Musashi* were conceived in a Japanese attempt to counter the growing strength of the US Navy in the Pacific. Acknowledging that American industry was capable of turning out greater volume in capital ships, the Japanese believed that investing in massive, heavily-armed battleships, substantially larger in size and firepower, would even the odds in a major naval engagement with their Western opponents. Therefore, Japan formally withdrew from the 1922 Washington Naval Treaty on December 29, 1934, with plans to build three super battleships of the Yamato-class.

While *Yamato* and *Musashi* were completed, the third battleship was later converted into the aircraft carrier, *Shinano*, the largest warship of her kind built during World War Two. The Yamato-class was authorised in 1937 in concert with an effort to modernise and improve existing battleships of the Japanese fleet, all of which had been originally built prior to 1921. For Japan, the expansion and modernisation of one of the world's strongest navies was a prerequisite to the waging of aggressive war in the Pacific and on the Asian continent, and then in establishing and maintaining a defensive perimeter against enemies.

Yamato was laid down at the Kure Naval Arsenal, Hiroshima, in November 1937. She was launched on August 8, 1940, and entered service on December 16, 1941, nine days after the Japanese attack on Pearl Harbor ignited World War Two in the Pacific. *Yamato* was the heaviest battleship ever built, displacing nearly 73,000 tons at full load. She was nearly 863ft long with a beam of almost 128ft, and draft of just over 36ft. She was powered by a dozen Kampon boilers that produced 150,000 shaft horsepower in conjunction with four Kampon steam turbines to deliver a top speed of 27kts.

The ship's complement aboard *Yamato* numbered more than 3,200 officers and ratings, while their floating fortress was protected by armour ranging from just over

ABOVE: Fires rage aft aboard the stricken *Yamato*, while a near-miss from an American bomb sends a geyser of water skyward on April 7, 1945. (US Navy via Wikimedia Commons)

16in at the belt to nearly 9in on armoured deck areas, and nearly 26in on the main gun turrets. She carried up to seven Nakajima E8N or E4N reconnaissance aircraft launched from two catapults.

ABOVE: The powerful Japanese battleship *Yamato* undergoes sea trials in the autumn of 1941.
(Hasuya Hirohata Government of Japan via Wikimedia Commons)

BELOW: *Yamato* (foreground) and *Musashi* at anchor off the Japanese base at Truk in the Caroline Islands, 1943.
(US Naval History and Heritage Command via Wikimedia Commons)

ABOVE: *Yamato*'s magazines erupt in a devastating explosion just before the battleship sinks during Operation Ten-Go. (US Navy via Wikimedia Commons)

ABOVE: *Musashi* reels under a fusillade of American bombs and torpedoes in the Sibuyan Sea on October 24, 1945. A Japanese destroyer, also under attack, is visible in the frame as well. (US Navy via Wikimedia Commons)

For all her heft, the most imposing aspect of *Yamato* was her armament. Her original main weaponry included nine 18.1in Type 94 naval guns in triple turrets along her centreline and near amidships. Secondary armament included a dozen 6.1in guns, six 5in, guns, eight triple-mounted 1-in anti-aircraft guns, and four twin-mounted 13.2mm anti-aircraft guns.

Yamato underwent sea trials until the spring of 1942, proving herself a stable and seaworthy gun platform, and was deemed combat ready in May. A month later she was at sea with Admiral Isoroku Yamamoto, Commander in Chief of the Combined Fleet, aboard during the pivotal Battle of Midway. As flagship of Battleship Division 1, she did not engage the enemy during the decisive defeat of the Imperial Navy.

For the next two years, *Yamato* sailed between the Caroline Islands and the home islands of Japan, at times in company with *Musashi*. On December 25,1943, the submarine USS *Skate* fired a spread of four torpedoes, scoring one hit and necessitating a return to Kure for repairs and some upgrades.

In October 1944, during the epic Battle of Leyte Gulf, *Yamato* served as the flagship of Admiral Takeo Kurita and Centre Force. She was slightly damaged in the Sibuyan Sea during the action that sank *Musashi* and later engaged elements of the US Navy's *Taffy 3*, covering the American landings on the Philippine island of Leyte. Her guns thundered during the so-called Battle off Samar on October 25, contributing to the sinking the escort carrier USS *Gambier Bay*

and the destroyer USS *Johnston* before she was driven out of the action by torpedoes from the destroyer USS *Heermann*.

Yamato's final sortie was undertaken during Operation Ten-Go in April 1945, as the Japanese attempted to disrupt American landings on the island of Okinawa. On the 7th, she was set upon by nearly 400 US Navy carrier-based planes. Under attack for nearly two hours, she took hits from at least ten torpedoes and seven bombs before capsizing. Her magazines exploded, and she sank in the East China Sea with 2,498 crewmen lost. Her wreckage was positively identified in 1984.

Although sisters, *Musashi* and *Yamato* were slightly different, in some aspects, when completed. *Musashi* was laid down on March 29, 1938, at the yard of Mitsubishi Heavy Industries in Nagasaki. She was launched on November 1, 1940, and commissioned on August 5, 1942. Primary structural differences involved secondary armament and internal layout. *Musashi*'s

complement was at times as high as 2,500 officers and ratings. Her sea trials and training exercises off Hashirajima through to the end of 1942 were followed by relief of *Yamato* as flagship of the Combined Fleet in February 1943. Much of her time at sea was spent between Truk, Brunei on the South China Sea, and the ports of Yokosuka and Kure in the home islands.

On March 29, 1944, *Musashi* was attacked in the Palau Islands by the submarine USS *Tunny*, which fired a

spread of six torpedoes. One of these struck home, tearing a gaping 19ft hole in *Musashi*'s bow. More than 3,000 tons of seawater poured in. Repairs and refitting to upgrade anti-aircraft capabilities were accomplished at Kure through April, and she participated in the Imperial Navy defeat at the Battle of the Philippine Sea as an aircraft carrier escort.

Musashi met her demise during the Battle of the Sibuyan Sea, a component of the Battle of Leyte Gulf, in October 1944. After leaving the harbour at Brunei on the 22nd with Admiral Kurita's Centre Force, she was assailed two days later by dozens of US Navy planes from the aircraft carriers *Franklin*, *Intrepid*, and *Cabot*. Under attack for four hours, *Musashi* sustained hits from an estimated 17 bombs and 19 torpedoes before sinking, taking 1,023 crewmen to watery graves.

The wreck of *Musashi* was found in 3,280ft of water in 2015 during an expedition led by former Microsoft co-founder Paul Allen.

ABOVE: This grainy image of the battleship *Musashi* was captured as she departed Brunei on her final war cruise on October 22, 1944. (Lieutenant Tobei Shiraishi - U.S. Navy photo via Wikimedia Commons)

U-47

One of the most spectacular feats of daring in all of World War Two occurred on the night of October 13-14, 1939, when Kapitanleutnant Gunther Prien and the crew of the Nazi submarine *U-47* torpedoed and sank the Royal Navy Revenge-class, World War One-vintage battleship HMS *Royal Oak*.

Sinking a British battleship was an accomplishment in itself; however, Prien and *U-47*, a Type VII-B U-boat of the Kriegsmarine, made history in the circumstances, penetrating safety nets and block ships sunk in the narrow channel of Kirk Sound to send *Royal Oak* to the bottom of the supposedly safe haven of Scapa Flow in the Orkney Islands of Scotland. Scapa Flow was the anchorage of the Royal Navy Home Fleet, and the news of the sinking sent shock waves through the Admiralty command establishment. The event also made Prien a national hero in Nazi Germany after *U-47* returned to the North Sea port of Wilhelmshaven, Germany, unscathed.

U-47 had undertaken her second war patrol on October 8, and six days later Prien managed to navigate through the barriers at the Scapa Flow anchorage. It was indeed a rare display of seamanship and willingness to accept incredible risk. Taking advantage of the high tide and winding into Kirk Sound, *U-47* steered a northward course, squeezing between the hulks of the block ships *Numidian* and *Seriano*, but scraping across a defensive cable strung from *Seriano* across the channel.

When Prien realised that *U-47* had been grounded by the tangle, the crew held its collective breath. The unperturbed officer ordered air pressure valves opened and flooded dive tanks to be blown. *U-47* shuddered and shook free, but adding

to the tension, the headlights of a taxi passing along a roadway that skirted the shoreline momentarily caught the intruders

ABOVE: Kapitanleutnant Gunther Prien commanded *U-47* during the attack on HMS *Royal Oak*.

(Creative Commons Bundesarchiv Bild via Wikimedia Commons)

ABOVE: This artist's rendering depicts *U-47* on the surface at sea with an accompanying Luftwaffe fighter plane.

(Creative Commons Paint-tekening U-47 via Wikimedia Commons)

ABOVE: Her crew standing topside, *U-47* returns to base at Kiel sometime in either 1939 or 1940. (US Naval History and Heritage Command via Wikimedia Commons)

in their beams. No alarm was raised, and the German submarine moved, silently submerged, further into the anchorage.

Just before midnight, the 28,240-ton *Royal Oak* was spotted at anchor about 4,400yds distant. The hull of a second ship, which Prien incorrectly identified as a Renown-class battlecruiser, was somewhat obstructed just behind. In fact, this was the seaplane tender HMS *Pegasus*.

At 12.58am, *U-47* unleashed a spread of three torpedoes. One of these struck the bow of *Royal Oak* but did minor damage – mainly severing the battleship's starboard anchor chain. Some sailors aboard *Royal Oak* thought an accident might have produced the muffled explosion. To most of those aboard, the impact was little more than a low thump. No appreciable response followed, and Prien was emboldened to continue his attack. He turned *U-47* about and fired another torpedo from his single stern tube. It missed.

His frustration probably mounting, Prien reoriented the U-boat again to the northward and then fired another spread of three torpedoes from his bow tubes. The time was 1.06am, and geysers erupted as *Royal Oak* was struck. She began to roll over as water poured inside through a terrible gash in the hull amidships. Ratings who had been asleep in their bunks were pitched onto the deck below. Electric power failed, and the entire ship went instantly dark.

Royal Oak sank in just 13 minutes. Open hatches and portholes had hastened the sinking, but it was standard practice to have them open when a ship was in its home anchorage. Casualties included 835 dead among her complement of 1,234.

Prien later remembered: "There was a bang and the next moment the *Royal Oak* blew up. The view was indescribable."

After making good their escape and returning to port on October 17, the entire crew of *U-47* received the Iron Cross 2nd Class. Adolf Hitler dispatched a plane to transport Prien to Berlin for a personal meeting and awarded the 31-year-old officer the Knight's Cross of the Iron Cross, the first for a submariner in World War Two. Prien was nicknamed the "Bull of Scapa Flow", and the snorting bull emblem was emblazoned on the conning tower of *U-47*, later becoming the emblem of the entire 7th U-boat Flotilla.

U-47 was a Type VIIB submarine of the Kriegsmarine. Through the war years, variants of the Type VII were the most numerous of all submarines produced in German shipyards. *U-47* was laid down at Germaniawerft, Kiel, on February 27, 1937, launched on October 28, 1938, and entered service on December 17 of that year. She was more than 218ft long with a beam of just over 20ft, and draft of nearly 16ft. A pair of diesel engines produced a top speed of nearly 18kts for surface

ABOVE: The World War One-vintage Revenge-class battleship HMS *Royal Oak* fires her main batteries in 1916, during the Battle of Jutland, in this painting by William Lionel Wyllie. (More Sea Fights of the Great War Cassell 1919 Public Domain via Wikimedia Commons)

ABOVE: The snorting bull became the emblem of *U-47* and the 7th U-boat Flotilla.
(Creative Commons Sahfi via Wikimedia Commons)

running, while electric batteries allowed submerged propulsion at a maximum of 8kts. Armament consisted of five 21in torpedo tubes, four in the bow and one in the stern, 14 torpedoes, a single 88mm deck gun, and a 20mm anti-aircraft gun.

Several U-boats were ordered to sea in August 1939, nearly two weeks before the Nazi invasion of Poland, to take up positions to strike enemy shipping as soon as possible in the event of a declaration of war. *U-47* departed Kiel on August 19, and her first war patrol took her around the British Isles to station in the Bay of Biscay. On September 5, she sank the British-flagged passenger liner and cargo ship *Bosnia* with a single torpedo after evacuating the crew. *Bosnia* was the second Allied ship to fall victim to a German U-boat in the war, after *U-30* had torpedoed the liner *Athenia* two days earlier. During her first patrol, *U-47* sank three ships for a total of 8,270 tons.

During her 21-month career, *U-47* conducted ten war patrols and became one of the most successful U-boats of the Kriegsmarine, sinking 30 ships totalling 162,769 tons, and damaging eight others. She was lost with all hands in the North Atlantic on March 7, 1941, sometime after torpedoing and damaging the British whale processing ship *Terje Viken*. Kapitanleutnant Prien was among the 45 men who died. He was posthumously promoted to Korvettenkapitän on March 18.

The circumstances surrounding the loss of *U-47* remain a topic of discussion today. For some time, it was believed that the U-boat was sunk in an attack by the British destroyer HMS *Wolverine* off the west coast of Ireland. However, an official records review has cast doubt on this conclusion.

ABOVE: The battleship HMS *Royal Oak*, sunk by *U-47* at Scapa Flow, is shown at anchor in 1937.
(Government of the United Kingdom via Wikimedia Commons)

IJN AKAGI

BELOW: After extensive modernisation in the mid-1930s, *Akagi* is shown in the waters of Sukumo Bay, off the home island of Shikoku, in the spring of 1939. (US Naval History and Heritage Command via Wikimedia Commons)

During the 1930s, *Akagi* was heavily involved in the formation of efficient air operations under the auspices of the navy's First Air Fleet, including the launch and recovery of waves of aircraft, fuelling and servicing, and co-ordination with other carriers that joined the fleet, including her partners in the Pearl Harbor attack, *Kaga*, *Soryu*, *Hiryu*, *Shokaku*, and *Zuikaku*. In the late 1930s, she participated in the Sino-Japanese War, her pilots gaining valuable combat and flight experience.

ABOVE: Looking the length of the *Akagi* flight deck, this photo was captured from an aircraft that has just taken off from the carrier in April 1942.
(Kure Maritime Museum via Wikimedia Commons)

Pounding through heavy seas, the mighty assemblage of the *Kido Butai*, the aircraft carrier strike group of the Imperial Japanese Navy, neared the predetermined launch point for its attack aircraft. The mighty armada had sortied from Hitokapu Bay in the Kurile Islands, on November 26, 1941, its mission to destroy the US Navy's Pacific Fleet anchored at Pearl Harbor, Hawaii.

On the bridge of his flagship, the aircraft carrier *Akagi*, Admiral Chuichi Nagumo ordered level bombers, torpedo bombers, dive bombers, and fighters into the air in the predawn hours of December 7, 1941. Flying from 200 miles north of the Hawaiian island of Oahu, the Japanese carrier planes attacked in two waves, inflicting serious damage on the Pacific Fleet, and plunging the United States into World War Two.

The Pearl Harbor strike seemed to validate the Japanese carrier aircraft doctrine developed largely in the 1930s

and championed by Admiral Isoroku Yamamoto, Commander in Chief of the Combined Fleet. The Japanese had amassed the awesome strength of six aircraft carriers for the heavy blow, a culmination of the concerted naval effort to fully utilise these evolutionary warships as offensive weapons.

The first of the Japanese fleet carriers, *Akagi* was in the vanguard of naval air doctrine development and execution. Laid down at the Kure Navy Arsenal in December 1920, she was originally designed as a 42,000-ton battlecruiser, sharing this common beginning with her future American opponents, USS *Lexington* and USS *Saratoga*. Conversion to an aircraft carrier configuration began on November 19, 1923, with a launch on April 22, 1925, and commissioning on March 25, 1927. *Akagi* measured 857ft long and displaced 27,300 tons upon completion. Three flight decks were installed, the longest at 624ft.

Akagi's beam was nearly 103ft, her draft almost 29ft, and 19 Kampon water tube boilers were teamed with four Kampon geared steam turbines to deliver 131,000 shaft horsepower, and a top speed of nearly 32kts. Three hangars were constructed to handle up to 60 aircraft, but no island was built for command or flight control. Between 1935 and 1938, Akagi underwent a major modernisation and refit at the Sasebo Naval Arsenal. An island was installed on the port side, while two of the flight decks were eliminated and the one that remained was lengthened to 819ft. The hangar decks were enclosed, a third elevator was installed, and aircraft capacity increased substantially to more than 80 modern planes.

After returning to Japan unscathed following the Pearl Harbor attack, *Akagi* sortied to the Indian Ocean in the spring of 1942 along with other Japanese aircraft carriers. During the Indian Ocean Raid, Japanese carrier planes wreaked destruction, attacking the British naval bases at Trincomalee and Colombo on the island of Ceylon, and sinking the old Royal Navy aircraft carrier *Hermes* in a hail of bombs, while the heavy cruisers *Cornwall* and *Dorsetshire*, the Australian destroyer HMAS *Vampire*, other warships and merchant vessels, were also sunk.

In early May, *Akagi* took part in the Battle of the Coral Sea off the Australian coast, launching air strikes during the first naval battle in history in which the opposing surface fleets did not visually contact one another. Planes from *Shokaku* and *Zuikaku* damaged the aircraft carrier USS *Lexington* (which later sank), and the carrier USS *Yorktown*. In exchange, American planes sank the Japanese light carrier *Shoho,* and damaged *Shokaku* heavily while *Zuikaku*'s air group was severely depleted.

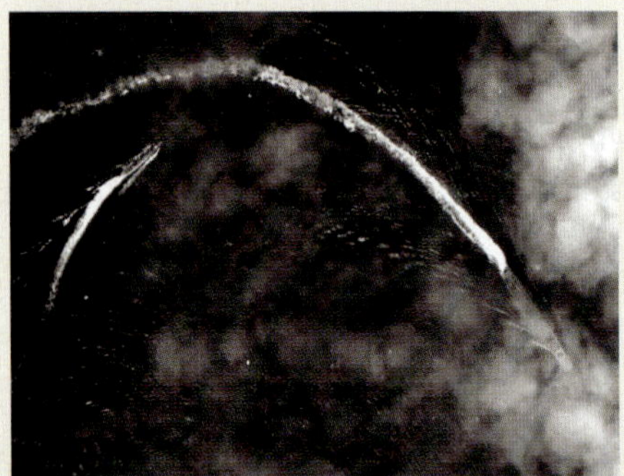

ABOVE: The Japanese aircraft carrier *Akagi* (on right) manoeuvres violently while under attack by US bombers on the morning of June 4, 1942.

(US Army Air Forces via Wikimedia Commons)

ABOVE: The Japanese aircraft carrier *Akagi*, with three Mitsubishi Zero fighter planes parked forward on the flight deck, steams in 1941. (US Navy National Museum of Naval Aviation via Wikimedia Commons)

nearby, as well as extended fuel lines, as the carrier's planes were being prepared for another mission.

Within minutes, secondary explosions rocked *Akagi* and fires raged out of control. The carrier blazed from stem to stern, and the billowing smoke from *Kaga* and *Soryu*, both also mortally stricken, could be seen in the distance. *Hiryu* was sunk in a later dive bomber attack. Damage control parties were unable to bring the fires aboard *Akagi* under control. She was abandoned as Nagumo, stunned by the lightning strike of destruction, transferred his flag to the light cruiser *Nagara*. Yamamoto ordered the blasted hulk of *Akagi* be sunk by Japanese destroyers, and the battered carrier slid beneath the waves on the morning of June 5 with the loss of 267 crewmen.

In a flash, the balance of carrier air power in the Pacific War had irreversibly shifted to the US Navy.

Meanwhile, Admiral Yamamoto planned a grand stroke aimed at capturing the American outpost at Midway Atoll, just 1,100 miles from Hawaii. Operation MI was intended not only to land Japanese troops at Midway, but also to lure the US Navy and its remaining aircraft carriers into a decisive naval battle that would result in their destruction.

The complex Japanese plan began to unfold as the *Kido Butai* weighed anchor on May 26, bound for waters off Midway. The US Navy, its carriers *Enterprise*, *Hornet*, and the hastily repaired *Yorktown*, committed in a desperate bid to halt Japanese expansion in the Pacific, were waiting. American commanders Admiral Frank Jack Fletcher and Raymond Spruance had been warned by codebreakers, at Station Hypo on Oahu, of the coming offensive and prepared to counter in the high-stakes battle.

With *Akagi* and the *Kido Butai* at the tip of the spear, Yamamoto was confident of victory. Admiral Nagumo led the Japanese carrier force of *Akagi*, *Kaga*, *Soryu*, and *Hiryu*, which launched air strikes against Midway. However, Nagumo became alarmed with the sighting of an unidentified American aircraft carrier. In the ensuing chain of events, the Kido Butai met a stunning reversal of fortune. All four Japanese aircraft carriers were destroyed by American dive bombers, while *Yorktown* was lost near the end of the four-day Battle of Midway, June 4-7, 1942, the turning point of the carrier war in the Pacific.

Around 10.26am on the morning of June 4, the Japanese carriers were steadily attacked. The first American bomb directed at *Akagi* either scored a hit on her starboard side or inflicted damage in a near-miss, while a second 1,000lb bomb dropped by US Navy pilot Lieutenant Dick Best penetrated *Akagi*'s flight deck at the aft edge of the centre elevator, exploding in the upper hangar and igniting ordnance stacked

ABOVE: Deck crewmen prepare Mitsubishi Zero fighter planes for launch on the flight deck of *Akagi* during operations against Pearl Harbor, December 7, 1941. (Government of Japan Public Domain via Wikimedia Commons)

ABOVE: Construction of the aircraft carrier *Akagi* proceeds prior to launching at Kure, April 1925.

(Kure Maritime Museum via Wikimedia Commons)

I-19

ABOVE: Flames engulf the aircraft carrier USS *Wasp* after she was struck by three Japanese torpedoes south of Guadalcanal on September 15, 1942.

(US Navy via Wikimedia Commons)

The waters off the island of Guadalcanal in the Solomons were a combat zone for months during World War Two. American landings on the island signalled the first US ground offensive of the conflict. The fight for possession of the island was long and bloody, and control of the surrounding seas was critical to its outcome.

On the afternoon of September 15, 1942, the aircraft carrier USS *Wasp* was escorting a convoy transporting troops and supplies to Guadalcanal. Always vigilant for Japanese submarines, a lookout shattered the relative calm with a startling warning at 2.44pm: "Three torpedoes…three points forward of the starboard beam!" *Wasp* took evasive action, but the helm responded too late. In seconds three deadly Type 95 torpedoes slammed home. *Wasp* erupted in flames and power was snuffed out, preventing effective damage control. A few hours later,

the carrier was scuttled by torpedoes from a US destroyer.

Wasp had gone down with the loss of 25 officers and 150 sailors.

The torpedoes had been fired by the Japanese submarine *I-19*, under Commander Takakazu Kinashi, and the spread of six underwater missiles wreaked havoc, not only with the sinking of *Wasp*, but also with damage to the battleship USS *North Carolina* and the destroyer USS *O'Brien*. At least one torpedo struck *North Carolina* 20ft below the waterline, gashing the port side of her hull with a hole 32ft wide and 18ft long. She was out of action until November. *O'Brien* sank a month after the incident en route to San Francisco for repairs.

Kinashi's daring attack had resulted in the most destructive single fusillade of torpedoes fired by a submarine in World War Two. *I-19* was a Type B1 submarine laid down at the shipyard of Mitsubishi Heavy Industries in Kobe on March 15, 1938, launched September 16, 1939, and commissioned in the spring of 1941. One of 20 Type B1 submarines built, *I-19* was 357ft long with a beam of 31ft and draft of nearly 17ft. She was powered by a pair of diesel engines for surface running and electric motors for submerged propulsion. Top speed was 16kts. With a complement of 94 officers and sailors, *I-19* was armed with a 140mm deck gun and carried a floatplane for reconnaissance. Her primary offensive weapon was the torpedo, and she carried 17 that were launched via six 21in forward tubes.

Prior to the fateful day off Guadalcanal, *I-19* had participated in Operation K, a reconnaissance mission to French Frigate

Shoals prior to the June 1942 Battle of Midway, and operations in the Aleutian Islands. On December 24, 1941, she torpedoed and damaged the freighter SS *Absoroka*. Afterwards, *I-19* was active with the nocturnal Tokyo Express supply and reinforcement runs through 'The Slot' (New Georgia Sound) to Guadalcanal.

From April to August 1943, *I-19* sank the cargo ships *Phoebe A. Hearst* and *William L. Vanderbilt*, damaged the *MH DeYoung* beyond repair, and also damaged the *William Williams*.

On the evening of November 25, 1943, the destroyer USS *Radford* picked up a contact with surface radar off Makin Atoll in the Gilbert Islands. When *I-19* submerged, the destroyer maintained contact, and dropped a pattern of depth charges that sank the Japanese submarine with all hands lost.

ABOVE: Emblazoned with the rising sun, the conning tower of *I-19* is shown while the submarine is docked.

(Government of Japan via Wikimedia Commons)

BELOW: The Japanese submarine *I-19* fired the most spectacular torpedo spread of World War Two off Guadalcanal on September 15, 1942. (Government of Japan via Wikimedia Commons)

BELOW: The sleek Balao-class submarine USS *Tang* rides on the surface of San Francisco Bay near Mare Island Naval Shipyard, December 1943. (US Navy via Wikimedia Commons)

USS *TANG*

During the course of World War Two in the Pacific, US Navy submarines played a vital role in severing the maritime lifeline of supplies, equipment, and troops to and from the home islands of Japan, and its far-flung empire. American submarines ranged across the vast ocean and inflicted enormous losses on enemy merchant shipping as well as assets of the Imperial Japanese Navy.

The most successful of the US submarines, USS *Tang*, is officially credited with sinking 33 enemy ships totalling 116,454 tons during five war patrols that spanned only nine months from January to October 1944, the highest tally of ships and tonnage sunk by an American submarine in the entire war. During her first patrol, *Tang* remarkably sank five Japanese ships while expending only 16 torpedoes, while on her third patrol alone her crew sank ten enemy ships, a US Navy record that still stands, totalling 39,100 tons.

Lieutenant Commander Richard H O'Kane, *Tang's* commanding officer, received the Medal of Honor for heroism during her final patrol, while the submarine's crew, typically up to ten officers and 80 sailors, earned a pair of Presidential Unit Citations along with four battle stars. During her second patrol along the approaches to the Japanese bastion at Truk in the Caroline Islands, Tang rescued 22 airmen shot down during raids against the enemy anchorage.

Tang's contribution to the war effort was substantial, which makes the circumstances of her demise difficult to reconcile. During her fifth patrol, she fired her 24th and last Mark 18 torpedo. A problem developed immediately as the torpedo broached from the waters of the Taiwan Strait and veered to port in a circular run. O'Kane ordered violent manoeuvres but to no avail. Twenty seconds after firing, the torpedo struck *Tang* near the aft torpedo room. She sank by the stern, and 78 crewmen were killed. Nine men, including O'Kane, survived

ABOVE: Sailors aboard the submarine USS *Tang* rescue downed airmen off Truk, in May 1944. (US Navy via Wikimedia Commons)

and were taken prisoner. Others escaped the submarine but were not located. Some of the sailors had used the mechanical Momsen breathing device to reach the surface.

A Balao-class submarine, *Tang* was laid down at Mare Island Navy Yard, California, on January 15, 1943, launched on August 17, and commissioned on October 15 of that year. She displaced 1,494 tons and stretched nearly 312ft long, with a beam of just over 27ft, and draft of almost 17ft. A diesel electric boat, she carried four Fairbanks-Morse, 9-cylinder diesel engines for surface propulsion, and four high-speed Elliott electric motors for running submerged. Her top speed was 20¼kts. Armament consisted of a single 5in deck gun along with 40mm Bofors and 20mm anti-aircraft guns, while ten 21-inch torpedo tubes were installed; six forward and four aft. When fully replenished, Tang carried 24 torpedoes.

Lieutenant Commander O'Kane survived the war and remained in the US Navy until 1957, reaching the rank of rear admiral. He died in 1994 at age 83, one of his country's most highly decorated World War Two veterans. In addition to the Medal of Honor, he earned three Navy Crosses, three Silver Stars, the Legion of Merit, and the Purple Heart.

An interactive exhibit at the National Museum of World War Two in New Orleans recounts the last war patrol of USS *Tang*.

ABOVE: USS *Tang* returns to port at Pearl Harbor after a war patrol in the spring of 1944. (US Navy via Wikimedia Commons)

USS *ARIZONA*

BELOW: The battleship USS *Arizona* is underway at sea in this photo taken prior to modernisation that began in the late 1920s. (National Archives and Records Administration via Wikimedia Commons)

ABOVE: A crowd gathers at the Brooklyn Navy Yard to celebrate the launching of USS *Arizona*, 1915. (National Archives and Records Administration via Wikimedia Commons)

On the morning of December 7, 1941, the battleship USS *Arizona* was quietly moored at Quay F-7 on Battleship Row in Pearl Harbor, Hawaii. In preparation for church services, awnings were stretched to mediate the morning sun, and a US Marine honour guard prepared to raise the flag of the United States.

Moored along Battleship Row with *Arizona* was the pride of the US Navy Pacific Fleet. The battleships *Tennessee*, *West Virginia*, *Maryland*, *Oklahoma* and *Nevada* lay nearby, while the repair ship *Vestal* was situated to the port side of *Arizona*. Just to the west, the battleship *California* was moored, while the flagship, USS *Pennsylvania*, was some distance away in Drydock No.1.

Just before 8am, the Marines of the honour guard aboard *Arizona* heard a strange sound. Crump! Crump! The first Japanese bombs had begun to fall around the seaplane hangar on Ford Island. The Sunday morning stillness was immediately shattered after the first wave of Japanese planes, launched from aircraft carriers some 200 or more miles off the Hawaiian island of Oahu, had cleared the mountains west of Pearl Harbor and begun bombing, torpedo, and strafing runs virtually unnoticed against the warships moored in the harbour, as well as other installations across the island.

The Marines hurriedly completed their task of raising the flag then ran to battle stations. Across the harbour, terrific explosions wracked both shore installations and ships. Within minutes, *Oklahoma* had taken several torpedoes and listed heavily, soon to capsize, trapping hundreds of sailors within her hull. *West Virginia* was gashed by torpedoes as well, but quick counterflooding allowed her to settle to the bottom of the harbour on even keel. *California*, *Maryland*, and *Tennessee* were on fire, while *Pennsylvania* was damaged and *Nevada*, the only American capital ship to get underway during the attack, was pounced upon by Japanese dive bombers and eventually beached. Every battleship of the Pacific Fleet sustained damage.

However, the most devastating blow came against *Arizona*. Commander Mitsuo Fuchida, leader of the Japanese air strike, watched in amazement at the drama below him unfolded. "As my group made its bomb run, American anti-aircraft from shipboard and shore batteries suddenly came to life," he later wrote. "Dark grey bursts blossomed here and there until the sky was clouded with shattering near misses that made our planes tremble…Suddenly, a colossal explosion occurred in Battleship Row. A huge column of dark red smoke rose to 1,000ft, and a stiff shock wave reached our plane. Studying Battleship Row through binoculars, I could see that the big explosion had been aboard *Arizona*. She was still flaming fiercely…"

The tremendous explosion Fuchida witnessed had indeed come from *Arizona*. Japanese bombers had scored two hits on the battleship, the first damaging air intakes and causing a thick plume of smoke to rise from her stacks. The second hit was catastrophic. A bomb modified from a shell, originally intended to be fired by a 14in naval gun, struck the battleship a mortal blow, penetrating slightly aft of Turret No. 2 through the main and second decks, crew quarters below, and exploding on the third deck directly over the powder magazines for the battleship's main 14in guns.

While an open hatch may have contributed to the conflagration, a fire ignited black powder that touched off six

ABOVE: The battleship USS *Arizona* transits the Panama Canal in 1921. Note the awning spread over the bow to provide shade. (Library of Congress via Wikimedia Commons)

ABOVE: After her modernisation is completed in the 1930s, USS *Arizona* ploughs through ocean waters. (US Navy via Wikimedia Commons)

magazines, each of which contained ten tons of the explosive propellant for the main guns, and then three more magazines, each filled with 13 tons of powder for the forward 5in secondary batteries. The resulting blast killed 1,177 men, and utterly destroyed the forward section of the battleship.

During the infamous Pearl Harbor raid, 2,403 American civilians and service personnel lost their lives. The greatest death toll by far had occurred aboard *Arizona*. Although portions of the battleship were salvaged, her great hull lies at the bottom of the harbour – stretched across it an iconic memorial dedicated in May 1962. Many of those who died remain entombed within the old hull, and the location is one of the American nation's most revered shrines.

The architecture of the *Arizona* Memorial is worthy of note, its ends upswept symbolically to represent the ultimate Allied victory during World War Two in the Pacific. But oil still seeps from the fuel bunkers of the battleship, and thousands come each year to pay their respects to those lost. Prefectures and cities of modern Japan have sent flower arrangements in homage to their one-time enemies.

Laid down on March 16, 1914, at the Brooklyn Navy Yard, USS *Arizona* was the second of two battleships of the Pennsylvania-class. She was launched on June 19, 1915, and commissioned on October 17, 1916. She was powered by a dozen Babcock & Wilcox boilers that delivered 33,376 shaft horsepower to a quartet of Parsons steam turbines that raised a top speed of 21kts. She displaced 31,400 tons, with a length of 608ft, beam of 97ft, and draft of nearly 29ft. Her armour protection ranged from 5in on main deck

areas to more than 13in at the belt, and 18in atop the main turrets. Her initial armament consisted of 12 14in guns arranged in triple turrets fore and aft, 22 5in guns, four single 76mm anti-aircraft weapons, and a pair of 21in torpedo tubes.

Sea trials were conducted off the Virginia Capes and Newport, Rhode Island, in the Atlantic, and then in the Caribbean Sea off Guantanamo Bay, Cuba. Although *Arizona* did not participate in World War One, she transported President Woodrow Wilson across the Atlantic to attend peace talks that concluded the terms of the Treaty of Versailles. She operated out of the home port of Norfolk, Virginia, and showed the US flag in the Mediterranean during the

1919 war between Turkey and Greece. By 1921, she had transferred to the Pacific, where she remained for the duration of her career. *Arizona* supported relief efforts at Long Beach, California, following a major earthquake in 1933.

A stately and majestic warship, *Arizona* was featured in the 1934 feature film *Here Comes The Navy*, starring James Cagney, Pat O'Brien, and Gloria Stuart. The battleship gained some measure of fame and came to be representative of US naval power in the Pacific, particularly during an era of rising tensions with the expansionist Japanese Empire.

ABOVE: A forward magazine explodes aboard USS *Arizona* after a devastating bomb hit during the attack on Pearl Harbor, December 7, 1941. (Naval History and Heritage Command Center via Wikimedia Commons)

Congressional budget tightening during the mid-1930s led to long stretches in port. However, by 1940, President Franklin D Roosevelt ordered the relocation of the Pacific Fleet from its home anchorage at San Pedro, California, to Pearl Harbor, 2,000 miles closer to potential areas of conflict should war erupt with Japan.

It was there that *Arizona* met her terrible fate on the Sunday morning that plunged the United States into World War Two.

ABOVE: The memorial to those who perished aboard the USS *Arizona* on December 7, 1941, spans the hulk of the battleship that rests on the shallow bottom of Pearl Harbor. (US Navy via Wikimedia Commons)

USS *LEXINGTON*

At the time that the 1922 Washington Naval Treaty went into effect, limiting the tonnage and number of capital ships among the great navies of the world, the United States had two battlecruisers under construction. *Lexington*, ordered in 1916, was at Fore River Ship Building Company, Quincy, Massachusetts, while *Saratoga* was being built at New York Shipbuilding Corporation in Camden, New Jersey.

Work was halted on both for a time in the early 1920s, but resumption was authorised with conversion of the two warships to aircraft carriers. The fact that both would displace about 33,000 tons, well in excess of the 27,000-ton treaty limit, did not deter progress. *Lexington* was laid down on January 8, 1921, launched on October 3, 1925, six months after *Saratoga*, and commissioned on December 14, 1927.

Developed amid the flurry of emerging aircraft carrier operational doctrine that began in the post-World War One years, and flourished through World War Two a generation later, *Lexington* and *Saratoga* were, for a time, the largest and fastest ships of their type in the world. Sixteen Yarrow boilers and four General Electric turbines provided 180,000 shaft horsepower and a top speed of slightly more than 33kts. *Lexington*'s unarmoured flight deck stretched 866ft, while her beam was 137½ft, and her fully loaded draft was 32½ft. An island with an immense single funnel was offset to the starboard side. A pair of elevators handled aircraft up and down from the cavernous 450ft, two-storey hangar deck. Constructed originally to carry 79 combat aircraft, her capacity was increased to 90 with the addition of a deck park. Early armament included 8in guns that were removed in 1942, 1.1in quad-mounts, and 20mm Oerlikon cannon.

After sea trials, *Lexington* was ordered to San Pedro, California, and later operated in

ABOVE: In October 1941, the aircraft carrier USS *Lexington* steams out of the harbour of San Diego, California. Note her single massive funnel. (US Navy via Wikimedia Commons)

ABOVE: Abandoned and burning, the aircraft carrier USS *Lexington* lists sharply to port on May 8, 1942, during the Battle of the Coral Sea. (US Navy via Wikimedia Commons)

the Atlantic and Caribbean. Nearly a decade prior to the outbreak of World War Two, she participated with *Saratoga* in Grand Fleet Exercise No. 4, a simulated air attack on the fleet anchorage at Pearl Harbor, Hawaii. Successfully executed, the February 7, 1932, simulation demonstrated that such an operation was indeed possible. No doubt, the Japanese took notice in planning their raid on Pearl Harbor on December 7, 1941.

Although the Japanese deemed their raid on Pearl Harbor successful, they failed to damage or sink, any of the American carriers that were at sea at the time. However, by the spring of 1942, the world's first carrier versus carrier naval battle was on the horizon. *Lexington* and her crew fought valiantly during the Battle of the Coral Sea, winning a strategic victory that turned a Japanese

invasion force away from intended landings to capture Port Moresby on the island of New Guinea.

The US Navy paid a steep price for the crucial triumph.

Coral Sea was the first naval battle in history in which opposing surface ships did not actually come in sight of each other. At one time the US and Japanese task forces were separated by only 70 miles of open water, each groping to find the other and launch air attacks.

On May 7-8, 1942, the two sides traded heavy blows. The Japanese light carrier *Shoho* was sunk, while the fleet carrier *Shokaku* was severely damaged, and the air contingent, pilots and planes, aboard the carrier *Zuikaku* were decimated. In turn, the carrier USS *Yorktown* was seriously damaged.

The greatest blow to the US Navy at Coral Sea was the loss of *Lexington*, which was set upon by Japanese dive bombers and torpedo planes at around 11.30am on the May 8. She was struck by two bombs and as many as four torpedoes, killing 65 sailors. For a time it appeared that "Lady Lex" might be saved, but internal explosions wracked the ship. She was abandoned and sunk hours later by torpedoes from a US destroyer. From her complement of 2,700, only 216 perished.

The wreck of *Lexington* was discovered during an expedition led by Paul Allen, co-founder of Microsoft, in 2018. She sits mostly upright in several sections at the bottom of the Coral Sea, a depth of 9,800ft.

USS *HORNET*

Before and during World War Two, US Navy aircraft carrier design continued to evolve. Following the early *Lexington*, *Saratoga*, and *Ranger* builds, the Yorktown-class deployed in the mid-1930s, and USS *Hornet* was next in line.

While the major navies of the world had agreed to restrict aircraft carrier tonnage, the US Congress passed the Naval Expansion Act in the spring of 1938, and two additional aircraft carriers, *Hornet* and *Essex*, were authorised and expected to total no more than 40,000 combined tons. *Hornet* was built along the lines of the Yorktown-class, with some modifications that place her there or in a category all her own, depending on the source consulted. *Essex*, ultimately built without the treaty restrictions that limited earlier blueprints and reaching a displacement of 27,000 tons, became the progenitor of a mighty class of fast carriers that dominated the later years of World War Two in the Pacific.

BELOW: Photographed shortly after completion in 1941, the aircraft carrier USS *Hornet* steams off the US east coast. (US Navy via Wikimedia Commons)

ABOVE: A US Army Air Forces B-25 Mitchell medium bomber takes off from the pitching deck of USS *Hornet* during the Doolittle Raid on April 18, 1942. (US Navy via Wikimedia Commons)

Hornet, however, achieved lasting fame in her own right. Laid down at Newport News Shipbuilding in Virginia on September 25, 1939, *Hornet* was launched on December 14, 1940, and entered service on October 20, 1941. Her flight deck extended 814ft, overall length was nearly 825ft, and her beam was just over 83ft. She displaced 25,909 tons fully loaded and made a top speed of 32½kts powered by nine Babcock & Wilcox boilers and four Parsons geared turbines generating 120,000 shaft horsepower. Three elevators shuttled planes to and from the hangar and flight decks, and she accommodated 72 aircraft. Her complement included about 1,300 officers and sailors.

After shakedown and training, *Hornet* was ordered to the Pacific, reaching Alameda Naval Air Station at San Francisco Bay in March 1942. Three weeks later, she embarked with 16 US Army Air Forces North American B-25 Mitchell medium bombers, their

crews under the command of Lieutenant Colonel James "Jimmy" Doolittle, and their mission – bomb Tokyo. On the morning of April 18, their clandestine mission perhaps compromised by a Japanese picket boat some 600 nautical miles off the home islands, *Hornet* turned into the wind and launched the bombers, which had never been intended for carrier operations.

When the raid was over, the Japanese military establishment was shocked, President Franklin D Roosevelt gloated that the planes had come from the mythical Shangri-La, and Doolittle was a national hero, receiving the Medal of Honor. *Hornet* and her consorts, including the aircraft carrier *Enterprise*, returned safely to Pearl Harbor, Hawaii.

Following the Doolittle Raid, *Hornet* and *Enterprise* formed Task Force 16 under Admiral Raymond A Spruance, which made rendezvous with Task Force 17, under Admiral Frank Jack Fletcher, aboard the carrier USS *Yorktown* at Point Luck about 325 miles northeast of Midway Atoll in early June. Tipped off by intelligence codebreakers, the Americans were

ABOVE: The aircraft carrier USS *Hornet* lists heavily after being badly damaged and abandoned on the afternoon of October 26, 1942, during the Battle of the Santa Cruz Islands. (US Navy via Wikimedia Commons)

prepared to meet a massive Japanese naval force intent on destroying the US carriers and seizing the tiny islets of Midway, just 1,100 miles from Hawaii. *Hornet*'s aircraft participated in the major US victory in which four Japanese carriers were sunk, and the gallant sacrifice of her air group, particularly Torpedo Squadron 8, is well known.

Hornet later moved to the Southwest Pacific to support American efforts to capture the vital island of Guadalcanal in the Solomons. For roughly six weeks, she was the only operational US aircraft carrier in theatre. Joined by *Enterprise* in August, she participated in the Battle of the Eastern Solomons. In October, *Hornet* was the immediate focus of Japanese attention during the Battle of the Santa Cruz Islands. Japanese aircraft attacked the American carriers just before 9am on August 26, concentrating on *Hornet*, which took a bomb hit on the flight deck aft, shuddered with the concussion of two near-misses, and was then rocked by three successive bombs. A Japanese pilot, realising his plane was heavily damaged, chose to dive into *Hornet*, and two torpedoes slammed into the carrier amidships on the starboard side.

Hornet lost all power but the fires that had raged were brought under control, and for a while it appeared the carrier might survive. Later in the day, however, another Japanese aerial torpedo struck home. Power was lost again, and *Hornet* was abandoned. Stubbornly, she would not sink when US destroyers tried to end her agony. Later, she was found adrift by Japanese destroyers and sent to the bottom. About 140 men were killed in the day's action.

Hornet's wreck was discovered in January 2019 during an expedition led by Microsoft co-founder Paul Allen.

USS *ENTERPRISE*

The sailors aboard the aircraft carrier USS *Enterprise* were full of fight in the autumn of 1942, and the sign they displayed stated the fact boldly: "*Enterprise* vs Japan."

Although USS *Hornet*, another vital carrier, had been sunk and their own *Enterprise* damaged by two bombs that killed 44 crewmen and wounded 75 in the October Battle of the Santa Cruz Islands, the sailors knew that their carrier would be charged with holding the line against the Japanese during a critical period of World War Two in the Pacific. After two weeks of repairs at New Caledonia, *Enterprise* returned to action, the only combat capable US Navy aircraft carrier in theatre.

Nicknamed the "Big E", *Enterprise* and her fighting crew went on to burnish their reputation for courage and grit as the carrier finally earned 20 battle stars, more than any other combat ship of the US Navy in the war. For good measure, she also received a Presidential Unit Citation and the Navy Unit Citation. Wounded grievously on more than one occasion, *Enterprise* survived the conflict, becoming one of the most storied warships in the history of the navy. However, postwar efforts to save her as a museum ship were fruitless.

In the throes of the Great Depression, US President Franklin D Roosevelt recognised the economic hardships that were extant; however, he also understood that navy construction programme would create jobs. As a former Assistant Secretary of the Navy, he further endorsed shipbuilding as a prudent defensive measure. In 1934, the US Congress authorised a multi-year construction program that included the two aircraft carriers of the Yorktown-class. The second of these, *Enterprise* was laid down at Newport News Shipbuilding in Virginia on July 16, 1934, launched on October 3, 1936, and commissioned on May 12, 1938. She was 769ft long at the waterline, with a flight deck that stretched 802ft, and a beam of nearly 109ft. She carried up to 90 aircraft,

ABOVE: A Japanese bomb explodes on the flight deck of the aircraft carrier USS *Enterprise* during the Battle of the Eastern Solomons, August 24, 1942. (US Navy via Wikimedia Commons)

and was built with two hangars and three elevators to service air operations.

Enterprise was powered by nine Badcock & Wilcox boilers that fed four Parsons steam geared turbines, with 120,000 shaft horsepower and top speed of 32½kts. Early anti-aircraft defences included single-mount 8in guns, quad-mounted 1.1in weapons, .50-calibre machine guns, and later 20mm Oerlikon cannon. Her complement grew from 2,217 to 2,900 after the US entered World War Two.

The Yorktown-class marked a leap forward in American aircraft carrier design, and Admiral James M Russell, a pilot who had served on earlier carriers, commented: "We fought for a lot of things…We put reclining chairs in the ready rooms, all facing in one direction with a blackboard, and a teletype information system that could be operated from a central point… air conditioning too…"

Early *Enterprise* wartime operations included launching air strikes against Japanese installations in the Gilbert and Marshall Islands in February 1942, just weeks after the enemy attack on Pearl Harbor. In April, *Enterprise* supported

ABOVE: In this photo taken from the light carrier USS *Bataan*, a Japanese kamikaze plane crashes into USS *Enterprise* in May 1945. (US Navy via Wikimedia Commons)

ABOVE: A near-miss from a Japanese bomb rocks the aircraft carrier USS *Enterprise* during the Battle of the Santa Cruz Islands, October 1942. (US Navy via Wikimedia Commons)

ABOVE: The historic aircraft carrier USS *Enterprise* (foreground) awaits transfer to the scrapyard in New York, June 1958. The attack carrier USS *Independence* is seen on the opposite side of the pier. (US Navy via Wikimedia Commons)

Hornet during the famed Doolittle Raid on Tokyo, which boosted American morale during the dark early days of the war. Her fighters flew air cover, while *Hornet* launched North American B-25 Mitchell bombers to attack the Japanese capital.

In June 1942, *Enterprise* played a pivotal role in the tremendous victory at the Battle of Midway, a turning point in the Pacific War. Her courageous pilots joined those of *Hornet* and *Yorktown* in sinking four Japanese carriers. By August, US ground forces had landed on the island of Guadalcanal in the Solomons, and *Enterprise* was offshore to support them, participating in two major carrier battles and at times fighting for her life.

On August 24, 1942, opposing carrier forces fought the Battle of the Eastern Solomons. At approximately 4.30pm, veteran Japanese dive bomber and torpedo plane pilots spotted *Enterprise*, which took the brunt of the heavy air assault. In two minutes, the Japanese scored three bomb hits on the carrier, the first striking the flight deck and penetrating three decks below before detonating, and killing or wounding more than 100 sailors. Fifteen feet away, the second Japanese bomb ignited fires and set off 5in ammunition, killing 35 more. The third bomb blew a 10ft hole in the flight deck. Amazingly, efficient damage control crews had *Enterprise* back on line and conducting flight operations within an hour.

In late October, the opposing carrier forces closed to within 200 miles of one another, and the second desperate encounter of *Enterprise*'s Solomons service ensued. During the Santa Cruz battle, *Hornet* took the heaviest punishment as

ABOVE: The combat veteran aircraft carrier USS *Enterprise* is shown at sea in September 1945. (US Navy Bureau of Ships via Wikimedia Commons)

Enterprise was partially obscured by a rain squall for a time. *Hornet* was struck by four Japanese bombs and two torpedoes, and was sunk later by Japanese destroyer torpedoes. Japanese losses were substantial, and the heavily damaged aircraft carriers,

Shokaku and *Zuiho*, were out of action for months.

Meanwhile, *Enterprise* made for New Caledonia. Subsequently, she took part in the November 1942 Naval Battle of Guadalcanal, which was primarily fought by surface ships and land-based aircraft.

After the Solomons campaign, *Enterprise* participated in the great US naval victories at the Battles of the Philippine Sea in June 1944, and Leyte Gulf in October. During the amphibious operations at Iwo Jima and Okinawa, her aircraft conducted air support, combat air patrol, and interdiction missions. In April and May 1945, she was twice damaged by Japanese Kamikaze suicide planes. When World War Two ended, *Enterprise* was at the Puget Sound Navy Yard in Bremerton, Washington, undergoing repairs and refit for subsequent participation in Operation Magic Carpet, the postwar effort to return US military personnel to the United States.

During the course of the Pacific War, *Enterprise* and her crew proved resilient time after time. On at least three occasions, Japanese propagandists were so confident that the carrier had been sunk that they announced the erroneous news of her demise. When word of the disinformation was received, she was given another nickname – Grey Ghost.

Although *Enterprise* was only about a decade old in 1945, her design had been eclipsed by the later Essex-class aircraft carriers. By 1947, she was decommissioned from the navy with plans to donate the ship to the state of New York for preservation. However, this idea failed to materialise. Further preservation efforts, and the endorsement of former officers and crew, failed to generate funding to purchase *Enterprise* from the navy. Thus, in one of the great travesties in the annals of the US Navy, this historic warship was sold to the Lipsett Corporation in 1958, and scrapped at Kearny, New Jersey. It was truly an inauspicious and unfitting end for a most gallant warship.

ABOVE: Her flight deck filled with navy aircraft, some of them biplanes, USS *Enterprise* is at sea in 1939. (US Navy via Wikimedia Commons)

PT-109

I t was pitch dark in Blackett Strait. For Lieutenant John F Kennedy and the crew of *PT-109*, the predawn hours of August 2, 1943, brought another patrol in the Solomons Islands of the South Pacific. Although it was eerie quiet, save the drumming of his own engines, Kennedy was wary as his boat swept along the southwest coast of the island of Kolombangara.

The World War Two campaign for possession of the Solomons was in full swing, and in company with three other Patrol Torpedo (PT) boats, the *PT-109* was prowling for Japanese shipping, probably destroyers, making rapid runs with resupply and reinforcements to be unloaded to their troops fighting on the nearby island of New Georgia.

Lieutenant Kennedy's command included 12 others, Ensign Lenny Thom, the boat's executive officer, third officer Ensign George Ross, and ten sailors. Their craft was diminutive but efficient, and tailor-made for the task at hand – it was also armed to the teeth. *PT-109* was an example of the US Navy's best coastal patrol craft, well-suited for inter-island waterways and the close quarters of the Solomons, where an encounter with the enemy could feel like a knife fight in a phone booth.

PT-109 and other such boats were the brainchild of Hubert Scott-Paine of the British Power Boat Company, who offered his design to Elco, the Electric Launch Company of Bayonne, New Jersey, and its naval division. The design was originally intended for fast air-sea rescue, but was highly adaptable as a weapon of war. A total of 531 PT-boats were built for the US Navy by Elco and Higgins during World War Two.

PT-109 was 80ft long, with a beam of nearly 21ft, and shallow draft of only 3½ft.

ABOVE: *PT-109* is strapped aboard the Liberty Ship SS *Joseph Stanton* en route to the Pacific on August 20, 1942. (US National Archives Bureau of Ships Collection via Wikimedia Commons)

She displaced 57 tons fully loaded, and three 12-cylinder Packard W-14 M2500 petrol engines, marine variants of standard aircraft powerplants, supplied a top speed of 41kts. Armament consisted of a single 20mm gun aft, a pair of twin Browning .50-calibre machine guns, a pair of depth charges, and four 21in torpedo tubes. For extra punch, Kennedy had ordered an old single shot 37mm anti-tank gun mounted on deck planking.

Kennedy was the son of a wealthy and politically connected New England family, who survived World War Two to become the 35th President of the United States. However, that night in Blackett Strait, the 26-year-old officer fought the fight of his life. The 15 PT-boats that sortied from their forward operating base on the island of Rendova had been divided into four groups under the command of Lieutenant Harry Brantingham aboard *PT-159*. For much

ABOVE: The coconut shell with Lieutenant Kennedy's plea for rescue was preserved as a paperweight. (John F. Kennedy Presidential Library via Wikimedia Commons)

of the night, they were unaware of the proximity of Japanese destroyers that had already deposited their cargoes at Vila

BELOW: With 94 survivors from the sunken cruiser USS *Northampton* aboard, *PT-109* enters the harbour of the island of Tulagi in the Solomons in December 1942. (US Government via Wikimedia Commons)

on the southern coast of Kolombangara, and then turned for the homeward leg of their mission.

PT-159 had become separated from the other boats and discovered the Japanese. Brantingham sent no warning message, attacked alone, and scored no hits. Meanwhile, Kennedy and *PT-109* were quietly cruising, the crew going about routine tasks. Suddenly, at 2.30am, Motor Machinist Mate Harold Marney spotted a large object off the port bow. From his .50-calibre gun mount, Marney shouted: "Ship at 2 o'clock!"

Kennedy ordered evasive action as the unidentified vessel steamed on a collision course. He remembered: "At first I thought it was a PT. I think it was going at least 40kts." There was no time to avoid impact. The Japanese destroyer *Amagiri* sliced through the wooden hull of *PT-109* and ignited the high-octane fuel in her tanks. *PT-109* was cut in half, and an explosion punctuated the fatal crash. *Amagiri* continued ahead, its wake dousing the fires.

Two American sailors were killed, probably in the collision. Kennedy called out to the crew, and six men responded. Two others were wounded in the water, one of them able to swim. Kennedy took the other in tow, pulling the straps of his life jacket and gripping them in his teeth as the group struggled towards the nearest land, Plum Pudding Island, more than three miles away. The gruelling swim took four hours, and the exhausted men had no food or water. At least there were no Japanese either.

Although aircraft flew overhead, frantic signals were unacknowledged, while back at Rendova no one believed there had been any survivors when *PT-109* was lost. Kennedy swam alone into Ferguson Passage, attempting to signal passing boats with a lantern salvaged from his sunken PT, but to no avail. The group then painfully relocated to Olsana Island

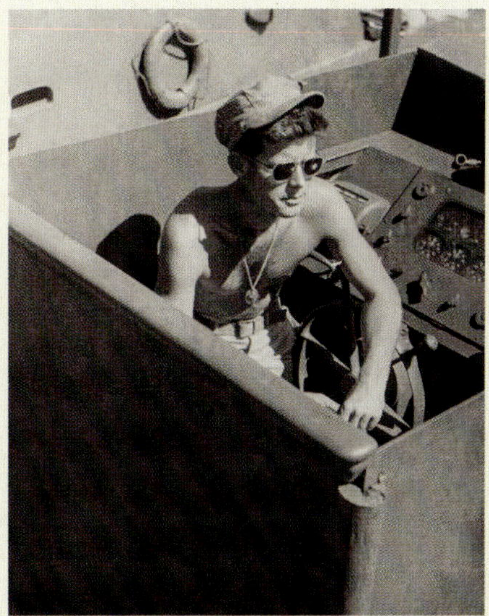

ABOVE: Shirtless Lieutenant John F. Kennedy sits next to the wheel aboard *PT-109* in 1943.
(US Navy via Wikimedia Commons)

on August 4, Kennedy again towing the wounded man. Kennedy and Ross swam on to Naru Island, where they found a wrecked boat, a box with Japanese writing on the lid containing candy, a container of water, and a one-man canoe.

While Ross rested at Naru, Kennedy returned to Olsana, where two teenage natives had appeared. The officer scratched a message on a coconut shell, handed it to the boys, and repeated the word "Rendova", hoping they would deliver the plea for rescue to the base. Meanwhile, Australian Sub-Lieutenant Reginald Evans had seen the explosion and fire when *PT-109* was destroyed. The coastwatcher sent natives to look for survivors but found none. Finally, Kennedy and Ross were brought to Evans on Gomu Island.

Evans alerted Rendova, and on the night of August 7, seven PT-boats set out on a rescue mission, picking Kennedy

ABOVE: The Imperial Japanese Navy destroyer *Amagiri* is moored in port in this 1930 photograph.
(Shizuo Fukui Government of Japan Public Domain via Wikimedia Commons)

up from a canoe. He guided the PTs to Olsana, where the rest of the survivors of *PT-109* were loaded aboard, and given sandwiches and brandy. Three hours later, they arrived at Rendova. It was 5am on August 8, and the ordeal had lasted nearly a week.

Kennedy was treated for cuts and abrasions from the sharp coral, and remained in the Pacific for several months, in command of *PT-59*. A severe back injury sustained in the collision plagued him for the rest of his life. He received the Purple Heart and the Navy and Marine Corps Medal, and was medically discharged from the US Navy in December 1944.

John F Kennedy was elected president in 1960 at age 46 with the story of *PT-109* contributing to his persona of youth, vigour, and heroism. He was assassinated on November 22, 1963.

ABOVE: The crew of *PT-109* smile for the camera, just days before the fatal encounter in Blackett Strait.
(Naval Historical and Heritage Center via Wikimedia Commons)

USS *JOHNSTON*

The pilot's warning was too incredible to believe. Admiral Clifton AF Sprague, commanding Taffy 3, a collection of escort carriers, destroyers and destroyer escorts supporting the American landings on the Philippine island of Leyte, asked for clarification.

The Battle of Leyte Gulf, the largest naval engagement of World War Two – and in naval history – was underway on October 25, 1944, and the pilot confirmed: "I can see pagoda masts, and I see the biggest meatball flag on the biggest battleship I ever saw!"

The Battle off Samar was about to begin. On paper, Sprague's command was massively outgunned by the Centre Force of the Imperial Japanese Navy under Admiral Takeo Kurita. Along with other battleships and cruisers, Kurita was aboard the super battleship Yamato, her big 18.1in guns dwarfing the 5in "pop guns" aboard the little Taffy 3 flotilla, but these were all that stood in the way of the Japanese. If they passed Taffy 3, Kurita's big guns could wreak havoc among the transports and cargo ships off the Leyte beachhead. They would be, as Kurita had described, "a hawk among chickens".

Sprague had been placed in this precarious position when Admiral William F "Bull" Halsey had been drawn northwards in pursuit of a Japanese decoy force that included enticing aircraft carrier targets, though their decks were devoid of enemy aircraft. Sprague called for help. His escort carriers sent their planes aloft. His destroyers and destroyer escorts answered the call, and did the only thing they could do against such a superior force – attack!

USS *Johnston* and her gallant crew were among the heroes of Taffy 3 on the morning

ABOVE: A forward 5in gun turret is depicted in this ghostly image of the wreck of USS *Johnston*. (Creative Commons Vivescovo via Wikimedia Commons)

of October 25, 1944. Laid down at Seattle-Tacoma Shipbuilding in Washington State on May 6, 1942, launched on March 25, 1943, and commissioned on October 27 of that year, USS *Johnston* was one of 175 Fletcher-class destroyers built for the US Navy during World War Two. These ocean-going greyhounds were versatile in escort duty, shore bombardment, anti-submarine operations, and other tasks. But they were not meant to slug it out in a surface battle with enemy capital ships.

Johnston displaced 2,134 tons, with a length of 376½ft, beam of nearly 40ft, and draft of almost 18ft. Her top speed of 38kts was delivered by four Babcock & Wilcox boilers

and a pair of geared steam turbines generating 60,000 shaft horsepower. Armament included five single-barrel 5in turreted main guns, five twin 40mm anti-aircraft guns, seven single-mount 20mm anti-aircraft guns, depth charges, and perhaps her most formidable weapon – two quintuple 21in torpedo tubes.

Admiral Sprague ordered his small warships to make smoke and attack with torpedoes. Immediately, *Johnston* and her companion destroyers, *Heermann* and *Hoel,* dashed forward, 5-inchers blazing. A torpedo from *Johnston* tore the bow off the Japanese cruiser *Kumano*, and the 5in shells from the game destroyers peppered the superstructures of the big Japanese ships. Aircraft strafed and dropped whatever ordnance they had on the enemy, one even loosing a depth charge. The escort carriers sought shelter in a rain squall.

After a while, the Japanese gunners began pounding their targets. The *Johnston* and *Hoel* were sunk in torrents of enemy shells, 6in, 8in, 14in, and 18.1in. The destroyer escort *Samuel B. Roberts* was sunk after firing more than 600 5in rounds at her tormentors. The escort carrier *Gambier Bay* was sunk, while *Kalinin Bay* took 15 hits but survived. Reportedly, some of the Japanese shells of heavy calibre passed through the thin skins of the escort carriers and straight out the opposite side without exploding.

Kurita was shaken. The boldness of the American defence convinced him that he was facing heavy units of the US fleet, battleships, and fleet carriers. His cruisers *Suzuya*, *Chokai*, and *Chikuma* were sunk, while *Kumano* and *Yamato* were damaged. With victory in his grasp, Kurita lost his nerve and ordered a general retirement.

Realising that he would live to see another day, an American sailor yelled: "Dammit boys! They're getting away!"

The wreck of USS *Johnston*, a tomb for 186 American sailors, was discovered in 2019 in the Philippine Sea at a depth of more than 21,000ft.

ABOVE: A year before her gallant fight off Samar, USS *Johnston* lies anchored at Seattle, Washington, October 27, 1943. (US Navy via Wikimedia Commons)

ABOVE: As Japanese shells churn the water, the little ships of Taffy 3 make smoke and prepare to launch torpedoes on October 25, 1944. (US Navy National Museum of Naval Aviation via Wikimedia Commons)

IJN *SHINANO*

ABOVE: The massive Japanese aircraft carrier *Shinano* during sea trials on November 11, 1944.
(Government of Japan Public Domain via Wikimedia Commons)

The largest aircraft carrier built during World War Two, *Shinano* of the Imperial Japanese Navy, was originally intended to be the third of the colossal Yamato-class battleships. However, the disastrous loss of four fleet carriers at the Battle of Midway in June 1942 prompted the Imperial Navy command establishment to change course.

Construction on the third Yamato-class battleship had been underway at Yokosuka Naval Arsenal since the keel was laid on May 4, 1940, but the order was issued to convert the hull into a super carrier named after the province of Shinano. With the conversion to a carrier, she was launched on October 8, 1944, and declared ready for sea trials just six weeks later.

Shinano was a massive flattop, displacing 65,800 tons at standard load and a staggering 73,000 tons at full load. Her length was slightly more than 872ft, while her beam was just over 119ft, and her draft approached 34ft. Her flight deck alone stretched 840ft and was supported by a pair of still pillars at either end. An island was built on sponsons on the starboard side and incorporated the funnel. The forward area of the hangar deck was designed for aircraft maintenance and storage, and a pair of elevators were positioned at either end of the hangar deck on the centreline of the ship. The carrier was powered by a dozen Kampon boilers and four geared steam turbines that produced an expected top speed around 27kts with 150,000 shaft horsepower. However, *Shinano* never achieved that speed during trials.

Shinano's defensive armament included 16½in Type 89 dual-purpose guns, a total of 105 25mm light anti-aircraft guns in 35 triple-mounts, and 12 launchers of 28 barrels for 120mm rockets. Her armour protection was more than 15½in at maximum waterline thickness, and up to 3in across the flight deck. *Shinano,* and the earlier *Taiho,* were the only Japanese aircraft carriers with armoured decks, but the horrific experience at Midway had been sobering. It was deemed necessary to provide enhanced protection against American bombs.

ABOVE: *Shinano,* is seen at upper right in this photo taken by a US bomber that coincidentally flew over Yokosuka on the date of the carrier's commissioning. It is one of only three images of *Shinano* known to exist.
(US Government Public Domain via Wikimedia Commons)

Capable of carrying 47 aircraft, *Shinano* was also intended to transport the rocket-propelled Ohka manned aerial suicide bomb and small Shin'yō suicide boats. Her complement included 2,175 officers and sailors.

At 6pm on November 28, 1944, Shinano embarked from Yokosuka with orders to put in at the naval base at Kure for final fitting. Captain Toshio Abe requested an extension of time at Yokosuka for the installation of watertight doors and hatches, plus testing of vital systems and internal components. When his request was denied, Abe ordered *Shinano*, crew, 300 shipyard workers, and 40 civilian technicians to sea. Many hatches and watertight doors that had been installed were left open, along with access spaces into her hull. Also aboard were 50 Ohka and six Shin'yō to be delivered to Okinawa and the Philippines once the work at Kure was completed. Abe had preferred to sail during daylight hours, but soon after leaving Yokosuka, darkness set in.

At 8.48pm, the submarine USS *Archerfish*, under Commander Joseph F Enright, made contact with the mammoth aircraft carrier, beginning a stalk of several hours. Just after 3am on November 29, *Archerfish* fired a spread of six torpedoes. Four struck the starboard side of the carrier causing substantial flooding, and a severe list that inexperienced damage control parties were unable to counter. Eight hours later, *Shinano* capsized and sank 160 nautical miles southwest of Tokyo Bay, taking 1,435 men with it.

Strangely, US naval intelligence could not confirm the existence of *Shinano* until after the war, doubting the claim that Enright made of sinking a Japanese aircraft carrier. After evidence was uncovered to support his assertion, the officer was awarded the Navy Cross.

ABOVE: The Balao-class submarine USS *Archerfish* rides on the surface of San Francisco Bay, June 5, 1945.
(US Navy via Wikimedia Commons)

HMS *ILLUSTRIOUS*

ABOVE: The aircraft carrier HMS *Illustrious*, platform for the famed air raid on Taranto, is shown in 1940. (Collections of the Imperial War Museums via Wikimedia Commons)

ABOVE: Damage control parties deal with a hole in the flight deck of *Illustrious* made by a German bomb on January 10, 1941. (Government of the United Kingdom via Wikimedia Commons)

By 1930, the British Admiralty had acknowledged that the aircraft carrier was reshaping the face of naval warfare. Two battlecruisers had been converted to aircraft carriers, and while these went to sea as HMS *Courageous* and HMS *Glorious*, at mid-decade the Royal Navy had begun building carriers of more practical design.

While the threat of war with Nazi Germany loomed, construction programes in 1936, 1937, and 1938 led to orders for the Implacable and Illustrious carrier classes. HMS *Implacable* was laid down at Fairfield Shipbuilders of Govan, Glasgow, Scotland, in February 1939. *Implacable* and the second carrier closely associated with her design, HMS *Indefatigable*, are sometimes categorised as "modified Illustrious-class" warships, along with HMS *Indomitable*, laid down at Vickers-Armstrong at Barrow-in-Furness, England, on November 10, 1937.

Preceding *Implacable* and *Indefatigable*, the immediate Illustrious-class carriers included HMS *Formidable* and HMS *Victorious*, laid down in the spring of 1937 at Harland & Wolff Ltd, in Belfast, Northern Ireland, and Vickers-Armstrong in Wallsend respectively. HMS *Illustrious* was laid down on April 27, 1937, at the Vickers-Armstrong yards at Barrow-in-Furness. She was launched on April 5, 1939, and commissioned on May 25, 1940. Completion had been delayed allowing the installation of Type 79 radar for distant aircraft warning, and *Illustrious* was the first carrier to mount this innovative technology. Anti-aircraft defences were upgraded through the years to include an ensemble of 2-pounder, 40mm Bofors, and 20mm Oerlikon guns.

HMS *Illustrious* displaced 23,369 tons. Powered by three Admiralty boilers and three Parsons geared turbines that generated 111,000 shaft horsepower, she was capable of a top speed of 31kts. She was 753ft long with a 650ft flight deck, beam of nearly 96ft, and draft of almost 29ft. Her armoured flight deck was complemented by a single armoured hangar serviced by two elevators. The armoured construction was included in response to the threat of air attack while operating in the confines of the English Channel, North Sea, or Mediterranean.

Though armour offered better protection against bombs, the trade-off was restricted aircraft capacity of 36 planes, roughly half that of earlier types without such armour above the waterline. These restrictions were addressed somewhat with HMS *Indomitable*, whose blueprint retained armour and added

ABOVE: Still operating with propeller-driven aircraft, HMS *Illustrious* steams at sea in 1954. (Creative Commons Municipal Archives of Trondheim via Wikimedia Commons)

a second hangar that raised the number of aircraft to 48.

After flight trials in the Firth of Clyde and sea trials during a voyage to Bermuda, *Illustrious* reached Scapa Flow in Scotland briefly and then deployed to the Mediterranean. Air operations were conducted against Italian installations in North Africa and the Greek Isles. By the autumn of 1940, however, the Admiralty had given the go-ahead for an ambitious air attack on the Italian Navy anchorage at Taranto, near the heel of the Italian boot, where the Regia Marina had amassed six battleships, seven heavy cruisers, two light cruisers, and eight destroyers.

On the night of November 11, 1940, a swarm of Fairey Swordfish biplanes of the Fleet Air Arm took off from the deck of HMS *Illustrious* to attack Taranto in two waves. The Swordfish achieved complete surprise, and inflicted embarrassing losses on the Italians, sinking one battleship while damaging two others, along with a cruiser. *Illustrious* engaged in convoy duty and further operations in the Mediterranean, absorbing damage from enemy bombs, and in the Indian Ocean during the coming years.

With the formation of the Royal Navy Pacific Fleet in November 1944, *Illustrious* joined five other fleet carriers on the other side of the globe. These carriers participated in air attacks on the Japanese home islands and elsewhere, their armoured decks and hangars proving their worth in defence against kamikaze planes.

One US Navy officer quipped: "When a kamikaze hits a US carrier, it means six months of repair at Pearl. When a kamikaze hits a Limey carrier, it's just a case of 'Sweepers, man your brooms.'"

After various post-war modifications and deployments, HMS *Illustrious* was placed in reserve in 1955. Sold for scrap a year later, she was broken up in 1957.

HMS *GLOWWORM*

The fog was dense and patchy on the morning of April 8, 1940, and the Royal Navy G-class destroyer HMS *Glowworm* had been detached from the force, covering minelaying operations in the Norwegian Sea to search for a man who had gone overboard in the stormy waters. Sometime later, *Glowworm* turned towards a rendezvous with the battlecruiser HMS *Renown*. However, when a pair of Nazi Kriegsmarine destroyers was sighted at a distance, one of the most heroic naval actions of World War Two was in the offing.

Glowworm had come upon the enemy destroyers *Z11* (*Bernd von Arnim*) and *Z18* (*Hans Ludemann*), heading for the coast of Norway along with the heavy cruiser *Admiral Hipper* to disembark troops during Operation Weserubung, the Nazi invasion of the Scandinavian country. The troop-laden German destroyers had become separated from *Hipper*, and when *Glowworm* commenced firing on *Z18*, a call for assistance was sent. Soon enough, Lieutenant Commander Gerard Roope, commanding officer aboard the British destroyer, turned his attention to *Z11*, which had already sustained damage amid the storm, causing a serious reduction in speed.

For an hour *Glowworm* and *Z11* exchanged fire without either side sustaining damage. But then, *Hipper* reached the scene of the action.

At 8.55am, *Glowworm* reported an unidentified ship. Moments later, the identity of the new contact was clear. Within

ABOVE: In this dramatic photo taken from the deck of the Nazi heavy cruiser *Admiral Hipper*, HMS *Glowworm* makes smoke and crosses the enemy bow, April 8, 1940. (Unknown Author European Union Public Domain via Wikimedia Commons)

eight minutes of acquiring *Glowworm*, Captain Helmuth Heye ordered *Hipper* to open fire with her main 8in guns at a range of 9,200yds. *Glowworm* made smoke, manoeuvring in and out of the cover, but took punishment when *Hipper*'s fourth radar-guided salvo found its mark. As the range closed sufficiently, the big German cruiser's secondary 105mm guns opened fire and inflicted serious damage to the game little destroyer's superstructure.

Roope launched torpedoes from 875yds, but all missed. However, when *Glowworm* turned again into the smoke, *Hipper* followed. Suddenly, the two ships were dangerously close and Roope ordered a swift turn to starboard,

knifing into the German cruiser's hull abaft of the anchor. The collision tore the bow off *Glowworm* but ripped a 130ft gash in the armour belt of the Nazi cruiser, which began to list and took on nearly 600 tons of seawater.

After ramming her tormenter, *Glowworm* was helpless, drifting away until her boilers exploded. She sank just before 10.30am. A total of 109 crewmen were lost with *Glowworm*, and Roope died when he could not hang onto a rope cast from *Hipper*, which rescued 40 British sailors. Roope was later to receive a posthumous Victoria Cross, partially

ABOVE: The stricken HMS *Glowworm* belches smoke and flame before sinking during the uneven battle with Admiral *Hipper* in the Norwegian Sea. (Unknown Author European Union Public Domain via Wikimedia Commons)

on the recommendation of Heye, who wrote to the Admiralty via the International Red Cross to tell of his opponent's gallantry.

The diminutive *Glowworm* had truly fought an enemy many times her size. *Hipper* displaced 17,820 tons, while the Royal Navy destroyer displaced only 1,370 tons. *Glowworm* had been laid down at the shipyard of John I Thornycraft & Company, Woolston, Hampshire, on August 15, 1934, and commissioned in January 1936. She had served on blockade duty during the Spanish Civil War, and then in the Mediterranean prior to the outbreak of World War Two in September 1939. She was 323ft long, with a beam of 33ft, and draft of nearly 13ft. Her top speed was 36kts driven by geared steam turbines that produced 34,000 shaft horsepower. In comparison to *Hipper*, her main armament was only a quartet of 4.7in guns, while secondary armament consisted of just .50-calibre machine guns. She also mounted a pair of 21in torpedo tubes and depth charge apparatus.

Outsized and outgunned in the Norwegian Sea, the captain and crew of HMS *Glowworm* nevertheless wrote a stout-hearted chapter in the history of the Royal Navy, demonstrating tremendous valour against long odds.

ABOVE: The G-class destroyer HMS *Glowworm* rides at anchor in this 1937 photo. (Collections of the Imperial War Museums via Wikimedia Commons)

USS *ESSEX*

The exigencies of World War Two made the international naval treaties of the interwar years essentially dead letters. When the United States entered World War Two in the Pacific, it was readily apparent that the aircraft carrier, rather than the revered battleship, would be the weapon of decision.

To that end, American aircraft carrier construction and development accelerated swiftly. The US Congress had passed the Naval Expansion Act in 1934, authorising the construction of two new aircraft carriers totalling 40,000 tons displacement. USS *Hornet* was the last carrier built under treaty restrictions, and the follow-on Essex-class at 27,000 tons – built unfettered by treaties – would become the war-winning carrier type of the Pacific War from 1943 to 1945, while its postwar service was critical in the 1950s, and its design influenced future carrier construction for more than a decade.

USS *Essex*, the lead ship of a remarkable 24 carriers, was laid down on April 28, 1941, at Newport News Shipbuilding in Virginia. She was launched on July 31, 1942, and commissioned on December 31 of that year. Designed with some of the enhancements debuted with *Hornet*, *Essex* was remarkable in its capacity to carry up to 90 aircraft of varied types, nearly three times that of contemporary carriers of the British Royal Navy. The Essex-class flight deck extended 862ft, while her beam was 93ft, and the ship was 148ft across at its widest point.

Two centreline elevators were 44ft long and 48ft wide, while a third elevator, held over from the design of the carrier USS *Wasp*, was installed on the edge of the flight deck for rapid deployment and recovery of planes from flight deck to hangar deck. This third elevator was 60ft wide and more than

ABOVE: This stern view of USS *Essex*, her deck filled with anti-submarine warfare aircraft, was taken in 1962, around the time of the Cuban Missile Crisis. (US Navy via Wikimedia Commons)

ABOVE: The crew of the NASA Apollo 7 space mission are welcomed aboard USS Essex on October 22, 1968. (National Aeronautics and Space Administration via Wikimedia Commons)

34ft long, and was built to fold for passage through the Panama Canal, facilitating the movement required of a two-ocean navy. *Essex* outweighed *Hornet* by 6,500 tons, and she was 10ft wider, and 40ft longer. When aircraft became heavier, design revisions introduced two catapults in Essex-class carriers under construction from March 1943.

USS *Essex* was powered by eight Babcock & Wilcox boilers that produced steam for four Westinghouse turbines, generating 154,000 shaft horsepower, and a top speed of 33kts. While *Essex* and her sister were smaller than the earlier battlecruiser conversion carriers, *Lexington* and *Saratoga*, they were more than a generation improved, with size, speed, and sustainable strike capability that could project US naval might across the entire expanse of

the Pacific Ocean, and eventually overwhelm the Imperial Japanese Navy during World War Two.

ABOVE: A ball of fire erupts aboard USS *Essex* as the carrier is struck by a Japanese kamikaze off the Philippines, November 25, 1944. (US Navy via Wikimedia Commons)

Her initial defensive armament included 12 5in dual-purpose guns, along with 30 40mm, and 46 20mm anti-aircraft guns.

Following sea trials and shakedown cruise, USS *Essex* was ordered to the Pacific theatre in May 1943, participating in carrier operations against Marcus and Wake Islands, and the Japanese fortress at Rabaul on the island of New Britain, while her aircraft supported the US Marine landings at Tarawa Atoll in the Gilbert Islands in November, and Kwajalein in the Marshalls through the balance of the year.

In early 1944, *Essex* continued to operate off the Marshall Islands, and her aircraft took part in crippling raids against the Japanese naval base at Truk in the Carolines in February. Her single wartime overhaul was accomplished in the early spring, and by May she was providing further air support for US Marines and army troops fighting for control of the Marianas at Saipan, Guam, and Tinian. She participated in the major battles of the Philippine Sea and Leyte Gulf, and was struck by a Japanese kamikaze suicide plane off the Philippines on November 25, 1944. The aircraft struck the flight deck on the port side among aircraft massed for take-off. The resulting fire and explosions killed 15 sailors and wounded 44.

Repairs were made quickly, and *Essex* rejoined Task Force 38 in Philippine waters, launching air strikes against targets in the Philippines, Formosa, and north to Okinawa. After entering the South China Sea, her planes struck enemy shipping and shore installations on the island of Hainan, mainland China, and the harbour of Hong Kong. During the final months of World War Two, *Essex* support operations against the islands of Iwo Jima and Okinawa, as well as the home islands of Japan.

With the end of the war, *Essex* returned to Puget Sound Navy Yard at Bremerton, Washington, on September 15, 1945. She was decommissioned and placed in reserve in January 1947. Recommissioned four years later during the Korean War, *Essex* had been modified with a more streamlined island. In September 1951, an aircraft accident killed seven men and caused damage that required repair at Yokosuka, Japan. Afterwards, her aircraft resumed strikes against communist forces in North Korea. By 1954, she was ordered to waters off the coast of Indochina during US diplomatic considerations of direct support for French forces fighting the

ABOVE: This photograph of the aircraft carrier USS *Essex* was taken in 1956 after completion of the SCB-125 modernisation project. (US Navy via Wikimedia Commons)

ABOVE: In 1967, after conversion to an anti-submarine warfare carrier, USS *Essex* is shown underway in the Atlantic Ocean. (US Navy National Museum of Naval Aviation via Wikimedia Commons)

communist Viet Minh. In 1955, under the SCB-125 modernisation programme, the carrier received an angled flight deck addition to facilitate jet aircraft operations.

Essex continued to serve through the Vietnam era of the 1960s and recovered the crew of the NASA space flight Apollo 7 mission, which splashed down near Puerto Rico in October 1968. She was decommissioned on June 30, 1969, at the Boston Navy Yard, and scrapped in 1973.

After US entry into World War Two, the completion of 19 Essex-class carriers followed the lead ship, built and commissioned from Newport News, the navy yards of Brooklyn, Philadelphia, and Norfolk, and the Fore River Shipyard in Quincy, Massachusetts. During their service lives, various Essex-class carriers underwent substantial modifications under at least five conversion and modernisation programmes. Wartime improvements included the augmentation of anti-aircraft

defences and the addition of clipper bows to some that led to designation as "long hull" carriers. No Essex-class carriers were lost to enemy action during World War Two, although several were seriously damaged, particularly by Japanese kamikazes.

Laid down at Brooklyn in May 1944 and commissioned in 1950, USS *Oriskany* was the last of the Essex-class carriers completed. Construction was temporarily halted in 1946 with *Oriskany* 85% complete, resuming the following year under the SCB-27 modernisation programme. *Oriskany*, therefore, served as a prototype for another 14 carriers completed in similar fashion between 1950 and 1955. Several of these were subsequently reclassified as attack carriers, from CV to CVA.

Four Essex-class aircraft carriers, including the second carriers named *Yorktown*, *Hornet*, and *Lexington*, as well as *Intrepid*, are preserved as museum ships today.

ABOVE: Her hull painted in wartime camouflage, USS *Essex* steams out of San Francisco Bay on April 15, 1944. (US Navy via Wikimedia Commons)

HMS *BELFAST*

BELOW: Located on the River Thames in London, the light cruiser HMS *Belfast* is a unit of the Imperial War Museum. (Creative Commons Alvesgaspar via Wikimedia Commons)

Built to treaty specifications in force at the time, HMS *Belfast* was the last of ten Town-class light cruisers constructed for the Royal Navy during the 1930s. Her 32 years of service spanned both World War Two and the Korean Conflict, and found her ranging over 500,000 miles.

Laid down at Harland & Wolff Shipyards, in Belfast, Northern Ireland, on December 10, 1936, HMS *Belfast* was the first Royal Navy warship to be named after the country's capital city. She was officially launched on St Patrick's Day, March 17, 1938, by Anne Chamberlain, wife of then-Prime Minister Neville Chamberlain, and commissioned on August 5, 1939. *Belfast* displaced 11,550 tons, with a length of 613½ft, beam of just over 63ft, and draft of nearly 20ft. Her four Admiralty oil-fired boilers and four Parsons geared steam turbines generated a top speed of 32kts.

HMS *Belfast* was armed with an array of multi-purpose weaponry, including main batteries of 12 6-inch guns in triple turrets fore and aft, 12 122mm dual purpose guns, 16 2-pounder (40mm) guns, eight .50-calibre anti-aircraft machine guns, and six 21in torpedo tubes. Armour protection ranged from 4½in on the main belt to 4in on the turrets, and 3in on armoured decks. In early configuration, she carried a pair of Supermarine Walrus reconnaissance aircraft.

When World War Two erupted in 1939, *Belfast* was assigned to the Home Fleet Cruiser Squadron at Scapa Flow in the Orkney Islands of Scotland, primarily responsible for the early economic and military blockade of Nazi port facilities. She captured the German passenger liner SS *Cap Norte* in October 1939, and that ship was interned in a British port. Just weeks later,

however, the light cruiser was transiting the Firth of Forth, en route to gunnery practice, when she struck a floating magnetic mine that broke her back. Initial damage assessment concluded she might be beyond repair, but the decision was made to try. Three years later, *Belfast* emerged ready for service once again.

After returning to active duty in 1942, *Belfast* served as flagship of the 10th Cruiser

ABOVE: The hull of HMS *Belfast* was severely damaged by a magnetic mine in 1939. (Collections of the Imperial War Museums via Wikimedia Commons)

Squadron, participating in escort duty for Arctic convoys to the Soviet ports of Murmansk and Archangel. On Boxing Day, December 26, 1943, she was active in the Battle of the North Cape in which a Royal Navy squadron, under the command of Admiral Bruce Fraser aboard the battleship HMS *Duke of York*, sank the German battlecruiser *Scharnhorst*, thwarting an attempted raid on Allied convoy traffic in northern waters.

Belfast was later detailed to lead the Royal Navy escort and fire support missions off Juno and Sword landing beaches in French Normandy on D-Day, June 6, 1944. Although she was to fire the first shot of the early bombardment, another ship's gunner inadvertently stole the moment and fired first. After five weeks on station, HMS *Belfast* made port at Plymouth. Soon thereafter, she was dispatched to the Far East, arriving after the surrender of Imperial Japan. She contributed to the relief of prisoners who had suffered in Japanese internment camps, and she remained on duty in Asia until the autumn of 1947.

After refit, *Belfast* returned to the Far East as flagship of the Fifth Cruiser Division, and following the outbreak of the Korean War, she spent 404 days in active service, including close-in fire support of United Nations forces ashore. She earned a reputation for extraordinarily accurate gunfire.

In August 1963, HMS *Belfast* completed her final cruise, this time in the Mediterranean Sea, and was placed in reserve. By the spring of 1971, she appeared to be headed for the scrapyard. However, she was rescued by a private trust organised by one of her former captains. In October of that year, she was opened to the public as a museum ship. Today, as part of the Imperial War Museum, she is a popular attraction, moored near Tower Bridge, on London's River Thames.

ABOVE: The light cruiser HMS *Belfast* lies off the naval base at Kure, Japan, in 1950. (US Navy via Wikimedia Commons)

MODERN ERA

With the end of World War Two in 1945, the character of naval warfare had changed dramatically. In every aspect, warship design, technology implementation, weapons accuracy, lethality, destructive capability, and the global projection of power were transformed.

Perhaps the most obvious change was the twilight of the battleship, the queen of the seas for centuries. No more would the Jutland-style face-off between opposing behemoths within sight of one another take place. The last exchange of fire between surface battleships had occurred at Surigao Strait in October 1944, during the Battle of Leyte Gulf. Afterwards, battleships were either relegated to reserve or scrapped in most cases, some to be revived later as shore bombardment platforms, or to provide launch pads for the Tomahawk cruise missile, for example.

ABOVE: In this 1986 photo, a Grumman F-14 Tomcat fighter prepares for take-off aboard USS *Saratoga*, one of the US Navy's last operational non-nuclear powered aircraft carriers. (US Navy via Wikimedia Commons)

In the battleship's place, the era of the aircraft carrier emerged. Its primacy proven in battle around the globe, the aircraft carrier became the focal point of the US Navy's post-war perspective. America had emerged as the world's foremost naval power, and its carrier task groups ranged the oceans in the projection of both goodwill and coercive influence. In partnership with the British Royal Navy, the US Navy became a primary instrument of Cold War era diplomacy. At the same time, American carriers performed their traditional roles in the Korean and Vietnam wars, while transitioning from propeller-driven planes to jet aircraft and helicopters. They were deployed in disaster relief and in hotspots from the Mediterranean to Southeast Asia, freedom of navigation cruises, and in-flight operations in the Balkans, the Gulf War, and operations during the Global War on Terror.

Meanwhile, technology evolved to include nuclear propulsion. In 1955, the USS *Nautilus* became the world's first nuclear-powered submarine. A few years later, the cruiser USS *Long Beach* became the world's first

ABOVE: The former Soviet Kirov-class battlecruiser *Frunze* of the Russian Navy sails under nuclear power. (US Navy via Wikimedia Commons)

nuclear-powered surface warship. In 1961, USS *Enterprise* became the world's first nuclear-powered aircraft carrier. Such propulsion systems extended the range of US naval assets and those of the UK, France, the Soviet Union, and the People's Republic of China.

A new arm race was initiated during the Cold War, not only in nuclear warheads, but also in delivery systems on land, air, and sea. Advancing technology created an entire doctrine of US Cold War foreign policy as nuclear-powered submarines, armed with ballistic missiles, became one leg of the so-called Nuclear Triad. The submarine supplied the key components of mobility and relative concealment. They evolved from tactical weapons that fired torpedoes to sink surface ships. With missiles aboard, they carried weapons of mass destruction.

Further technological advances included guided missile capabilities, enhanced sonar and radar equipment, autonomous weapons systems, and unprecedented intelligence gathering proficiency, among others.

Strategy and tactics have matured as well. A division of labour has arisen among ship types to include those intended for surface activity, air operations, amphibious assault, nuclear warfare, and anti-submarine operations, to name a few. Smaller, more versatile warships such as the destroyer and frigate, have supplanted the battleship in the composition of the modern naval task group.

In conclusion, while the flexing of naval power has evolved in the modern era, its relevance remains the same. And, just as in the old days, a fleet at sea is an awe-inspiring sight.

ABOVE: The Royal Navy nuclear ballistic submarine HMS *Vanguard* returns to Her Majesty's Naval Base Clyde, Scotland, after a patrol. (United Kingdom Open Government License via Wikimedia Commons)

SUBSCRIBE TODAY!

Aviation News is renowned for providing the best coverage of every branch of aviation.

Combat Aircraft Journal is renowned for being America's best-selling military aviation magazine.

/collections/subscriptions

Free 2nd class P&P on BFPO orders. Overseas charges apply.

USS *MADDOX*

ABOVE: The 5-inch guns of USS *Maddox* shell targets in North Vietnam in August 1968. (US Navy via Wikimedia Commons)

US government and the communist regime in North Vietnam were strained amid the growing Viet Cong insurgency and civil unrest in South Vietnam. *Maddox* became a direct participant in the so-called Gulf of Tonkin incident, which escalated US involvement in the Vietnam War, earning lasting notoriety in the process.

Sailing in the gulf, *Maddox* was in international waters on August 2, 1964, according to official reports. However, the destroyer was within the 12-mile offshore territorial limit that was generally acknowledged by most countries. Radar indicated the approach of three small craft that were believed to be P-4 torpedo boats of the North Vietnamese Navy. The communist boats had been shadowing the US Navy destroyer, but then appeared to be assuming an offensive posture.

ABOVE: In this photo circa 1960, USS *Maddox* is shown underway in the Pacific. (Naval History and Heritage Command via Wikimedia Commons)

USS *Maddox*, a Sumner-class US Navy destroyer, was ordered from the Bath Iron Works in Bath, Maine, during a period when the volume of American warship construction was at its zenith. The demands of World War Two in the Pacific required as many of the versatile, swift greyhounds of the ocean as possible.

Maddox was laid down on October 28, 1943, launched on March 19, 1944, and commissioned on June 2, 1944, beginning a service career that extended more than four decades. Following her shakedown cruise and anti-submarine drills, *Maddox* left Boston harbour for Norfolk, Virginia, and then the Pacific for assignment to Fast Carrier Task Group 38.1 of the US Third Fleet. She was struck by a Japanese kamikaze suicide plane in the East China Sea, off Formosa, in January 1945, and underwent repairs at Ulithi in the Caroline Islands before returning to duty off Okinawa, later to serve off the home islands of Japan in picket, escort, and air-sea rescue duty.

During the Korean War, *Maddox* served as an escort for US Navy and Royal Navy aircraft carriers, and participated in the blockade of the North Korean port of Wonsan. She remained in the Pacific afterwards, deploying from the US West Coast to the Far East at various times.

USS *Maddox* displaced 2,200 tons. She was 376½ft long, with a beam of 40ft, and draft of nearly 16ft. Her 34kts top speed was provided by four boilers and General Electric geared turbines. She was armed with six 5in main guns in double turrets, 20mm and 40mm anti-aircraft guns, depth charges, and ten 21in torpedo tubes.

From mid-1955 to the spring of 1962, *Maddox* completed six deployments to the Far East, and trained with units of the Japanese Maritime Self-Defense Force and the South Korean and Taiwanese navies. On July 31, 1964, she began the first phase of her patrol activities off the coast of Vietnam in the Gulf of Tonkin. Tensions between the

ABOVE: This decommissioned torpedo boat is similar to the North Vietnamese craft involved in the Gulf of Tonkin incident. (Creative Commons ד"ר אבישי טייכר via Wikimedia Commons)

ABOVE: In this photo taken aboard USS *Maddox*, three North Vietnamese Navy torpedo boats are seen aggressively moving towards the destroyer on August 2, 1964. (US Navy via Wikimedia Commons)

ABOVE: The destroyer USS *Turner Joy*, involved in the Tonkin Gulf incident, is shown at sea on May 9, 1964. (US Navy via Wikimedia Commons)

commander of USS *Maddox* during the critical moments in the Gulf of Tonkin. Therefore, with the support of McNamara, National Security Advisor McGeorge Bundy, and other key cabinet members and military officers, Johnson ordered retaliatory air strikes against targets in North Vietnam, an oil storage facility with 14 large tanks, and units of the "aggressor" North Vietnamese Navy, which totalled only 50 patrol and torpedo boats.

Hours later, Johnson took to the airwaves at home. In a nationally televised address to the American people, he asserted: "The North Vietnamese have decided to attack the US. This fact is plain for all the world to see. If we do not challenge these attacks, they will continue." The president proceeded to ask the US Congress for a joint resolution authorising the chief executive to take any action deemed necessary to counter additional threats to forces of the United States or allied countries in Southeast Asia.

The Gulf of Tonkin Resolution passed the House of Representatives without a single dissenting vote, while the US Senate approved 89 to two. It is likely that few, if any of the lawmakers, were aware that *Maddox* and *Turner Joy* had been engaged in an intelligence gathering mission on behalf of the government of South Vietnam at the time of the incident. Further, it is unlikely that some knew US advisors were already working with South Vietnamese Army troops in clandestine operations inside Vietnam, or that there were serious doubts surrounding the accuracy of the reports of North Vietnamese aggression.

After the Gulf of Tonkin incident, American involvement in the Vietnam War increased exponentially, and lasted nearly a decade until the last US soldiers and prisoners of war came home.

USS *Maddox* was stricken from the navy roll in 1972 and given to the navy of the Republic of China. She served until 1984 under the name *Po Yang* and was scrapped the following year.

Believing he was under attack, the destroyer captain ordered three warning shots to be fired in the direction of the small boats. The communists responded with torpedoes and machine-gun fire. A single bullet struck *Maddox* in the brief exchange, and all three of the P-4s sustained some degree of damage. They were driven off by fire from *Maddox* and planes launched from the nearby aircraft carrier USS *Ticonderoga*, with three North Vietnamese sailors killed, and six more wounded.

President Lyndon B Johnson was informed of the incident, responding that such patrols of the North Vietnamese coast would continue, and ordering another destroyer, the Forrest Sherman-class USS *Turner Joy*, to the vicinity. A second attack supposedly occurred on the night of August 4, when radar aboard *Turner Joy* detected what appeared to be more North Vietnamese torpedo boats. Both destroyers opened fire, but there was no indication of damage to any vessel in the area. Sceptics immediately began to question whether there had been any North Vietnamese attack at all and years afterwards, further analysis concluded that the American radar operators had been mistaken, identifying the sonar signatures of large waves in the Tonkin Gulf as communist patrol boats. There were radio messages that had once indicated the presence of the North Vietnamese, but these were also debunked.

Despite early indications that the fire of the destroyers on August 4 had been directed at a phantom enemy, President Johnson used the extension of the Gulf of Tonkin incident as a pretext to increase American participation in the civil war in Vietnam. Evidence later indicated that Secretary of Defense Robert McNamara may have suppressed the text of communications between President Johnson and the

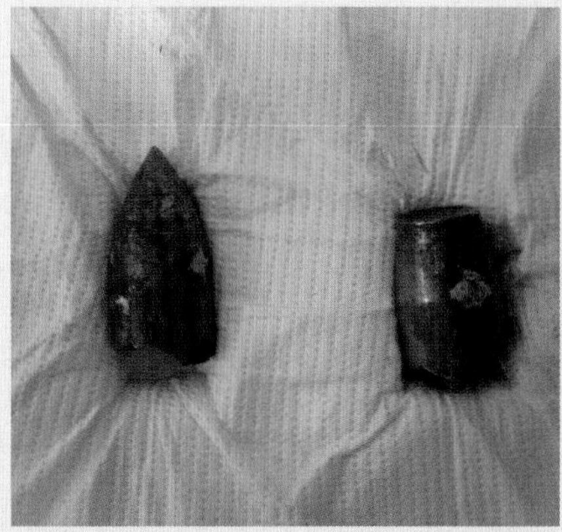

ABOVE: The fragmented North Vietnamese machine-gun round that struck USS *Maddox* in the Gulf of Tonkin has been preserved. (Creative Commons Naval History and Heritage Command via Wikimedia Commons)

USS *LONG BEACH*

The first warship in history to utilise nuclear power, the cruiser USS *Long Beach* was an example of longevity within the US Navy, serving nearly 34 years. *Long Beach* was also the first US cruiser to be designed and built after World War Two. Originally intended as a smaller frigate, she was also the last warship to be constructed on the wartime cruiser hull style, typically identified with a long, narrow design with a relatively high freeboard allowing for good speed and stability, often with a pronounced 'clipper bow' for better seakeeping, and with a heavily armoured belt along the waterline to protect vital machinery.

USS *Long Beach* was ordered as a conventional light cruiser in October 1956 and then reclassified as nuclear powered. Laid down at Bethlehem Steel Company's Fore River Shipyard in Quincy, Massachusetts, on December 2, 1957, she was launched on July 14, 1959, and commissioned on September 9, 1961. Her initial frigate design was expanded to fit the cruiser hull, and her superstructure was readily identifiable with its box-like construction. Just aft, an open area was made available first for the Regulus nuclear cruise missile, and then for the four tubes needed to launch the two-stage, solid fuel Polaris ballistic missile.

Long Beach was just over 721ft long, with a beam of 71½ft, draft of nearly 31ft, and displacement of 15,540 tons. The propulsion system included two C1W nuclear reactors powering a pair of General Electric turbines that delivered 80,000 shaft horsepower, and a top speed of 30kts. With the nuclear power aboard, the guided missile cruiser's range was essentially unlimited. Her reactors were replenished during refits in 1966, 1970, 1980, and 1992.

At first, *Long Beach* was designed to carry only missile armament; however, on orders from President John F Kennedy, two 5in gun mounts were added amidships. Missile armament included a pair of twin Mk-10 Terrier surface-to-air launchers that were later supplanted by the Standard Extended Range surface-to-air system. A twin Mk-12 Talos missile launcher was later removed in favour of box launchers for eight Tomahawk cruise missiles, while a single ASROC anti-submarine launcher was installed. Additionally, a pair of Mk-15 Vulcan 20mm close-in weapons systems (CIWS) were aboard, along with two triple 12¾in anti-submarine torpedo tubes.

ABOVE: USS *Long Beach* is shown under construction at the Fore River Shipyard in the summer of 1959.

(US Navy Bureau of Ships via Wikimedia Commons)

ABOVE: During Operation Sea Orbit in 1964, USS *Long Beach* sails between USS *Enterprise* and USS *Bainbridge*.

(US Navy via Wikimedia Commons)

Launchers for a suite of eight Harpoon anti-ship missiles were later added. USS *Long Beach* carried state-of-the-art radar and sonar apparatus that were modernised regularly during her career.

Originally, *Long Beach* was assigned to that Atlantic Fleet at Norfolk, Virginia. She trained later in the Caribbean, and then took part in peacekeeping missions in the Mediterranean with the Sixth Fleet during the 1960s. On May 13, 1964, she joined the aircraft carrier USS *Enterprise* and frigate USS *Bainbridge* to form the world's first all nuclear-powered task group. During Operation Sea Orbit, the task group departed Gibraltar and sailed around the world, demonstrating the sustainability of a nuclear-powered naval task group of the US Navy. *Long Beach* sailed more than 30,000 nautical miles in 58 days without reprovisioning or refuelling.

After training and maintenance, *Long Beach* was reassigned to the Pacific Fleet at Long Beach, California. She was deployed to the Far East in November 1966 and took up station in the northern Gulf of Tonkin during the Vietnam War, spending most of her time as a Positive Identification Radar Advisory Zone (PIRAZ) ship with responsibility for determining the identities of aircraft returning from missions to prevent communist planes from infiltrating. During a second deployment in 1968, her missile defences claimed two Soviet-made MiG-21 fighters shot down.

USS *Long Beach* was recognised for her service in the Vietnam War and remained active through the 1990s. A planned upgrade to the Aegis combat system was cancelled amid rising operational costs, and *Long Beach* was decommissioned and stricken from the navy roll on May 1, 1995. *Long Beach* was sold at auction for recycling in 2012, and her hull and reactor compartment were placed in storage at Puget Sound Naval Shipyard, Bremerton, Washington.

ABOVE: The guided missile cruiser USS *Long Beach* sails in Hawaiian waters off the island of Oahu on May 9, 1973.

(US Navy via Wikimedia Commons)

USS *ENTERPRISE*

The world's first nuclear powered aircraft carrier, USS *Enterprise* (CVN-65) was laid down February 4, 1958, at Newport News Shipbuilding in Virginia. With an estimated construction cost of $444 million, she was launched on September 24, 1960, and commissioned on November 25, 1961. Her eight nuclear reactors went live on the same day. She was deactivated in 2012, and decommissioned in February 2017.

Enterprise was constructed on a modified design based on the preceding USS *Kitty Hawk*. Changes included a distinctive island structure to accommodate billboard radar antennae and an angled funnel to prevent carrier exhaust from interfering with aircraft landings. At 1,123ft she was the longest naval vessel in history. Her displacement at full load was 94,781 tons, with a beam of nearly 133ft, and draft of 39ft. At launching, she was considered the largest warship in the world. Her Westinghouse A2W nuclear reactors and four Westinghouse geared steam turbines produced 280,000 shaft horsepower, and a top speed of nearly 34kts. Her projected cruising range, without refuelling, was more than 200,000 nautical miles.

ABOVE: With a portion of her air wing on the flight deck, USS *Enterprise* was photographed in 1967. (Creative Commons Bill Larkins via Wikimedia Commons)

Enterprise was intended as the lead ship of six in her class, however, spiralling costs led to the cancellation of the other five. Literally, the 'Big E' was in a class by herself. Her complement typically numbered as many as 4,800 officers and sailors, including personnel of attached air wings, and maximum aircraft capacity was up to 90 planes. No guns were installed for aircraft defence, and the originally planned Terrier anti-aircraft missile system was discarded in favour of the Sea Sparrow Mark 25 missile in 1967 with improved Sea Sparrows, and the Phalanx close-in weapons system (CIWS) upgrades following.

During her lengthy career, *Enterprise* underwent four major refits. One of the

ABOVE: During replenishment in the South China Sea, *Enterprise* sails with the fleet oiler USS *Hassayampa*. (US Navy via Wikimedia Commons)

most extensive was conducted at the Puget Sound Naval Yard in Bremerton, Washington, from 1979 to 1982. Her air traffic control capability, radar, and communications equipment were upgraded.

From August to October 1964, *Enterprise* sailed with the nuclear-powered guided missile cruiser USS *Long Beach* and the nuclear-powered frigate USS *Bainbridge* as Task Force 1 during Operation Sea Orbit. As the world's first nuclear powered naval task force, the trio circumnavigated the globe in 64 days, sailing 32,600 nautical miles without replenishing fuel or provisions. The following year, *Enterprise* became the first nuclear-powered warship to enter combat service, reaching Yankee Station in the Gulf of Tonkin off the coast of Vietnam. During a single deployment from the Philippines to Yankee Station, December 15,

1966, to June 20, 1967, *Enterprise* pilots and aircrew flew 13,400 missions in 132 days of combat operations.

From 1965 to 1975, *Enterprise* made six deployments to the Far East, either in support of Yankee Station air operations or with Task Force 71 amid rising tensions with North Korea following the seizure of the intelligence ship USS *Pueblo* in January 1968. By the mid-1980s, *Enterprise* had been ordered to the Mediterranean to take part in Operation El Dorado Canyon, the bombing of terrorist camps and other targets in Libya in retaliation for the terror bombing of a nightclub in Berlin, Germany. In 1988, her aircraft sank one hostile frigate of the Iranian Navy and damaged another during the "Tanker War" in the Persian Gulf.

In the 1990s, *Enterprise* assisted with the enforcement of "no-fly" zones in Bosnia during Operation Joint Endeavor, and Iraq during Operation Southern Watch. Her aircraft struck targets in Saddam Hussein's Iraq during Operation Desert Fox, intended to degrade offensive and chemical weapons capabilities.

Following the Al Qaeda terror attacks of September 11, 2001, *Enterprise* conducted air operations for three weeks, hitting terrorist targets in Iraq and Afghanistan. When word of the September 11 tragedy reached *Enterprise*, she was in the Indian Ocean returning from an Operation Southern Watch deployment. Without higher authorisation, her captain ordered a 180° turn towards the Arabian Sea to reach a position to launch 700 airstrikes in support of Operation Enduring Freedom.

During her 51-year career, *Enterprise* completed 25 deployments. She was the eighth warship of the US Navy to bear the name, and the ninth, a Gerald R Ford-class nuclear carrier, is currently under construction at Newport News.

ABOVE: The world's first nuclear powered aircraft carrier, USS *Enterprise,* is shown underway in the Atlantic on June 14, 2004. (US Navy via Wikimedia Commons)

BELOW: The aircraft carriers USS *Nimitz* (left) and *Independence* sail in the Sea of Japan in 1997. (US Navy via Wikimedia Commons)

USS *NIMITZ*

The lead ship of a class of ten nuclear powered aircraft carriers built for the US Navy, USS *Nimitz*, named after famed Fleet Admiral Chester W Nimitz, was laid down at Newport News Shipbuilding, Virginia, on June 22, 1968. She was the navy's second nuclear-powered carrier and, with the retirement of USS *Enterprise* in 2012, became the world's oldest aircraft carrier in active service.

USS *Nimitz* was launched on May 13, 1972, and commissioned on May 3, 1975. According to recent reports, her deactivation is scheduled to begin in 2026, to be completed the following year at a cost of more than $18 million. After a six-month maintenance programme was completed at the Puget Sound Navy Yard in Washington State in 2024, *Nimitz* returned to her home port at Naval Base Kitsap, Washington, where she was to remain until the USS *Ronald Reagan* completed her scheduled maintenance, and returned as the sole navy aircraft carrier stationed in the Pacific Northwest. At that time, USS *Nimitz* was to proceed to Newport News to begin the deactivation process.

During a career that spanned half a century, *Nimitz* has made more than 30 deployments. *Nimitz* and her accompanying air wings completed a 144-day stay in the Indian Ocean during the 1979 Iran Hostage Crisis, and completed a 1981 freedom of navigation cruise in the Mediterranean in which F-14 Tomcat fighter planes flying from her deck shot down a pair of hostile Libyan Soviet Sukhoi Su-22 fighters. She took up station in the eastern Mediterranean in the mid-1980s during terrorism unrest in Lebanon, and with the hijacking of TWA Flight 847. *Nimitz* provided security off the coast of South Korea during the 1988 Summer

ABOVE: USS *Nimitz* enters the harbour at San Diego, California, to moor at Naval Air Station North Island in 2009. (US Navy via Wikimedia Commons)

Olympic Games, and later escorted re-flagged Kuwaiti oil tankers through Middle Eastern waters during the so-called Tanker War of the late 1980s.

In the 1990s, *Nimitz* enforced the "no-fly" zone over Iraq during Operation Southern Watch and participated in international fleet exercises. She also deployed to the Persian Gulf during Operation Iraqi Freedom and Operation Enduring Freedom from 2003 to 2005.

The ten Nimitz-class carriers were completed during a 35-year span until 2009. The nine that followed the lead ship include *Dwight D Eisenhower*, *Carl Vinson*, *Theodore Roosevelt*, *Abraham Lincoln*, *George Washington*, *John C Stennis*, *Harry S Truman*, *Ronald Reagan*, and *George H Bush*. Design changes sometimes lead to identification of sub-classes of Nimitz, Theodore Roosevelt, and Ronald Reagan, which was intended as a transitional design for the US Navy's newest Gerald R Ford-class carriers, the lead ship being commissioned in 2017.

USS *Nimitz* displaces over 100,000 tons loaded with a length of 1,092ft, beam of 134ft, and top speed of 31½kts, with 260,000 shaft horsepower delivered by two Westinghouse

A4W nuclear reactors and four steam turbines. Her aircraft capacity includes more than 60 fixed-wing planes and helicopters. The ship's complement approaches 6,000, including attached air wing personnel. Originally projected for a service life of 50 years, her reactors have been refuelled only once, during her midlife overhaul from 1998 to 2001 at Newport News. Along with anti-submarine countermeasures, *Nimitz* carries Sea Sparrow and RIM-116 missile systems, Phalanx close-in weapons (CIWS) systems, MK 38 25mm autocannon, and mounts for .50-calibre machine guns.

Nimitz and her sisters are engineering marvels. From keel to mast, *Nimitz* is 244ft tall, equivalent to the height of a 24-storey building. More than 3,000 televisions and 2,500 telephones were originally aboard, while the 2,250-ton air conditioning capacity is sufficient to cool 500 average-size homes. On deployment, *Nimitz* carries enough food to feed 6,000 people for 70 days, while more than a million pounds of mail are processed through her post office annually.

The latest of the Nimitz-class aircraft carriers are expected to continue operating into the mid-21st century.

ABOVE: During her first deployment, the aircraft carrier USS *Nimitz* sails with the cruisers California and South Carolina in 1976. (US Navy via Wikimedia Commons)

HMS *INVINCIBLE*

ABOVE: HMS *Invincible* is shown at sea in 2005. Note her flight deck ramp. (Open Government License Government of the United Kingdom via Wikimedia Commons)

t appeared that the deal was done. The aircraft carrier HMS *Invincible* was to be sold to Australia.

By the spring of 1982, senior officers at the Admiralty and elsewhere were reeling under the repercussions of a 1981 Defence White Paper principally authored by Secretary of State for Defence John Nott amid the financial constraints of a persistent recession. Nott had concluded that the military must tighten its belt, and the reductions specified for the Royal Navy included the sale of *Invincible,* along with the aircraft carrier *Hermes,* to India, the elimination of the Royal Marine amphibious force, reduction of 10,000 personnel, retirement of nine destroyers and frigates, and other cuts.

Admiral John 'Sandy' Woodward noted: "We argued our best, but our arguments had not been listened to, because however sound they may have been, they were certainly not convenient. John Nott possessed the cool heart of a career banker, and this was not offset by the cool brain of a military historian, much less any knowledge of things maritime."

Then, the unthinkable happened. The military junta that governed Argentina occupied by force the Falkland Islands, sovereign British territory in the South Atlantic, roughly 8,000 miles from the British Isles. Suddenly, the Royal Navy aircraft carrier became starkly relevant once again. Both *Hermes* and *Invincible* were directed with a hastily assembled task force to eject the Argentines from the Falklands.

Admiral Woodward took command during Operation Corporate, and the carriers formed the heart of the air-sea strike contingent that contributed mightily to

ABOVE: The aircraft carrier HMS *Invincible* churns through the waters of the South Atlantic during the Falklands War. (Ken Griffiths Public Domain via Wikimedia Commons)

the success of the largest British military operation since World War Two.

HMS *Invincible* was the lead ship of her class of three aircraft carriers, including the follow-on HMS *Illustrious* and HMS *Ark Royal*. Originally configured to counter technologically advances in Soviet submarines, she functioned as a standard carrier during the Falklands War, operating the versatile VSTOL (vertical short take-off and landing) Sea Harrier jump jet and Sea King helicopter, a full complement of 22 total aircraft. On deployment to the Falklands, *Invincible* carried eight Sea Harriers and ten Sea Kings, while *Hermes* brought 16 Sea Harriers of the Fleet Air Arm, ten ground attack Harriers of the Royal Air Force, and ten Sea Kings. *Invincible* carried ten nuclear depth charges in the Falklands, standard munitions for her anti-submarine role; these were removed during the deployment.

Laid down at Vickers Shipbuilding Limited at Barrow-in-Furness, England, in July 1973, HMS *Invincible* was launched on May 3, 1977, and commissioned on July 11, 1980. She displaced 22,000 tons fully loaded

with a length of 689ft, beam of just over 118 ft, and draft of nearly 29ft. Her top speed of 28kts was achieved with four Rolls-Royce Olympus TM3B gas turbines that generated 97,000 shaft horsepower. Defensive armament included the Goalkeeper CIWS (close-in weapons system) and GAM-B01 20mm close-range guns.

British ship designers had long been innovators, and *Invincible* was built with an upward sloping flight deck, nicknamed the ski-jump ramp, to assist the Harriers in take-off.

Following the victory in the 74-day Falklands War, *Invincible* returned to a hero's welcome at Portsmouth. The sale to Australia was officially nullified in July 1983. She underwent a major refit from 1986 to 1989. During the 1990s, she participated in "no-fly" zone enforcement, and other operations in the Balkans and the Middle East. She was decommissioned in 2005, retained in reserve until 2010, when she was stricken from the reserve roll and sold to a Turkish firm for recycling the following year.

ABOVE: HMS *Invincible* receives a tumultuous welcome, steaming through the Solent toward Portsmouth after the victory of Operation Corporate, spring 1982. (Royal Navy Open Government License via Wikimedia Commons)

HMS QUEEN ELIZABETH

Although the British Royal Navy was long an innovator in aircraft carrier design, construction, and operations as steam catapults, mirrored landing sites, angled flight decks, and ski jump ramps originated with it, for a time, the great fleet was without an operational carrier of its own.

The last of the Invincible-class carriers, HMS *Illustrious*, was withdrawn from service in 2014, years after plans for the construction of a new class of large carriers had been quashed during the 1960s. However, experience such as the deployment to the Falklands during the war of spring 1982 had indicated the need to reevaluate the future of the aircraft carrier in the Royal Navy.

By early 1998, a government-sponsored Strategic Defence Review related that aircraft carriers provide "capability to operate offensive aircraft when foreign basing may be denied; all required space and infrastructure – where foreign bases are available, they are not always available early in a conflict and infrastructure is often lacking; and a coercive and deterrent effect when deployed to a trouble spot."

The report concluded with a strong endorsement for carrier construction, commenting: "The emphasis is now on increased offensive air power and the ability to operate the largest possible range of aircraft in the widest possible range of roles. When the current carrier force reaches the end of its planned life, we plan to replace it with two larger vessels. Work will now begin to refine our requirements, but present thinking suggests that they might be of the order of 30,000-40,000 tonnes (33,600-44,800 tons) and capable of deploying up to fifty aircraft, including helicopters."

The result of this pronouncement bore a marked difference in the estimated and actual size of the two new aircraft carriers,

ABOVE: The bulbous bow of HMS *Queen Elizabeth* is visible during construction in this 2011 photo.
(Creative Commons PuzzleScot via Wikimedia Commons)

and the 65,000-ton Queen Elizabeth-class construction programme did not get underway until 2009. *Queen Elizabeth* entered service with the Royal Navy in 2017, while the second carrier of the class, HMS *Prince of Wales*, was commissioned in late 2019. The carriers were built by the Aircraft Carrier Alliance, a partnership that was concluded between the UK Ministry of Defence and contractors BAE Systems, Thales Group, Babcock International, and A&P Group.

Although there are subtle differences in their construction, the two aircraft carriers are quite similar in build. Both carriers were built in separate sections then transported

ABOVE: A Merlin helicopter flies alongside the aircraft carrier HMS *Queen Elizabeth* in 2017.
(Open Government License United Kingdom via Wikimedia Commons)

ABOVE: An F-35B fighter lands aboard the aircraft carrier HMS *Prince of Wales* in 2023. (US Navy via Wikimedia Commons)

ABOVE: The Royal Navy aircraft carriers *Queen Elizabeth* and *Prince of Wales* sail together for the first time on May 19, 2021. (Open Government License United Kingdom via Wikimedia Commons)

to Rosyth Dockyard, Scotland, for assembly. Their overall length is 932ft with a ski jump (VSTOL assist) flight deck length of nearly 919ft, and width of 230ft. Their draft is 36ft, and they carry up to 72 aircraft, including the advanced Lockheed Martin F35 fighter jet. Propulsion is provided by two massive Rolls-Royce Marine Trent MT30 gas turbine engines and four Wärtsilä diesel generators that produce a top speed of more than 25kts, with a range of 10,000 nautical miles. Nuclear power was considered but discounted due to prohibitive cost.

The design includes a pair of islands on the starboard side, the forward responsible for navigation while the latter controls flight operations, housing the flying control centre, or "flyco". The type includes nine decks from hull to flight deck with seven decks in each of the islands. The two carriers are the largest warships ever constructed for the Royal Navy, and the ships' complement includes 679 officers and ratings.

Announcement of the Queen Elizabeth-class construction programme was made in the summer of 2007, but reorganisation among companies in the British shipbuilding industry and delays caused by cost overruns, contributed to a substantial interval between conceptualisation, and actual deployment. While original estimates of construction expense totalled £3.9 billion, the cost to complete *Queen Elizabeth* soared to £6.1 billion, and £7.6 billion with *Prince of Wales*.

The Carrier Air Wing aboard the two warships varies depending on deployment objective and includes approximately two dozen advanced F35s, anti-submarine and airborne early warning AgustaWestland Merlin helicopters, and light Wildcat AH1 transport and reconnaissance helicopters, Chinook airlift helicopters, and Apache attack helicopters. Changes were made to original blueprints for HMS *Prince of Wales* to install catapult and arrestor systems specifically to accommodate the F-35C, carrier variant of the fighter, but these were reverted to the original systems with the

announcement that the F-35B (VSTOL) version would be procured.

At times during the last 20 years, the disposition of HMS *Prince of Wales* appeared to be an open question. Ideally, while one carrier was in port for refit, the other would take its place to provide continual operations capability. However, there was discussion surrounding the sale of *Prince of Wales* to a friendly nation, and the fostering of a co-operative air programme. A Strategic Defence and Security Review in

ABOVE: HMS *Queen Elizabeth* is shown under construction in the summer of 2014.
(Open Government License United Kingdom via Wikimedia Commons)

2010 asserted that only one aircraft carrier would be completed; however, further analysis indicated that the cancellation of HMS *Prince of Wales* would be more costly due to contract obligations.

Queen Elizabeth completed a global seven-month maiden voyage, returning to her homeport of Plymouth in December 2021 after sailing 49,000 miles with multi-national components of Carrier Strike Group 21. At the time, Chief of the Defence Staff Admiral Sir Tony Radakin commented: "Throughout the past seven months HMS *Queen Elizabeth* and her Strike Group have been furthering the UK's interests and strengthening our partnerships around the globe. With involvement from across the Armed Forces, and our allies integrated throughout, this deployment has been a truly joint, truly international endeavour, which represents the very best of Global Britain."

HMS *Prince of Wales* has participated in several exercises in co-operation with allied naval units since being declared fully operational in October 2021, including trials with unmanned drones and NATO's Steadfast Defender Exercise in early 2024. During that deployment, *Prince of Wales* replaced *Queen Elizabeth*, which was experiencing mechanical issues with a propeller shaft.

Queen Elizabeth and *Prince of Wales* have both seen mechanical breakdowns of some magnitude. Most of the problems relate to the propulsion system, and these have resulted in either delayed or cancelled deployments. For example, just one day after setting sail for the United States in 2022, *Prince of Wales* broke down at sea with a propeller shaft problem. She has also experienced flooding on at least two occasions.

Resolution of these mechanical challenges, augmentation of suitable Royal Navy escort ships, and the increased availability of aircraft, must be resolved for the Royal Navy aircraft carriers to fully achieve their mission of delivering modern carrier strike capability.

ABOVE: A Lockheed Martin F-35B fighter takes off from HMS *Queen Elizabeth* during trials in 2020.
(Open Government License United Kingdom via Wikimedia Commons)

HMS CONQUEROR

The message was clear and succinct: "From CTG [Commander Task Group] 317.8, to *Conqueror*, text priority *flash* – attack Belgrano group."

It came from Admiral John 'Sandy' Woodward aboard the aircraft carrier HMS *Hermes*, commanding Royal Navy forces during Operation Corporate, the military expedition to reclaim sovereign British territory from Argentina during the Falklands War of 1982. Although Woodward was in immediate command, control of the nuclear-powered fleet submarines in the area around the Total Exclusion Zone belonged to Admiral Sir John DE Fieldhouse, Commander-in-Chief, Fleet, and Admiral Peter GM Herbert, Flag Officer, Submarines, at Northwood headquarters in suburban London, thousands of miles from the South Atlantic.

Woodward held the opportunity to break one arm of a pincer movement undertaken by the Argentine Navy and minimise the threat to his ships posed by the French-made Exocet missiles that could be launched by the enemy at any time. A change in the rules of engagement would have to come from Prime Minister Margaret Thatcher, yet there was no time for such protocol. The fleet submarine HMS *Conqueror* was taking up a firing position on the Argentine cruiser *General Belgrano*, and Woodward had to act. He sent the order, which was picked up via satellite in London and quickly removed. But it had served its intended purpose, and a rapid change in the rules of engagement was received.

Meanwhile, on the morning of May 2, 1982, HMS *Conqueror*, under Commander Chris Wreford-Brown, fired a spread of three Mark VIII World War Two-vintage torpedoes at *General Belgrano*, which had begun her naval career decades earlier as the US Navy cruiser USS *Phoenix* and survived the attack on Pearl Harbor on December 7, 1941. The 55-year-old torpedoes hissed away, the first blowing the cruiser's bow

off, the second striking the engine room, and touching off an explosion that destroyed crew mess and leisure areas. The third torpedo missed, striking the destroyer *Hipolito Bouchard* a glancing blow, before failing to explode.

General Belgrano sank in 20 minutes, taking 321 of her complement of 1,093 to the bottom. HMS *Conqueror* had become the only nuclear-powered submarine in naval history to sink an enemy warship with torpedoes. Afterwards, Argentine surface warships remained largely sidelined during the 74-day Falklands War, wary of another engagement with Royal Navy submarines. Although questions arose surrounding the sinking, which occurred outside the Total Exclusion Zone and while *General Belgrano* was steaming away from the submarine, postwar analysis vindicated the attack and Woodward's decision to shoot. Even the captain of the Argentine cruiser and his government deemed it a legitimate act of war.

HMS *Conqueror* was one of three nuclear-powered fleet submarines of the

ABOVE: HMS *Courageous*, sister of HMS *Conqueror*, is shown open to the public in 2002.
(Creative Commons Chris Allen via Wikimedia Commons)

ABOVE: Admiral Sandy Woodward, pictured in 2012, ordered HMS *Conqueror* to attack *General Belgrano*.
(Creative Commons Elizabeth Massey via Wikimedia Commons)

Churchill-class. Designed by Vickers Shipbuilding and constructed at Cammell Laird in Birkenhead, she was laid down on December 5, 1967, launched August 28, 1969, and commissioned November 9, 1971. She displaced just over 5,100 tons, with a length of nearly 287ft, beam of more than 33ft, and draft of 27ft. Her complement included 103 officers and sailors. Top speed of 28kts was supplied by a single Rolls-Royce PWR nuclear reactor and two English Electric geared turbines generating 20,000 shaft horsepower. She carried Mark VIII and Mark 24 acoustic torpedoes with six 21in tubes, and the Harpoon anti-ship missile.

After the Falklands War, HMS *Conqueror* continued in Cold War-era service, participating later in 1982 in Operation Barmaid along with US Navy units, successfully snatching a Soviet-made sonar device from a Polish-flagged vessel in the Barents Sea. In 1988, HMS *Conqueror* was involved in a collision with a training yacht, sinking the latter while four sailors were rescued. She was decommissioned in 1990 and remains in storage.

As for that fateful day in May 1982, Admiral Woodward later commented: "There was but one fast solution. I had to take out one claw of the pincer…There was the *Belgrano* and two destroyers armed with Exocet missiles milling around in the southern ocean. I knew from experience that while they were within 200 miles of our ships, they could have us overnight. So, I wanted them removed, didn't I?"

ABOVE: The fleet submarine HMS *Conqueror* (right) is shown moored alongside HMS *Warspite* at Devonport in 2006.
(Adrian Jones Public Domain via Wikimedia Commons)

ADMIRAL *KUZNETSOV*

The Russian and earlier Soviet concept of the aircraft carrier has differed markedly from that of Western nations during the past half century. Early Soviet naval air forays included two Moskva-class helicopter carriers of the 1960s, prior to a reorientation towards their aircraft-carrying missile cruisers designed and commissioned between 1975 and 1990.

While these warships were capable of carrying a substantial complement of fixed-wing and rotary aircraft, their primary mission of support for ballistic missile submarines, aircraft with anti-ship missiles, and other surface ships was more tactical rather than serving as a strategic global projector of air power. Nevertheless, by Western standards they have regularly been classified as aircraft carriers.

The Kiev-class aircraft-carrying missile cruisers were completed in the 1970s and decommissioned by 1993, and the lead ship was sold to China's Tianjin Binhai Aircraft Park for conversion to a tourist attraction.

Admiral Kuznetsov, one of two intended aircraft-carrying missile cruisers of its type, was laid down at the Black Sea shipyard in Mykolaiv, Ukraine, on April 1, 1982, launched on December 6, 1985, and commissioned in December 1990, although she was not fully operational for another four years. *Admiral Kuznetsov* displaces 43,000 tons, with an overall length of 1,001ft, ramped flight deck, and beam of 236ft. Powered by eight turbo-pressurised boilers and steam turbines that produce 200,000 shaft horsepower, her top speed is 29kts. Her air complement totals up to 52 aircraft, including fixed wing multi-role fighters and tactical support planes, as well as multi-purpose helicopters. Her primary armament includes close-in weapons defence systems and the P-700 Granit long-range cruise missile.

Making her first deployment, from December 1995 to March 1996, into the Mediterranean, *Admiral Kuznetsov* conducted extensive flight training and

ABOVE: The Russian aircraft-carrying missile cruiser *Admiral Kuznetsov* is shown with attending vessels in 2017. (Creative Commons Mil.ru Ministry of Defence of the Russian Federation via Wikimedia Commons)

observed the 300th anniversary of the Russian Navy. A scheduled overhaul was suspended in 1997 due to a funding shortage, and after returning to the fleet in the November 1998, the warship remained idle until 2000 when the loss of the nuclear submarine *Kursk* cancelled a Mediterranean deployment, and *Admiral Kuznetsov* participated in rescue operations. Further routine fleet exercises followed in 2008.

A crewman was killed in an onboard fire off the coast of Turkey in January 2009, and in 2012 the aircraft-carrying cruiser lost all propulsion and required the assistance of the tug *Nikolay Chiker* to reach her home port of Severomorsk, from the Bay of Biscay. In the autumn of 2016, *Admiral Kuznetsov* conducted air strikes against Islamic State and Al-Nusra terror groups then operating in Syria. With the conclusion of her mission, the warship had launched more than 400 sorties against 1,252 targets.

Early expectations were that the service life of *Admiral Kuznetsov* would extend to approximately 2030; however, in 2017 a modernisation programme was undertaken to add 25 years to her career. For some time, she had been the only active "aircraft carrier" in the Soviet or Russian Navy. The second of her class, *Varyag*, was under construction with the collapse of the Soviet Union, and her hull was sold to China, while the supercarrier *Ulyanov* was scrapped in 1992 when just 20% complete.

As for the modernisation programme undertaken in 2017 at the 25th Ship Repair Plant in Murmansk, *Admiral Kuznetsov* has seen financial difficulties, mechanical issues, and accidents. In October 2018, the largest drydock in Russia sank, causing a crane to topple and gouge a 200sq ft hole in the flight deck. In 2019, a fire killed two workers and injured 14 while causing extensive damage. Again in 2022, fire damaged the ship. Deadlines for completion of the project in both 2023 and 2024 were not achieved.

In the autumn of 2024, news reports indicated that *Admiral Kuznetsov*'s crew of about 1,500 had been transferred to the Russian Army for service in the war with Ukraine, raising the possibility that the cruiser's modernisation might be abandoned. Meanwhile, the Russian government has announced plans for another aircraft carrier project, the *Storm*, with anticipated service entry in the late 2020s. However, the project may still be in the preliminary stage.

ABOVE: The Russian aircraft carrier *Admiral Kuznetsov* sails in the Mediterranean south of Italy with the destroyer USS *Deyo* nearby. (US Navy via Wikimedia Commons)

ABOVE: *Admiral Kuznetsov* sails off the UK coast while being watched by the destroyer HMS *Dragon*, 2014. (Open Government License Royal Navy via Wikimedia Commons)

ABOVE: The People's Liberation Army Navy aircraft carrier *Liaoning* plies the East China Sea in 2020. (Creative Commons 日本防衛省・統合幕僚監部 via Wikimedia Commons)

LIAONING

The implications are clear. The People's Republic of China is committed to the establishment and operation of a blue water navy capable of projecting air power at least in a regional capacity throughout the Indo-Pacific. As Admiral Song Xue, Deputy Chief of the People's Liberation Army Navy (PLAN), declared some years ago via the state-run news agency Xinhua: "We won't have just one carrier."

During the early 1990s, the People's Republic of China embarked on its development programme that may see as many as four operational aircraft carriers on the high seas by the early 2030s. With the collapse of the Soviet Union, plans for that country's naval expansion stalled. The original Soviet plan to commission the new Admiral Kuznetsov-class aircraft carrying missile cruiser *Riga*, later renamed *Varyag*, halted abruptly. Launched in December 1988, *Varyag* was still under construction in Ukraine when her hulk, stripped of most equipment and proprietary technology, was sold in 1998 to the People's Republic nearly a decade after the demise of the Soviet Union.

Four years after the sale, the hulk was towed to the Dalian naval shipyard in

ABOVE: *Liaoning* undergoes aircraft carrier modification at Dalian in 2012.

(Creative Commons CEphoto Uwe Aranas via Wikimedia Commons)

northeast China for conversion to the Type 001 aircraft carrier *Liaoning*, named after a province in that region. *Liaoning* displaces 43,000 tons light and nearly 61,000 tons fully loaded. Her overall length is more than 1,000ft, with a ski-jump take-off assist ramp built into the flight deck, and her beam is just over 244ft. Eight KVG boilers and a quartet of steam turbines generate 200,000 shaft horsepower and a top speed of 32kts.

The aircraft complement of *Liaoning* is reported at 32 planes and helicopters. These included updated variants of the J-15 multi-role fighter, Changhe Z-18 transport helicopter, Kamov airborne early warning helicopter, Harbin Z-9 utility helicopter, and perhaps the J-35 stealth fighter that is being modified for use with catapult launch systems. *Liaoning* carries onboard defences including the 1130 CIWS (close-in weapons system) and the HQ-10 short-range surface-to-air missile.

Liaoning underwent a series of sea trials from August 2011 to July 2012. Shortly afterwards, aircraft were taken aboard and flight operations trials were conducted for the next two years. Reports of overall performance indicated that a steam malfunction in the propulsion system had resulted in a loss of power and partial evacuation of the ship at some point during the trials; the severity of the incident and its duration are unknown to Western observers. People's Liberation Army Navy (PLAN) communications and Chinese state media released periodic updates on the progress of air training aboard *Liaoning*, including announcements of successful touch-and-go

ABOVE: The Chinese aircraft carrier *Liaoning* lies in waters off Hong Kong in 2017. (Creative Commons Baycrest via Wikimedia Commons)

landings, arrested cable landings, and other progressive operations until mid-2013.

Formal commissioning to the PLAN took place on September 25, 2012, and *Liaoning* was designated a training ship until 2018 as air operations testing and evaluation required the anticipated four or five years of development and implementation. Her home port has been reported as Yuchi Naval Base in Shandong Province, in east China, south of the capital of Beijing. Unquestionably, the presence of *Liaoning*, whether as a training ship or in an active fleet role, may influence the course of diplomatic events in the Indo-Pacific, particularly in regard to the future of Taiwan, and the threatened reunification with the People's Republic by force.

In the spring of 2018, *Liaoning* participated in a large naval exercise in the South China Sea, and military assets used live-fire drills to demonstrate combat readiness and capabilities. That summer the carrier was reported to have begun its initial refit since commissioning six years earlier. It was completed in six months and *Liaoning* returned to service in January 2019. Since 2021, various sightings and

ABOVE: This aerial view of *Liaoning* with fighter aircraft on her flight deck was taken in 2022. (Creative Commons 日本防衛省・統合幕僚監部 via Wikimedia Commons)

surveillance reports have placed the carrier in the Miyako Strait or Kerama Gap between Okinawa and Miyaka Island, with escorting destroyers, frigates, and supply ships, as well as sailing in the Western Pacific, Yellow Sea, and East China Sea.

In the spring of 2022, *Liaoning* and its task group were observed by elements of the Japanese Maritime Self-Defence Force conducting exercises, while a Japanese destroyer shadowed the carrier strike group during a deployment in the Philippine Sea in the autumn of 2024. Positions and activities were documented during operations midway between Japan's Okinotorishima Atoll, Taiwan, and Guam, a US territory located in the Marianas archipelago. At the same time, PLAN warships were carrying out a second round of exercises with the Russian Navy, after docking at the port of Vladivostok.

Meanwhile, the second PLAN aircraft carrier to become active, the Type 002 *Shandong*, was reported to have successfully completed a training mission and returned to her home port at Yulin Naval Base on the island of Hainan. During her deployment, *Shandong* operated in the Western Pacific and South China Sea. *Shandong* displaces more than 60,000 tons, carries a complement of up to 36 multi-role fighter aircraft, and a dozen helicopters. Commissioned in December 2019, *Shandong* was reported to have reached basic operational readiness in October 2020, perhaps an indication of the rapid evolution and implementation of efficient PLAN aircraft carrier operations.

A third PLAN aircraft carrier, *Fujian*, was laid down by 2016 and launched on June 17, 2022. As of 2025, she was undergoing early sea trials and was expected to reach operational status by the end of the year. *Fujian* is designated a Type 003 aircraft carrier with aircraft capacity of more than 50 planes and helicopters.

PLAN officials have indicated that a fourth aircraft carrier is currently under construction.

ABOVE: The former Soviet *Varyag* bound for China is under tow off Istanbul, Turkey, in 2001. (US Navy via Wikimedia Commons)

ABOVE: A J-15 multi-role fighter takes off from *Liaoning* in the spring of 2022. (Creative Commons 日本防衛省・統合幕僚監部 via Wikimedia Commons)

USS *WISCONSIN*

ABOVE: Her main 16in batteries prominent in this view, the battleship USS *Wisconsin* sails the open sea circa 1990. (Naval History and Heritage Command via Wikimedia Commons)

One of four Iowa-class battleships ordered for the US Navy from 1939 to 1940, USS *Wisconsin* was the last battleship on active duty in the world when she was last stricken, along with USS *Iowa,* from the navy's roll, on March 17, 2006. During the 62 years from her commissioning on April 16, 1944, she was decommissioned and returned to service three times.

USS *Wisconsin* was laid down at the Philadelphia Navy Yard on January 25, 1941, and launched on December 7, 1943, two years to the day after the Japanese attack on Pearl Harbor that launched World War Two in the Pacific. The battleship displaced 45,000 tons light and more than 58,000 tons fully loaded. She was more than 887ft long, with a beam of over 108ft, and draft of about 38ft. Her top speed of 32½kts was supplied by eight Babcock & Wilcox boilers generating 212,000 shaft horsepower, and four General Electric geared steam turbines. Armour protection ranged from more than 12in at the waterline belt to 14½in on bulkheads, 19½in on turrets, and more than 6in on armoured portions of the deck.

Original armament included nine 16in main guns in three triple-mount turrets, two fore and one aft, ten twin-mounted 5in dual-purpose guns, 20 quadruple-mount 40mm and 49 single mount 20mm anti-aircraft guns. The configuration changed in the 1980s to include eight armoured quadruple box launchers for the BGM-109 Tomahawk cruise missile and a capacity of

32 missiles, four quadruple launchers for the RGM-84 Harpoon anti-ship missile, and the 20mm Phalanx CIWS (close-in weapons system).

USS *Wisconsin* completed initial sea trials off the Virginia Capes and concluded her shakedown cruise off the British West Indies. She joined the Pacific Fleet in October 1944 and participated in the actions at Iwo Jima, Okinawa, and the bombardment of the Japanese home islands. She sailed into Tokyo Bay on September 6, 1945, four days after the Japanese surrender that ended the Pacific War, then took part in post-war Operation Magic Carpet, the repatriation of US service personnel to the United States.

Wisconsin served as a training ship and visited various ports of call prior to deactivation on July 1, 1948. Reactivated in 1951, she completed a tour of duty during the Korean War from November of that year through April 1952. While serving as the flagship of the Seventh Fleet, her heavy guns executed numerous shore bombardment missions against communist positions along the North Korean coast. She returned to home waters and served as a training ship while participating in several fleet exercises. USS *Wisconsin* was the last active battleship of the US Navy prior to decommissioning in 1958.

The next 30 years were spent in fleet reserve. However, in October 1988, *Wisconsin* was reactivated during the execution of President Ronald Reagan's build-up to a 600-ship navy. Modern weapons and other systems were installed with the subsequent upgrade. From January 15 to February 27, 1991, *Wisconsin* served during Operation

Desert Storm, bombarding Iraqi artillery positions, shore installations, and communications sites with her 16in guns, launching cruise missiles at distant targets, and damaging or sinking as many as 15 Iraqi patrol boats, and other vessels.

By the early 1990s, the cost of maintaining USS *Wisconsin* had become prohibitive, and naval austerity resulted in decommissioning in September 1991. She was stricken from the naval roll in 1995, moved from the Philadelphia Navy Yard to Norfolk the next year, returning to the roll in 1998. Both *Wisconsin* and *Iowa* were ordered to be maintained with the reserve fleet under the National Defense Authorization Act of 1996, but the cost to modernise for further duty was later deemed excessive.

In 2000, *Wisconsin* was berthed in Norfolk at Nauticus, The National Maritime Center. She was opened to the public the following year as a museum ship.

ABOVE: The battleship USS *Wisconsin* lies moored beside the salvaged battleship USS *Oklahoma*, sunk during the 1941 Japanese raid on Pearl Harbor, in this November 1944 photo. (US Navy via Wikimedia Commons)

ABOVE: *Wisconsin* operates off the coast of North Korea in 1952 in company with the destroyer USS *Buck* (left) and the cruiser USS *Saint Paul*. (US Navy via Wikimedia Commons)

USS NAUTILUS

ABOVE: The world's first nuclear submarine, USS *Nautilus* is underway in the mid-1950s. (US Navy via Wikimedia Commons)

The world's first operational nuclear-powered submarine, USS *Nautilus,* was the product of the latest propulsion technology developed during the burgeoning Cold War. She went on to establish numerous other 'firsts' during her distinguished career in the US Navy – she was the first vessel to reach the North Pole, completed the first submerged voyage transiting the North Pole, the longest submerged cruise by a submarine, as well as the highest sustained submerged speed.

The US Atomic Energy Commission played a key role in the development of USS *Nautilus* as a group of research scientists and engineers, led by future Admiral Hyman G Rickover, designed a nuclear propulsion system while working under the auspices of the commission's Naval Research Branch. Rickover championed nuclear propulsion and later earned the nickname 'Father of the Nuclear Navy'.

Nautilus was laid down on June 14, 1952, at the General Dynamics Electric Boat Division shipyard in Groton, Connecticut. Launched on January 21, 1954, and commissioned on September 30 of that year, she was nearly 324ft long, with a beam of almost 28ft, draft of 22ft, and displacement of 3,522 tons. Her complement included 105 officers and sailors, and she was armed with six 21in torpedo tubes located in the bow, and a capacity of 26 torpedoes.

The nuclear propulsion system set *Nautilus* apart, and it consisted of the Westinghouse S2W pressurised water naval reactor that generated heat through splitting atoms. In turn, a heat exchanger produced steam which powered geared turbines to generate a top speed of 23kts. When *Nautilus* cast off all lines and Commander Eugene P Wilkinson ordered her to sea on the morning of January 17, 1955, the commanding officer signalled a message that revolutionised modern naval operations: "Underway On Nuclear Power."

During her first cruise, *Nautilus* sailed from Naval Base New London in Groton to Puerto Rico, a total of 1,300 miles. She was submerged the entire transit, establishing the distance record, and achieved the speed record at the same time. For months, *Nautilus* participated in rigorous trials and testing of endurance and equipment that rendered much of the anti-submarine technology of the day obsolete. Representing a new generation of submarine, *Nautilus* also took part in numerous naval exercises.

ABOVE: A crowd gathers to witness the launching of USS *Nautilus* in 1954. (US Navy via Wikimedia Commons)

President Dwight D Eisenhower was eager to bolster support for a programme to develop submarine-launched ballistic missiles and authorised an ambitious mission for *Nautilus* – Operation Sunshine – to become the first vessel to reach and transit the North Pole. In April 1958, Commander William R Anderson and her crew began training for the mission, and on June 9 she departed Seattle, Washington. However, she was forced to turn back from the Bering Strait ten days later due to deep ice. In the second attempt, *Nautilus* departed Pearl Harbor, Hawaii, reaching the Bering Sea on August 1, and the North Pole two days later. During the next 96 hours, *Nautilus* cruised 1,590 nautical miles under polar ice, surfacing northeast of Greenland. She sailed on to Isle of Portland, Dorset, and became the first US Navy ship to receive the Presidential Unit Citation during peacetime.

Following an overhaul undertaken in May 1959 at Portsmouth Naval Shipyard, Kittery, Maine, *Nautilus* joined the Sixth Fleet in the Mediterranean in August 1960. She established another record in the spring of 1966 after logging 300,000 miles underway. *Nautilus* participated in a variety of fleet exercises, tests, and evaluations that supported the design and development of future nuclear submarines.

Nautilus was decommissioned on May 3, 1980, at Mare Island Naval Shipyard, California, after 25 years of active service and cruising more than half a million miles. Two years later, the submarine was designated a national historic landmark. After conversion, *Nautilus* was towed to Groton, where she is explored by thousands of visitors each year at the Submarine Force Museum.

ABOVE: After retirement, USS *Nautilus* is assisted en route to Naval Base New London. (US Navy via Wikimedia Commons)

USS *LOS ANGELES*

In the US Navy the role of the attack or hunter-killer submarine is to sink enemy submarines and surface warships, deploy Tomahawk cruise missiles at designated targets, provide intelligence and surveillance, deploy mines and special operations forces as needed, and to protect the surface fleet from hostile forces.

Growing concerns over improved Soviet technology and submarine capabilities gave rise to the development of the Los Angeles-class nuclear attack submarine in the mid-1960s. The Los Angeles-class succeeded the Sturgeon-class, another Cold War workhorse, that was in production from 1963 to 1975. US designers and engineers undertook the groundwork for the Los Angeles-class in 1967, and the namesake was laid down at Newport News Shipbuilding in Virginia on January 8, 1972, launched April 6, 1974, and commissioned November 13, 1976.

By 1996, a total of 62 Los Angeles-class submarines were completed at Newport News and the General Dynamics Electric Boat Division in Connecticut. Through the course of the programme, production costs rose from $225 million, when funding began in 1970, to $900 million in 1990 and beyond, as both enhanced operational capabilities and inflation contributed to the increase. As of late 2024, a total of 24 Los Angeles-class submarines were still in active service, constituting roughly half the strength of the US Navy's hunter-killer submarines. The others include the three boats of the Seawolf-class first commissioned in 1997, and the Virginia-class, which entered service in 2004. The last Sturgeon-class boat was retired in 2005.

The Los Angeles-class submarines displace 6,900 tons, with a length of 360ft, beam of 33ft, and draft of nearly 31ft. A

ABOVE: The nuclear attack submarine USS *Los Angeles* ploughs through the open sea. (US Navy via Wikimedia Commons)

single S6G nuclear reactor and two turbines provide a top speed of more than 25kts, with virtually unlimited range since the reactor requires refuelling at estimated 30 years of service. Submersion test depth reached 1,480ft. The class carries four 21in torpedo tubes in the bow for the MK-48 torpedo, Harpoon anti-ship missiles, and the Tomahawk cruise missile, with a total available ordnance of about 25 torpedo-fired units. Crew complement includes 16 officers and 127 sailors.

Functioning in several offensive and defensive roles, including strike capability, escort, and carrier battle group support, the Los Angeles-class offered enhanced sound suppression and a larger propulsion system in comparison with the Sturgeon-class. The last 23 Los Angeles-class submarines completed were designated 'Improved 688s', with more advanced fighting systems, reinforcements to the steel hulls for ice breaking if needed, and quieter running characteristics. In addition to horizontal launching of cruise missiles through the torpedo tubes, the Improved 688s carry a dozen vertical launch tubes for the Tomahawk.

The longest serving Los Angeles-class submarines are approaching 40 years of active duty, and the record of the lead boat is noteworthy. Before decommissioning in

February 2011, USS *Los Angeles* deployed to the Mediterranean Sea and received a Meritorious Unit Citation in 1977. Permanent assignment to the Pacific Fleet and Submarine Squadron 7 followed. With her home port at Pearl Harbor, Hawaii, *Los Angeles* completed 17 deployments during the next 32 years, participating in major training events such as the Rim of the Pacific exercises, and visited numerous ports of call throughout the region.

The debut of the Seawolf-class brought quieter performance, weapons capacity of up to 50 units, eight torpedo tubes, displacement of 9,138 tons, and some with a 100ft hull extension described as a multi-mission platform to house additional payload capacity and advanced technology.

ABOVE: The aft end of the control room aboard the Los Angeles-class hunter-killer submarine USS *Jefferson City* reveals some of her advanced technology.

(Creative Commons Hobit via Wikimedia Commons)

ABOVE: The Los Angeles-class submarine USS *Santa Fe* lies moored with her vertical Tomahawk cruise missile doors open. (US Navy via Wikimedia Commons)

TYPHOON CLASS

The largest warships of their kind ever built, the Typhoon-class ballistic missile submarines were the frontline of the Soviet and Russian naval nuclear arms component for decades. Six of the originally planned seven Typhoons were built between 1976 and 1989 at the Severodvinsk shipyard in northern Arkhangelsk Oblast, Russia.

The Typhoons were built to fulfil a single strategic mission, to counter the US Navy's Ohio-class ballistic missile submarine, to serve as stealthy, mobile platforms for the launch of ballistic missiles carrying multiple nuclear warheads. They were constructed with the capability to remain submerged for lengthy periods, estimated up to 120 days in the event of nuclear war. Typhoons operated in waters around the globe, with careers that spanned five decades until the *Dmitriy Donskoi* (TK-208) was retired in February 2023.

Dmitriy Donskoi was indeed the first and last of the Typhoon-class, laid down at Severodvinsk on June 30, 1976, launched in September 1980, and commissioned on December 29, 1981. Western intelligence indicated that *Dmitriy Donskoi* became operational in February 1982, and participated in several exercises and submarine-launched ballistic missile (SLBM) firing drills. She was responsible for a series of test launches, both successful and unsuccessful, of the Bulava SLBM during the 2000s, while serving as a weapons testing

ABOVE: The sheer size of the Typhoon-class submarine is apparent in this image of *Arkhangelsk* (TK17) at sea. (Bellona Foundation via Wikimedia Commons)

platform, before decommissioning ended her career of slightly more than 40 years.

The massive size of the Typhoon-class led to its designation as a heavy cruiser with the designation TK, as opposed to the standard K or cruiser designation of other Soviet and Russian submarines. The Typhoons displaced 48,000 tons, with a length of more than 574ft, beam of 75½ft, and draft of over 39ft. The propulsion system included two OK-650 pressurised water nuclear reactors, a pair of geared steam turbines, and four turbogenerators that delivered a top surface speed of about 22kts, and a top submerged speed of 28kts. Two diesel generators were installed as a secondary source of propulsion. The submarine was

constructed with multiple hulls, including five inner hulls positioned inside the superstructure of two parallel main hulls. Sound quelling tiles were applied to the superstructure, and reinforced areas allowed for penetration of ice if necessary. The ship's complement included 160 officers and sailors.

Armament included six torpedo tubes located in the upper part of the bow, four of them 24.8in and two 21in, with a total of 22 anti-submarine and anti-ship torpedoes of varying types. The torpedo room was situated in the upper part of the bow, and the tubes were also capable of deploying mines. Twenty R-39 or RSM-52 (NATO designation) SLBMs were carried in vertical launch tubes within the two main pressure hulls. The missiles contained up to 200 multiple independently targetable reentry vehicle (MIRV) warheads.

ABOVE: The Typhoon-class ballistic missile submarine *TK-202* sits surfaced in arctic waters with ice covering her exterior. (Bellona Foundation via Wikimedia Commons)

Typhoons were outfitted with both satellite and radio communications systems, electronic countermeasures, active/passive sonar, and surface target detection radar. Maximum diving depth was more than 1,300ft.

The Typhoon-class was developed under Project 941 as the Akula or Shark class, but should not be confused with the NATO-designated Akula-class attack submarine type. NATO assigned the designation *Typhoon* to the ballistic missile submarine.

In 1999, the Typhoon-class submarine *TK-202* was withdrawn from service, and its nuclear fuel was removed with US financial assistance. Two more, *Arkhangelsk* (TK17) and *Severstal* (TK-20), were decommissioned by 2006. *TK-13* and *Simbrisk* (TK-12) were withdrawn and scrapped by 2009. The Typhoon-class has been succeeded by the Borei-class ballistic missile submarine.

ABOVE: This view of a Soviet-built Typhoon-class ballistic missile submarine includes an inset of an American football field (100yds) for length comparison. (US Navy via Wikimedia Commons)

AKULA CLASS

ABOVE: An Akula-class nuclear attack submarine of the Russian Navy rides at her moorings. (Creative Commons Источник — VL.ru via Wikimedia Commons)

The appearance of the Soviet-built fourth generation Akula-class attack submarine startled the Western military establishment. Designed in response to the US Navy's Los Angeles-class attack submarine, the Akula entered service with the Soviet Navy in 1986, and a 13-year building programme led to the completion of 16 of an originally planned 20 Akulas by 1996.

Soviet intelligence reports had indicated enhanced stealth qualities with the Los Angeles-class and prompted the development of the Akula to incorporate quieter running and acoustic features, such as advanced propeller designs and the installation of tiles that minimised the risk of echo. The overall design featured a stealth oriented propulsion system, hydrodynamic hull design, and towed sonar apparatus. While the Los Angeles-class was considered a significant advancement in submarine design, Western analysts had concluded that the Soviets could not produce a comparable hunter-killer submarine for at least another decade; therefore, the appearance of the Akula, preceded by the Victor and Sierra classes, in the mid-1980s was a sobering development.

The Akulas were built in the Soviet and Russian shipyards at Severodvinsk and Komsomolsk-on-Amur, and entered service with the Northern and Pacific fleets of the Russian Navy. Until the late 1990s, they remained the most technologically advanced submarines in the Russian fleet. To date, it is believed that three of the original seven Akula-class submarines remain in service, and together with the Victor-class, they provided the bulk of the Russian attack submarine force into the 21st century.

The Akula was designed at the Malachite St Petersburg Central Design Bureau, which then had more than a half century of experience in submarine development, and was responsible for the first Soviet attack submarines of the November-class. Chief Designer Georgy Tchemyshev and Chief Navy Supervisor Igor Boganchenko led the project. The original Akula-class submarines displaced 8,140 tons, with a length of 362ft, beam of 45ft, and draft of 32ft. Variants have exhibited similar dimensions.

ABOVE: This Akula-class submarine was photographed on Russian Navy Day in 2009.

(Creative Commons Alex omen via Wikimedia Commons)

The Akula-class is powered by a 190-megawatt OK-650B/OK-650M pressurised water nuclear reactor, two steam generators with seven steam pumps, and a single OK-7 steam turbine delivering a top speed of 35kts submerged, and 10kts on the surface. A pair of retractable OK-300 electric motors provide alternative propulsion with minimal noise at low speeds of 4kts, submerged or on the surface.

The Akula armament package includes eight torpedo tubes situated in the bow, four 25.6in and four 21in, to accommodate a total of 40 torpedoes and cruise missiles. Among these are the first Soviet Navy torpedoes capable of being fitted with nuclear warheads, while the largest conventional high-explosive torpedoes carry 1,100lb warheads. Six 15¾in external tubes are carried for the deployment of countermeasures. The cruise missiles are of the SS-N-21 Granat (NATO code name *Sampson*) type, and are similar to the US submarine-launched Tomahawk, intended for land targets. The Strela-3 surface-to-air missile system is also utilised for anti-aircraft defence. In action, the crew of an Akula-class submarine is expected to fire a missile or torpedo on 15 seconds' notice, with a second salvo in only six minutes.

ABOVE: An Akula-class submarine churns the waters in the open sea in this mid-1990s photo. (US Department of Defense via Wikimedia Commons)

Through the years, Akula-class submarines have been reported performing escort and training missions, and participating in fleet exercises with the Soviet and Russian navies. Their successful activities in tracking and surveillance of US Navy ballistic missile submarines has raised concerns at times in the West, while the Akulas are known to have operated off the East Coast of the United States and in the Gulf of Mexico.

The Yasen-class attack submarine, successor to the Akula-class, entered service with the Russian Navy in 2014, and to date it is believed that five Yasen-class boats are operational, with more to be commissioned by the 2030s.

USS *VIRGINIA*

ABOVE: After completing her first sea trials, USS *Virginia* returns to the General Dynamics Electric Boat shipyard in Groton, Connecticut, July 2004. (US Navy via Wikimedia Commons)

By the late 1990s, the programme to construct the successor to the long-serving Los Angeles-class nuclear attack submarines of the US Navy was well underway. The contract to construct the lead submarine of the Virginia-class was awarded to General Dynamics Electric Boat Division in Groton, Connecticut, on September 30, 1998.

To date, at least 21 Virginia-class hunter-killer submarines have been completed by Electric Boat and Newport News Shipbuilding in Virginia. The two shipyards have co-operated in the construction process, with Electric Boat handling engine room and control room specifications, while Newport News constructs the bow, stern, crew areas, machinery spaces, torpedo room, and sail. Work on the nuclear powerplant, final assembly, testing, and delivery is alternated between the two companies. Recent plans included final construction of 34 submarines of the class, while construction may be extended in the future for sales to the Royal Australian Navy.

This most advanced submarine class is perhaps best known for its stealth capabilities with hull design and acoustic suppression enhancements that reduce the boat's submerged signature, allowing it to operate virtually undetected. The Virginia-class is 377ft long, with a beam of 34ft, draft of 30½ft, and displacement of 7,460 tons surfaced. The single pump-jet S9G nuclear reactor's operation minimises noise, and delivers a top speed of 25kts surfaced and 35kts submerged. The ship's complement includes 15 officers and 117 sailors.

USS *Virginia* was laid down at Electric Boat on September 2, 1999, launched on August 16, 2003, and commissioned on October 23, 2004. She participated in the Global War on Terror, first deploying in 2005, and then covering 37,000 miles in a six-month deployment that concluded in 2010. The class is expected to make up to 15 deployments during an anticipated service life of 33 years, and a programme of modifications has been designed to deliver on that expectation.

Along with increases in stealth capabilities, the Virginia-class submarines also exhibit enhanced manoeuvrability and firepower. The class was designed to provide coastal fire support and surveillance if needed, while considerations were given to use in special operations for transport of personnel and equipment required for long land deployments. Armament includes four 21in torpedo tubes to accommodate the Mk-48 torpedo or Harpoon anti-ship missile. The Tomahawk cruise missile is fired via the vertical launch system (VLS), 12 tubes located in the bow within the hull. Improvements are introduced through a progression of Blocks, and the Block III Virginia-class submarines already include two large diameter Virginia Payload Tubes (VPT) capable of firing multiple Tomahawks at the same time, eliminating the need for the dozen tubes of the VLS.

Block III improvements were successfully tested with the USS *North Dakota* during sea trials in 2014, and were included on all Virginia-class boats completed between 2008 and 2013. Block V submarines, including ten boats completed from 2019 to 2023, were expected to be fitted with the Virginia Payload Module (VPM) which includes

ABOVE: Commissioning ceremonies are conducted aboard the Virginia-class hunter-killer submarine USS *North Carolina*. (US Navy via Wikimedia Commons)

four large diameter payload tubes capable of carrying seven Tomahawks each, augmenting the type's collective cruise missile capacity by 28 with each VPM addition.

During the implementation of the Virginia-class programme, the use of modular construction, readily available commercial-grade components, open floorplans, and other cost containment measures, have been stressed to control expense and facilitate the introduction of continually improving technology and systems.

ABOVE: A Virginia-class submarine fires a torpedo in this artist's rendering. (Department of Defense Graphic Ron Stern via Wikimedia Commons)

USS GERALD R. FORD

ABOVE: After a week of sea trials in the spring of 2017, USS *Gerald R Ford* returns to her homeport at Norfolk, Virginia. (US Navy via Wikimedia Commons)

With the service lives of the Nimitz-class aircraft carriers lengthening, the US Navy's first wholly redesigned warships of their kind since the mid-1960s, began to take shape with the turn of the 21st century.

The Gerald R Ford-class aircraft carriers, incorporating some construction and technological improvements, integrated with the USS Ronald Reagan subclass of the Nimitz class, represent the most advanced carriers in naval history, as well as the most expensive. Intended to extend the capabilities of the US Navy's capital ships beyond the 2070s, the first carrier of ten planned was influenced heavily by the CVN (X) programme, which evaluated innovations that improve performance and space utilisation, while reducing the required number of crew, and saving an estimated $4 billion in operating costs during an anticipated service life of 50 years.

The Gerald R Ford-class aircraft carriers feature the Electromagnetic Aircraft Launch System (EMALS) rather than the steam catapult system of earlier types, which reduces wear and tear on the aircraft and improves operational efficiency. Other improvements include advanced arresting gear that enhances the reliability and safety in aircraft recovery, advanced weapons elevators to carry ordnance more safely and efficiently, a 20% reduction in required manpower, electrical generating capacity to facilitate future systems that include direct energy weapons, such as lasers, and adaptability for operations with forthcoming aircraft types. The Gerald R Ford class is further capable of carrying unmanned aerial vehicles, a critical component of warfare technology in the modern era.

Completed at a cost of $13.3 billion, about a 30% overrun from original estimates, most of these expenditures were related to construction timeline delays and performance issues with the munitions elevators, nuclear propulsion system, and EMALS. Such issues combined to delay the delivery of the USS *Gerald R Ford*, lead

ABOVE: This view of the bow of the aircraft carrier *Gerald R Ford* was taken during construction in 2013. (US Navy via Wikimedia Commons)

ABOVE: An Evolved Sea Sparrow anti-aircraft missile is launched during testing. (US Navy via Wikimedia Commons)

ABOVE: The aircraft carrier *Gerald R Ford* (lower) sails the open sea alongside the Nimitz-class carrier *Harry S Truman*.
(US Navy via Wikimedia Commons)

ship of the class, from the original date of February 2016 to the spring of 2017. The comprehensive delay from beginning of construction to commissioning amounted to about three years.

The keel of USS *Gerald R. Ford* was laid at Newport News Shipbuilding in Virginia on November 13, 2009. She was launched October 11, 2013, handed over to the US Navy on May 31, 2017, and commissioned July 22 of that year. To date, three additional carriers of the Gerald R Ford class are in various stages of completion. The second carrier, USS *John F Kennedy*, is slated for delivery to the navy in 2025, while the third, USS *Enterprise* is expected to be in service by 2028, and the fourth, USS *Doris Miller*, under construction as early as 2026. While the sheer cost of the class has given both US government officials and the American public pause, there is truly no alternative for the maintenance of the global obligations envisioned for the US Navy in the future. Still, the per-ship savings are some salve to the up-front costs, which will surely increase due to inflation, and other pressures.

"We had 23 new technologies on that ship, which quite frankly increased the risk of delivery and cost – of delivery on time and cost right from the get-go," explained Admiral Michael Gilday, Chief of Naval Operations in 2021. Much of the advanced technology and construction innovation with the Gerald R Ford class is owed to the decommissioned Kitty Hawk-class aircraft carrier USS *America*, which was utilised as a test bed as early as the spring of 1995. Although a strong movement attempted to preserve USS *America* as a floating museum, the carrier was subjected to live-fire evaluations, underwater explosions, and other stresses, and she was sunk when these evaluations were completed.

USS *Gerald R Ford* displaces about 112,000 tons, with a length of 1,092ft, beam of 134ft, and a flight deck with a width of 256ft. The carrier comprises 25 decks and a height of 250ft above the waterline. The ship's complement, 700 fewer than the Nimitz class, totals roughly 4,500 personnel, including an attached air wing. She can carry 75 aircraft

of varied types, and efficiencies derived from the new air operations technology are expected to place aircraft in the air at a 33% higher rate than the preceding Nimitz class. During routine operations, the carrier is capable of sustaining 160 air sorties per day, while emergency surge capability expands substantially to 270 sorties per day.

The Gerald R Ford's nuclear powerplant includes a pair of Bechtel A1B reactors producing steam for four electric turbines that generate a top speed of 30 kts. The A1B reactor is smaller and more efficient design than the A4W reactors of the Nimitz class, while the system further delivers three times the electric power. Refuelling is not anticipated until the carrier's complex mid-life overhaul after 25 years of service.

The defensive armament suite aboard the USS *Gerald R Ford* includes the RIM-162 Evolved Sea Sparrow Missile for anti-aircraft protection, and the RIM-116 Rolling Airframe Missile (RAM), a light, quick reaction missile intended to defend against incoming anti-ship missiles. Further defences include the Phalanx CIWS (close-in weapons system), the Mk 38 25mm machine gun system, and the reliable M2 Browning .50-calibre machine gun.

ABOVE: This three-dimensional graphic depicts the USS *John F Kennedy*, second of the Gerald R Ford-class aircraft carriers. (US Navy via Wikimedia Commons)

USS *Gerald R Ford* embarked on her first deployment in March 2021 to take part in Ready For Operations exercises with the Italian aircraft carrier *Cavour* in the Atlantic. The carrier participated in NATO exercises in the autumn of 2022, while making her first international port calls at Halifax, Nova Scotia, Canada, and Stokes Bay, near Gosport, on the western edge of Portsmouth harbour. In May 2023, the carrier left her homeport of Norfolk, Virginia, for NATO exercises with the US Sixth Fleet, then sailing to the Mediterranean for further exercises with Italian Navy units in the Ionian Sea. She took up station in the eastern Mediterranean to reinforce the US naval presence in the wake of the October 2023 Hamas attack on Israel.

After eight months at sea, the USS *Gerald R Ford* returned to Norfolk after an eight-month deployment that covered 83,476 nautical miles, with 10,396 air sorties supported.

ABOVE: The aircraft carrier USS *Gerald R Ford* leaves Newport News Shipbuilding in April 2017.
(US Navy via Wikimedia Commons)

ABOVE: This artist's rendering from 2019 depicts a Columbia-class ballistic missile submarine underway. (US Navy via Wikimedia Commons)

COLUMBIA CLASS

For more than 40 years, the Ohio-class ballistic missile submarine has been at the front line of the US Navy 'boomer' force, projecting nuclear power around the world. Longevity, in the context of advancing technology and the changing demands of naval preparedness as a component of the US nuclear triad, is a valued commodity and the Ohio-class has delivered. However, its projected retirement in the years from 2027 to 2040 necessitated a replacement programme that was initiated several years ago.

The result is the Columbia-class ballistic missile submarine, at this time destined to be the most mission-capable submarine in history, with attributes of stealth and quiet running never seen before. Twelve of these cutting edge 'boomers' are anticipated for deployment in the coming years, and the first of these, USS *District of Columbia*, is under construction at this time in the General Electric Boat yard at Quonset Point, Rhode Island. Identified as the ballistic submarine of the future since 2013, her keel was laid on June 5, 2022, and launch is expected in 2029, with completion in 2030, and service entry the following year, although delays have impacted the original production

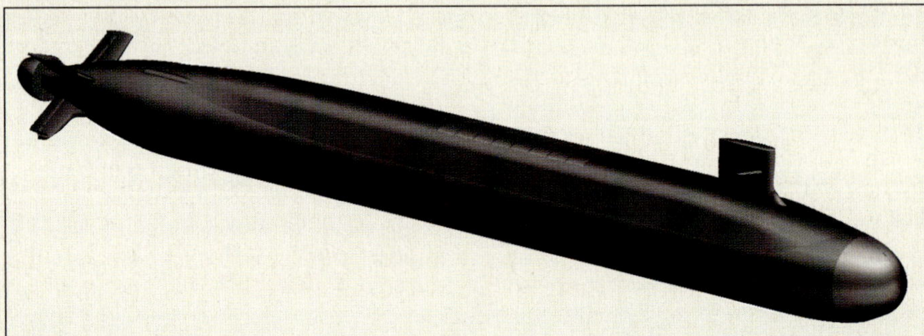

ABOVE: This drawing of the Ohio replacement concept submarine was produced in 2012. (US Navy via Wikimedia Commons)

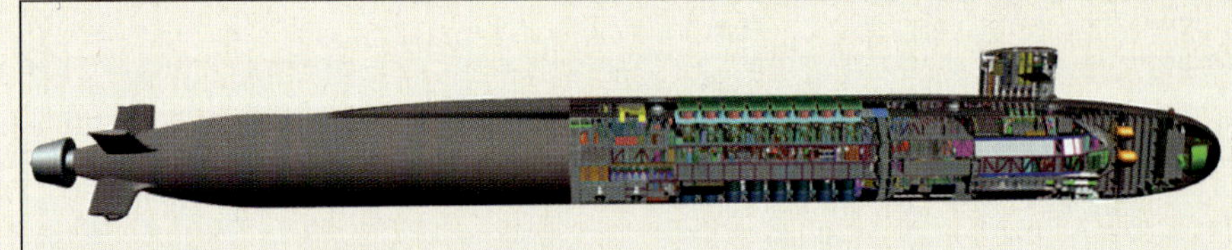

ABOVE: This cutaway view reveals some of the interior of the future Columbia-class ballistic missile submarine. (US Government via Wikimedia Commons)

schedule. Issues with suppliers, labour shortages, and the inherent difficulties of inter-company relationships, have all contributed to the setbacks.

Budgeted expenditures for the first submarine are estimated at $15.2 billion, while the second, USS *Wisconsin*, is projected at $9.3. Construction has been undertaken in a joint venture between General Dynamics Electric Boat Division of Groton, Connecticut, and Newport News Shipbuilding in Virginia, similar to their

ABOVE: This 2012 drawing shows what was then known as the Ohio replacement submarine firing a ballistic missile. (US Navy via Wikimedia Commons)

co-operation in the modular construction of the Virginia-class hunter-killer submarines.

During the keel laying ceremonies, Admiral Daryl Caudle, commander of US Fleet Forces Command remarked: "Laying the keel of the future USS *District of Columbia* truly is a historic occasion – not only for the countless designers, welders, metal workers, electricians, and master craftsmen whose unmatched expertise, ingenuity, hard work, and dedication will bring this modern marvel to life – but for the future sailors who will prowl the deep inside her hull, protecting our nation, deterring strategic attacks, and ensuring our freedom and way of life for decades to come."

Indeed, when the dozen submarines of the Columbia-class replace the 14 operational boats of the Ohio-class, they will carry 70% of the deployed US nuclear weapons arsenal. Each new submarine is planned to carry 16 state-of-the-art nuclear weapons in the form of the UGM-133 Trident II D5LE ballistic missile. The Trident missiles are stored in 87in diameter launch tubes called Quad Packs, and the four aboard the Columbia-class submarines are located in the middle section of the boat in an area designated the Common Missile Compartment (CMC).

In addition, the Columbia-class will be equipped with the latest available technology in every area of operation. Her S1B pump-jet nuclear reactor, developed by the Navy Nuclear Propulsion Program, is intended to operate for the duration of the submarine's service life, with no requirement for refuelling. The life of the reactor core is expected to be 42 years, and with the projected service life of the Columbia-class submarines in tandem, USS *District of Columbia* and her sisters should serve as the tip of the US Navy's nuclear spear into the 2080s.

In the meantime, the operation of the nuclear reactor is expected to produce no more acoustic signature or energy than a 20-watt lightbulb, and electric drive reduces noise in comparison to the steam turbines of the Ohio-class, rendering Columbia-class ballistic missile submarines virtually undetectable by existing sonar and sound apparatus. In addition, the Columbia-class

ABOVE: A submarine-launched Trident II ballistic missile breaks the surface of the sea during a test. (US Department of Defense via Wikimedia Commons)

will be designed and equipped to launch the Tomahawk cruise missile against land targets, as well as deploy special operations forces if needed. Such multi-role capability adds capacity to the fleet's overall strength and response time.

The Columbia-class submarines are projected to displace 21,140 tons submerged and 16,800 tons on the surface, with a length of 560ft, beam of 43ft, and draft of 38ft. Range is virtually unlimited due to nuclear power, and top speed is 15kts surfaced and 20kts submerged. These are the largest submarines ever built for the US Navy. The ship's complement is projected at 15 officers and 140 crewmen.

Stealth features have been integral components of the Columbia-class submarines from the beginning. In addition

ABOVE: The ballistic missile submarine USS *Ohio*, lead ship of her class of 14 boats, is commissioned in November 1981. (US Navy via Wikimedia Commons)

to features that will minimise the class's acoustic signature, the boats incorporate an X-shaped stern to minimise sound, while improving safety, manoeuvrability, and operating efficiency. Sail-mounted dive planes, anechoic coating, Large Aperture Bow (LAB) sonar system, and technically advanced sensors of various types, will enhance stealth performance as well.

The second and third Columbia-class ballistic missile submarines, *Wisconsin* and USS *Groton*, along with the fourth in the class, were originally scheduled for delivery to the navy by 2033, with successive deliveries to follow one per year until the entire class of 12 is completed. However, these dates are likely to be revised, considering the delays experienced in the construction of the lead boat.

Speaking at a November 2024 Naval Submarine Symposium, Matt Sermon, Executive Director of the Program Executive Office Strategic Submarines, declared: "Shipbuilders out there, supply chain, major mechanical equipment out there, stakeholders out there, we're going to have *District of Columbia* on patrol in 2030."

However, experience during the construction of USS *District of Columbia* indicates that the timeline from keel laying to service entry for future boats might in fact be eight years rather than the originally projected seven years.

CONCLUSION

Often majestic but always menacing, the world's greatest warships have left their lasting impression on the course of history.

From the days of seafaring peoples in the Mediterranean Basin to the earliest of Far Eastern ocean-going vessels, and the evolution from oar to sail, to steam and the nuclear reactor, the explorers, the raiders, the pirates, seekers of wealth and adventure, explorers, and the navies of the world have etched their names in the annals of time. Their exploits are the stuff of legend, at times a blend of fact and fiction, but always compelling.

One anonymous seaman of old summed up his lifetime of experience: "The sea is a mighty enemy, and the sailor is always a man of war." Surely, there is truth in the statement. Whenever there is conflict, shores and seas to be defended, the mighty clashes of arms on the oceans of the Earth have settled the question for better or worse. But even when there is no human foe, the rise and fall of the waves, the pounding surf in a gale force wind, the blazing sun, and the ice-bound poles challenge "those who go down to the sea in ships".

The heroes of naval warfare remain enshrined in the halls of the gallant. Across the centuries of conflict, they stand among the most fearless of men. Lord Nelson, who fell at Trafalgar in 1805, admonished his lieutenants to close with the enemy quickly. He declared: "No one makes a mistake by bringing his ship alongside that of his enemy." It was such an order that cost

ABOVE: Lord Nelson personally engages in close combat with the Spanish enemy in 1797.

(Richard Westall Royal Museums Greenwich via Wikimedia Commons)

ABOVE: Already on fire, the Japanese aircraft carrier *Shoho* takes a torpedo hit from a US Navy plane during the Battle of the Coral Sea, May 1942.

(US Navy via Wikimedia Commons)

Nelson his life, but the daring deeds of his fleet won the day and established Britain's naval supremacy for more than a century while ensuring the country would not be invaded by Napoleonic France. At the same time, modern combat has required a steely resolve. At Jutland, Admiral Sir Horace Hood was killed aboard the battlecruiser HMS *Invincible* as he charged toward the battleships of the German High Seas Fleet.

A generation later, the Battle of the Coral Sea became the first naval fight in which the surface ships of either combatant never came within sight of one another. From over the horizon, waves of aircraft were launched to drop bombs and torpedoes in an effort to strike a mortal blow against the enemy's capital ships. The dawn of the dominance of the aircraft carrier had eclipsed the battleship and the broadside in the modern naval battle.

From there, the Nuclear Age brought depth and breadth to the endurance of fleets around the globe. And in the undersea game of cat and mouse that the Cold War superpowers played, the hunter was also the hunted, while submarines became the transporters of weapons of mass destruction – ballistic missiles, dozens of them with multiple warheads capable of unleashing catastrophic destructive force.

This volume of the *World's Greatest Warships* has presented a glimpse into the careers of a relative few of those vessels that have influenced the fates of nations in the past and those that will continue to do so in the future. Thanks for reading!

ABOVE: The USS *John C Stennis* aircraft carrier strike group sails with warships of the South Korean Navy during exercises in 2016. (US Navy via Wikimedia Commons)